850

D1557570

DEAN MARTIN

Recollections

BERNARD H THORPE
and ELLIOT THORPE

Grosvenor House
Publishing Limited

Front cover art by Steve Caldwell www.steve-caldwell.co.uk

This book is published by
Grosvenor House Publishing Ltd
Link House
140 The Broadway, Tolworth, Surrey, KT6 7HT.
www.grosvenorhousepublishing.co.uk

A CIP record for this book
is available from the British Library

ISBN 978-1-78623-365-3

"How would I like to be remembered? Well, I guess that I did my best to hopefully please everybody; that I was a nice guy, and that's about it. What more could anyone want? It's been a grand life."
DEAN MARTIN

"*Cool is as cool does*. Dean Martin was the epitome of that statement. A distinctive vocal ability and effortless grace have made Dean an icon for the ages."
MICHAEL BUBLÉ

"Why do you go on about this Dean Martin chap, son? He's never likely to ever contact you. It's just a phase you're going through. You'll forget all about him in a few months."
HENRY THORPE (*circa* 1956)

Acknowledgements

The authors wish to thank their family and:

Mark Adams, Steve Caldwell, Vincenzo Carrara, John Chintala, Rhea Dingess, Barnaby Eaton-Jones, Kent Edens, Hal Espinosa, the team at Grosvenor House Publishing, Rich Little, George Daniel Long, Linda Nagle, Mathew Todd;

BBC Essex, Michael Bublé, Croydon Advertiser, Roger de Courcey, Tony Fisher, Luke Foxwell, Del Fuller, Ian Gallagher, Robert Hammond, Nicholas Hollands, Jayne Kempsey, Danny Kissane, Sharon Reid, Emerian Rich, Steve Scruton, Michael Tingley, Rosemary Tingley, Uckfield FM, Uckfield News, Tony Williams, Andy Worden;

All of the record, film, television, and production companies, artists, producers, managers, and directors who have ever worked with Dean Martin over the decades...all the other organisations and people (who are too numerous to mention individually) who have assisted us and the Dean Martin Association (and vice versa) over the years;

The Dean Martin Family - thank you for all that you have done and continue to do.

Dedications

For Dino. In memoriam.

Bernard H Thorpe also dedicates this work to his wife Irene and his children Carole & Elliot and to the memories of his grandparents Maria & Don Pasquale Verrechia and to those of his parents Florinda & Henry.

For my parents. In memoriam.
It is an honour and a privilege to have taken the baton, Dad. Thank you.

Elliot Thorpe also dedicates this work to his children Alexi & Eliza, his sister Carole and to the memories of Dean Martin and Jerry Lewis.

Contents

Part One

Just Dino

Written by Bernard H Thorpe
with Elliot Thorpe
Edited by Linda Nagle

Dino

Dear Bernard:

I must admit that I have not taken much interest in anyone
writing about me, but I guess there must be something there
for you to have been my club President for so many years.
So, I hope your writing will be successful, remember, save a
copy for me.

Your friend

Dino *Dino*
Beverly Hills,
March 1995

Introduction

There is a comment written on a Dean Martin album sleeve that goes like this: *Turning an ear in the direction of the mellow Martin voice is like lifting your face to catch a breeze off the sea on a sweltering day; it beguiles and refreshes and relaxes you.*

Everyone has their own idea of what Dean's voice does – no matter who they are. But there is much more to him than just his voice. He created himself, his own persona. And in the eyes of the public, that persona is uniquely Dean Martin. This is the public willing enough to support and acclaim any artist, but one equally cruel and critical as to quickly discredit them. It's a risk in show-business that what starts as a loving gathering of admirers can so easily turn the other cheek and destroy a career.

But let us not forget that the positive proof of success in Dean's business is not to receive acclaim just once or twice, but to maintain that success in order to stay at the top.

That takes some doing, especially with modern media. So often nowadays, celebrities are created from reality television and that, in many ways, perhaps waters down the skills of truly talented people out there. In Dean Martin's day, that was never an issue – in fact, then, to succeed meant you had to exceed.

Of course, he had as many failures as successes with his share of great happiness and sadness along the way. That's the nature of life, and is not just restricted to the entertainment industry.

There has been much said about how glorious this person or that person is; who can do no wrong; who is perfection personified…all the false accolades that are bestowed upon such personalities as Dean Martin.

But when it all comes to the final reckoning, it's the genuine personality of Dean that shone through - in both his public and private lives.

All people have good and bad attributes that they present to the world, but in his case, he expressed sincerity and kindness in his work, allowing his personal feelings to take their place exactly as they should have done, correctly and diplomatically.

Dean Martin was an expressive, underrated, but sincere vocalist. He was sure there were better singers out there (he name-checked Gigli, Pavarotti and Caruso as those who *could* sing) and was also of the opinion that he himself didn't have the best singing voice there was.

But, sales of his recordings proved otherwise: he had the voice that sold and even today, years after his death, he still has.

Not every song met with resounding success, but Martin tasted a glorious cross-section that gave him the first-hand experience he needed to survive in the hard and fast business of entertaining the fickle public. He had consistency: he sang every song as if it had been written especially for him; in fact, you could never mistake that voice, or think him similar to anyone else. He behaved with cool professionalism on movie sets, cabaret stages, on radio, on television and in recording studios, as if he had done all of those things a million times before.

Yes, it is said that he was not the greatest in the world, but how many personalities had such a wide variety of talents - all packaged into one man?

Dean Martin was the ultimate personality, the total entertainer.

He worked with panache, and had talent and good looks that paid handsomely. That magnetic charm of his, coupled with his attitude to life, certainly attracted many to him.

Dean Martin was never a 'pop' star in the way we've come to understand the term; he didn't have that 'bobbysoxer' or 'swooning' type of adulation in his career, although he did have a large proportion of passionate admiration from millions of people around the world, almost since the day he started.

There has always been that certain amount of quiet sophistication, a gentle, if you like, support and appraisal from his global admirers. And while musical tastes and style have come and gone, returned, and gone yet again, Dean remained a popular choice throughout it all.

He sang just about every song that was offered to him in those early days, presenting them in his own inimitable style. He found his comedy style taking shape as he began a film career with Jerry Lewis. Once that partnership ended, Dean tried all types of parts and characters, choosing a different film company almost every time he made a movie.

Thus, he gained much more practical knowledge, confidence and training, experiencing the moods, methods and ideas of his peers, and the continuation of his regular cabaret and club appearances meant he still had that link with a live audience.

But there was only ever apple juice in that glass.

Dean preferred cabaret work above all else, Vegas being his main focus. The seats were always full and, long after he had left the stage as his theme 'Everybody Loves Somebody' played out, his audience clamoured for more.

He had a high demand on television, his weekly series for NBC garnering viewing figures in their millions, with screenings (including syndication re-runs) virtually every week of the year.

With such saturation, it was very telling that Dean himself projected, in contrast, a laid-back air of sheer relaxation.

"The thing is not to try too hard," he told me. "If there is a chance you can be relaxed and assured in front of your audience, then they will come to accept you and the act you are delivering."

The greatest proof of this was Dean's success; he was someone who made it by working hard while appearing to have a distinct devil-may-care attitude.

"If you are too firm and scripted, there's a danger that you may give off an air of insincerity. The result of that, then, is that perhaps your public will dismiss you for being just too serious. You've got to have fun - otherwise you might as well let them throw dirt on you."

He was not known for hanging around for small talk after his work was completed. He rarely socialised with anyone he was working with, a stance which made getting to know Dean Martin virtually impossible.

"The *real* Dean Martin? Well, this is me just as you see me, I don't put on any act. I can't. This is the real person you see here."

Yet Dean remained, for his entire life, one of the most enigmatic characters imaginable. "Look, I'm not trying to prove anything whatsoever with anyone. I'm singing, working, having a good time and getting paid well for it. Isn't that enough? I do the best I can, I can't do any more than that. I'd like to be remembered as a guy who did his best, pleased a damn lot of people and I hope that'll be what I'll always be remembered for. I sang some songs, acted here and there, but no way would I call myself exceptional. I just hope I did *do* my best for my audiences."

Behind the façade, the public persona, he deplored changes of routine. He had long-term personal managers and staff with whom he kept a very close and exclusive bond. Rightly or wrongly, they shielded from him the burden of problems, of finance and business, allowing him the freedom to enjoy his work and his beloved golf, only matched by his adoration for watching television. It also, in some way, fueled his naivety.

His face was without expression if he was ever hurt or displeased with someone or something. If anyone gained Dean's confidence, it was never questioned, but should the reverse ever have occurred, it came swiftly. That said, he was not given to recrimination with anyone, any issues were dealt with quickly.

He gave the impression that he was aloof, cold and distant: but this is a distortion of the facts. Dean never confided *in* anyone or passed opinions *on* anyone and he flatly resented those who would attempt to spill out their troubles to him.

But where he became aware of a genuine difficulty, he would assist the person in the best way he knew, without any fuss and preferably without anyone ever knowing about it.

He rarely showed appreciation to associates, friends, or even family members. Away from the cameras he seldom shook hands (but when he did, his grip was tremendous), kissed on the cheek or patted on the back. But his loyalty is legendary and his working staff proved that by the long-serving devotion they showed over the years - and this is written from personal experience. The rewards that were not necessarily visible by working for him were truly gratifying and pleasing. When he did something for you, he never expected a thank you, rather he did not *want* to be thanked. Whether this was down to insecurity or embarrassment, only Dean knew.

But I *do* thank Dean. His legacy stands proud, even all these years later, amongst his peers, and that has to be the best tribute to anyone.

Having collected an almost diary-like mass of material on Dean's life since around 1952, many suggested over the years that I should write such a book on his life and career. I had always thought about it, wondering if I could do Dean justice. In 1994, with some trepidation, I finally decided that once I had received Dean's consent that I would try, but knew I, or he, didn't want a 'warts and all' sensationalist, scandal-filled exposé. There is enough of that in the tabloids already and Dean himself had been the target of much ridicule and scorn.

I simply wanted to tell his life story, directly and respectfully.

I was greatly privileged to be supported by this fine person and entertainer. I was immensely proud to call him my friend and this book is my way of saying thank you to him for all of that genuine time and friendship he gave me.

BERNARD H THORPE

1

The crossing was long, arduous, and the Atlantic a cruel mistress at the best of times, but the view from the steamships as they began their final stretch towards the L'isola delle lacrime must have been as exhilarating as it was nerve-wracking.

L'isola delle lacrime: the place the Italians knew as the Island of Tears, and which was known to all as Ellis Island. But while this appeared to convey a sense of despair, for many Italian immigrants it was the beginning of a new life.

One immigrant in particular arrived in 1913, alone but for his professional status as a barber to bring him fortune. Having left Pescara (a fishing village on the north-east coast of Abruzzi, Italy) some weeks before to escape economic hardship, Gaetano Crocetti was just nineteen years of age. His elder brothers Archie and Joseph had already made the journey some years before.

The immigrant officials ordered Gaetano to stand in one line with other men while the women and children stood in another. Unnerving to him and the other new arrivals, many of whom could only speak Italian, it was this strict crowd control that had become a necessity in one of the world's busiest immigration stations.

The medical inspection followed, a harsh but certainly effective method by which to filter the sick, quarantine them, and return them to the immigration process once they were fit and well.

Crocetti had no such concerns. He passed the medical, and the US Public Health Service cleared him for the next stage of the process to become an American citizen, the immigration inspection itself.

This was a far more detailed procedure, almost an interrogation in some ways. Federal Law excluded convicted criminals and extreme radicalists and it was a requirement to understand the person's intention.

With this stage cleared, Gaetano was free to join his brothers in one of the nation's big steel towns, Steubenville. At that time, it was a thriving community and work was readily available.

Before the Great War, the US had moulded itself into a land of freedom and happiness, and all who had passed through the conveyor belt on Ellis Island now looked for that large pot of gold at the end of the stars-and-stripes rainbow.

But Steubenville wasn't quite the land of plenty that Gaetano had hoped for. It wasn't by accident that it was nicknamed 'Little Chicago'. It was rife with gambling, prostitution and illicit liquor. Those in the mills worked hard and played harder; to survive, Gaetano had to adapt to this harsh way of living.

Yet his chosen trade meant he could position himself in the community as a reliable, much-needed figure. The barbershop that ultimately employed him, charging 25¢ for a haircut and shave, gave him the stability he needed.

Avoiding as much as he could the darker side of the town, one that stretched along the banks of the Ohio River, Gaetano, who by now was calling himself Guy in a bid to Americanise himself, met Angela Barra.

Although she was studying in the town's convent at the time of their first date, she had no strong allegiance to her faith that would mean she would ever enter a truly celibate life.

Guy's English was broken and he lacked the confidence to speak his adopted tongue fluently. Conversely, Angela could not speak a word of Italian, even though her parents had arrived on Ellis Island towards the end of the 19th century.

Irrespective of the language barrier, their love didn't so much bloom as explode and, besotted, they married soon after.

By 1914, and with Guy bringing home a respectable $30 a week, Angela gave birth to a son, William.

Life in the US for the Crocettis was comfortable, and both Guy and Angela had managed to accept and understand the American way of life, markedly different to that back in Pescara. Their home at 319 South Sixth Street was their place of solitude

11

as the years went by; as their marriage strengthened, Angela became pregnant again.

But this time, it wasn't so straightforward.

On June 7th, 1917, Angela went into labour, prematurely and with some difficulty. The child was not expected to live and so was baptised almost immediately at St Anthony's church.

Whereas Bill had been given his moniker to reflect his parents' absorption into American society, his new baby brother Dino Paul was so-named to show pride in their Italian heritage.

2

"I was pretty cocky and a mischievous kid." Growing up was tough for Dino, not because of any difficulties in his home life but because the poor neighbourhood was challenging for kids and adults alike. "I felt I had to be."

As a result, times were hard, and not many of the family's possessions were new. Toys and even household items were sometimes hand-me-downs from friends or perhaps from another family they knew.

Further, Dino hated school. He simply couldn't see the point in it. He much preferred playing in the streets and on his bike. True, he could not hold a proper conversation and wasn't Grant Junior High's best student at reading or writing (whenever he ordained to turn up), but somehow - with a lot of assistance from his patient and attentive parents - he made it to Wells High School and, by the age of fourteen, had also attained a height of six feet with a fairly substantial frame. He wasn't your average-looking school boy and, together with dark wavy hair and a typical Roman nose, found that he was turning heads, too.

"I told my father one day that I wanted to leave school. He was pretty bewildered, even though he knew I didn't always go."

Guy, naturally, wanted to know why, and asked if young Dino thought he knew more than the teachers. "Yes," came the determined response, and Guy begrudgingly agreed to pay for his son's initial enrolment at a barber's training school.

"But I wasn't interested in spending the rest of my life cutting hair six days a week."

So instead, after he had left his school in his Tenth Grade in June 1936, his Uncle Joseph gave him his very first job: as an assistant on his milk round.

Five weeks later, he'd had enough and tried his hand in a soda store but boredom quickly set in again and he found a position as a gas station attendant. With more gasoline on the ground and over the vehicles than in them, he soon walked away.

Somewhat desperate, his brother William (although everyone called him *Bill*) managed to wrangle him into the Weirton Steel Mill in West Virginia, quite a drive from Steubenville. Dino tried not to let Bill down and seemed to settle into a routine for a few months.

"A four-ton coil of hot steel narrowly missed me one day. I didn't know if it was me not paying attention or something the other guys had done by accident, but I got out of there like a shot and never went back."

Now unemployed and with little opportunity to earn any income, he fooled around with his old school pals, playing pool, swimming in the Ohio river, with snatches of basketball whenever he had the chance.

But he was very restless, still wandering around town looking at the way the gamblers worked in the bars, and he fell in with a crowd that taught him the ways of pettiness. This society that he found alluring led him to the circle of amateur boxing, specifically under the tutelage of Tony Romano, a small-time time fight manager who convinced Dino there was good money in boxing. Persuaded, nineteen-year-old Dino became a prize-fighter with some enthusiasm, earning the name 'Kid Crochet' in the process. Winning twenty-four out of his thirty bouts as a welterweight, he'd worked himself up as a semi-professional for about ten to twenty dollars a match.

But a bent nose, wrecked hands (his manager knew nothing of properly binding his hands under the gloves) and the misconception that being a boxer would more easily win him girls, fired the restlessness within Dino once more.

He moved to a steady capacity as a delivery boy, but it was bootleg whisky he was carrying around town and occasionally to Canonsburg, Pennsylvania. Dino doesn't recall if his parents truly knew what it was he was doing.

"I prayed a lot in those days," he said, supporting the family's Catholic faith, "and I'm sure they would have called in the priest had they found out, so I got myself a job as a clerk."

But the Rex Cigar Store that employed him was a front for one of Steubenville's biggest gambling houses. It was considered almost routine then that a tobacco store would have a gambling concession and, aside from his normal capacity, Dino would go into the back rooms and watch the big players gamble. He'd stay around and play with the chips and the roulette wheel, learning very quickly how to deal and play cards with expertise. When the store realised that he was beating them at their own game, they made him a croupier.

If you ever saw Dino playing cards or dealing at the tables in Las Vegas or in a film you could see that precise expertise on display.

With his skill at the time, he was earning enough each week to enable him to help pay off his parents' extended mortgage and to get his brother into college. But still, he looked beyond what he had, still pining for something that was missing in his life, leaving him unfulfilled.

Dino used to sing on many an occasion (even during those rare times when he assisted his father in the barbershop), at home or wherever he could - even while at the cigar store.

"Several of my pals used to encourage me to sing almost anywhere and they even would persuade me to sing a song or two at parties. Damn it, it was terrifying but I got up there and did it."

It was these tentative steps in the early 40s that made Dino realise singing was a way to express himself, backed by a small combo that always played at these places, usually at Reeds Mill Roadhouse or Walker's Nightclub.

With his pleasant baritone style, it wasn't long before a bandleader called Ernie McKay offered Dino the position as regular vocalist at Walker's. However, he was in no way impressed or attracted by this offer. "Why would I be? I was already collecting a lot more that the $50 he was offering me."

A combination of legitimate earnings plus those 'extras' he was earning at Rex's cigar store meant he was fetching home in the region of $125 a week.

But his refusal only fuelled a streak of depression.

For the first time, he'd realised what he wanted to do but saw no financial gain in it, instead living day-to-day in a job that was unfulfilling and directionless.

"I didn't want to talk to anyone or anybody. And before I knew it, no one wanted to talk to me. I hated it. It took me a while to start talking to my buddies again and they told me I'd been a fool to not accept McKay's offer. And what they'd been planning behind my back I wasn't happy about but I got around it and accepted it."

Between them, his friends, namely Izzy McGregor, Dom Gilbertoni, Tony Tarantino and Harry Barbra, had been working out a deal in which they would support Dino's singing career, providing he would give them a cut from any future earnings.

"How could I turn that down? I went back to McKay and said yes. But he told me I needed a new name. Nobody could say Crocetti right so Ernie said I was now going to be Dino Martini. I wasn't happy with that but I guess he knew what he was doing."

He stayed with McKay for six months on inland tours and it was on one of those stop-overs that Dino was spotted by another bandleader, Sammy Watkins, who offered him a cool $100 a week.

In a precursor of Dino's future management choices, he signed the contract without reading the small print (much to McKay's chagrin) and was now committed to a seven-year stretch with 10 per cent of his earnings to pay agent fees. Further, Watkins didn't like 'Dino Martini' and wanted a more American-sounding and easier to remember moniker. So, in a change that stayed with him for the rest of his life, 23-year old Dino Crocetti became, to the world, Dean Martin.

One of the Sammy Watkins Band appearances took them to the Hollenden Hotel in Cleveland and it was here that another chapter of Dean's life would begin.

"I just couldn't believe it. There was this girl in the audience. Man, her eyes just sparkled."

Elizabeth Anne McDonald was staying at the hotel with her father and, intent on finding out who she was, Dean purposely kept bumping in to her: in the hotel lobby, down a corridor, in and out of the entrance, just anywhere he could catch a glimpse and even try and talk to her. But Elizabeth, or just Betty, was coy, annoyed and seemingly uninterested in this Italian lounge singer.

"She told me to go away and that I was annoying her. I don't think she ever said she would tell her father! But I saw something behind her brashness and so I just asked her out on a date. She said yes."

Dean and Betty saw much of themselves in each other. They both had a shy confidence about them and didn't hold back in telling people what they thought. She was a few years younger than him and was Irish-born to a liquor manufacturer in Morion, Pennsylvania, and had not travelled very much in her life up to that point, so a mere chance meeting at The Hollenden started off an intense romance.

They'd been dating for three months when Dean told Betty that the band was about to take to the road on a long tour on one-night appearances across the country. This seemed to point to their romance being doomed from quite early on.

Naturally needing the money, Dean had no choice but to prepare himself for working away from home, spending indefinite periods in hotel rooms, on the road, with late nights and all the unaccustomed routines that would come with his new and chosen career and lifestyle.

For Betty, she wanted perhaps more than Dean was able to give her, a settled home-life and stability. But she saw his passion when he was up on stage, and knew that she couldn't suppress him.

For these two lovers, parting seemed like the end of the world. Dean's work was inevitably to stand in their way, and he had chosen his future. However, he wanted Betty so very much, and there was only one solution, however drastic it proved to be.

They went back to Steubenville and Dean promptly showed Betty off to his stakeholder friends who had continually convinced him he was a better singer than he thought he was. With their approval of the dark, Irish girl on his arm, he went home to tell his parents he was getting married.

Mama and Papa Crocetti fully approved of her.

With only a handful of days left before the band started their tour, Dean had another problem: the Catholic Church insisted on the wedding bands being posted for at least six weeks before the ceremony. But luck was on their side and Betty's own priest gave special dispensation for the couple to have an immediate ceremony. The families, friends and the complete Sam Watkins Band all gathered together for the joining of husband and wife the very next day, on October 2nd, 1940 at St. Ann's Church in the McDonalds' home town of Cleveland.

Dean's mother made the bride's dress, and the reception was a fairly grand affair for those days, considering neither party were high earners.

While desperately in love, Betty was not sure of the future herself. Would her new husband be a success? Would he really want to stay in this business? She could obviously not see the course they were both to take but she saw he was happy and accepted the life she had chosen as a band-wife, following Dean around the country, their first stop being Louisville, Kentucky. His attention to the band, however, more often than not overrode his matrimonial responsibilities and he would often stay behind after shows playing cards in his dressing room. Nevertheless, Betty announced to Dean one evening late October 1941 that she was pregnant. Her news didn't make him change his approach and she began to feel somewhat isolated, and that there was only one person truly in the marriage.

Craig was born on June 29th, 1942, but from then on things became increasingly difficult for Betty: Dean was always away on tour, and the little home they'd set up in Cleveland was mostly absent of a father. He was travelling frequently now and even if he was able to go home after a night's performance, he would normally roll in in the small hours, the allure of card-playing never leaving him. Gambling and drinking seemed much more preferable – and fun – than being the family man.

3

One night in 1943, Dean was playing cards with Merle Jacobs, the MCA agent who always organised the band's bookings. He suggested that Dean went out on his own: he was convinced that the days of the Italian-American crooner were not yet at their peak.

"After all, that skinny kid from Hoboken had just made it at the Riobamba so perhaps Merle was on to something," Dean told me. As a result of 'that skinny kid"s success, agents and managers were all scurrying around looking anywhere for Italian 'baritones', ballad singers who could throw a good tune. Merle told Dean he was excellent material for nightclubs.

Dean was convinced, and Merle suggested he tried something in the New York area; he wanted to get known and, after all, if he made it there, he could make it anywhere.

Like most young male singers of that period, he could carry a tune reasonably well and did imitations of Bing Crosby and other popular radio singers, but at the same time developed a pleasant and easy-going style of his own.

Anxiety almost getting the better of him, he did nevertheless go to Club Riobamba at 151, East 57th Street, New York City, taking the stage not long after the same skinny kid had finished his set. The kid was, of course, Frank Sinatra.

That first evening was indelibly engraved on Dean's mind: "I still remember what I was wearing: a light blue dinner jacket and a maroon tie. Damn, I was so nervous that I imagined the audience thought I was singing a rhumba and had castanets hidden in my knees." To make things worse, it was celebrity night and the audience was almost entirely composed of celebrities. "Wherever I looked I saw these famous people looking right back at me. I felt like a fraud."

Unknownst to him, however, a small-time performer was sitting at the bar to avoid the cover charges on the tables. There to watch Sinatra, he was known for miming along to records, an act that didn't seem to show any particular signs of remuneration or recognition. Jerry Lewis was his name and he'd missed Sinatra's performance, not aware that the running order had changed. He didn't ask for his money back.

Instead, he watched, entranced by the sight of this unknown who could sing to an audience so easily and with what seemed such confidence.

Then, sometime later, whilst appearing at Loew's Theatre (where Jerry was also on the bill), Dean was seen to be clutching something in his hand. Curious, Jerry, who had already finished his act and wanted to watch this new singer again, wondered what it was. He later found out that it was a little white crucifix.

In the next few months, Dean and Jerry occasionally crossed paths on their way to dressing rooms or exiting theatres. Jerry was quite taken with this laid-back, easy-going Italian, and Dean often found messages from Lewis scrawled on various dressing-room walls, mirrors, or even on make-up dressers.

'Hi, Dean, I was here, hope you do well,' he would write from time to time.

During Dean's time at the Club Riobamba, Irving Zussman, a public relations man, spoke to him at length and suggested he stay in the New York area for work, meaning he would receive a steady $400 a week, allowing him to move his wife and son into rented accommodation at the London Terrace apartments, some of the finest buildings in Lower Manhattan.

The reviews in the New York press of Dean's Riobamba appearances were abominable. One reported that he wore an ill-fitting tuxedo, had a reasonably fair voice but had a lot to learn, and would seem to be lost without a microphone - and this was one of the kindest.

His audiences dwindled and, after a few weeks, Dean found himself out of work, debts growing, and Betty pregnant for a second time.

They moved to cheaper accommodation but he owed the London Terrace so much in back rent that they claimed a minimum of $30 a week until it was cleared.

Dean sent Betty and Craig to her parents in Pennsylvania to have their second baby. When Claudia was born, her father was appearing in Montreal and unable to get home. He was singing in second-rate clubs (also on the East Coast) and worked his way around numerous venues for months whilst Betty stayed with her parents.

With less than $200 a week coming in now, he was seriously in debt to MCA and everyone else with his cards, gambling and the occasional gratification with women, in no way allowing him to live any sort of reasonable life. He was beginning to wonder if this was all worth the trouble and stress.

Lou Perry, an independent agent of Italian descent, saw Dean at the Riobamba and was sure that this young man had a bright future. A fellow Italian, Dean said that Lou "...was the only guy who seemed to have this idea about me or any faith in me at all."

Dean was tied by contract to MCA but Lou Perry found out that they were only too pleased to dispose of this person from their roster; he was a chain around their neck and they were more than willing to sell Dean to the highest bidder.

Lou's faith was indeed so strong that decided he would buy out Dean's contract, and paid off his debts to clear him completely from MCA.

But Dean had no bookings anywhere, was hopelessly in debt with so many people (including his friends back in Steubenville) and had nowhere to live. Further, his devotion to Betty, Craig and Claudia was far from perfect.

Lou Perry lived in the Bryant Hotel on the corner of 54th Street & Broadway, a low-class hovel of a building catering for the lower-bracket performers in showbusiness. Perry's part of the building was one room with just a double bed and a table, the full sum total of Lou's belongings, but he still took pity on Dean and invited him to share the room. Dean at least now had a roof over his head.

Every so often, devoted Betty would come and see her husband and share some time with him. Lou would discreetly disappear for a while, allowing them to spend a few hours together, but other than the occasional visit, she would see little of her husband.

She was living a sad life, hardly ever seeing Dean, and managing to survive mainly because she happened to be at her parents' home. Her husband only managed to send sporadic amounts by borrowing money from Lou, who was also paying for all of Dean's food, laundry and anything else needed for his day-to-day existence.

But deep down, Lou believed there was talent there, that Dean had that *something*, but needed that stroke of luck to get him going. He stood by Dean, willing to make sacrifices.

"I didn't get what he saw. I was a bum."

One thing Lou thought could improve this young man's looks even more was an operation on his nose. Dean was a reasonably handsome guy, but his nose was rather large and it had seen some action back when he was Kid Crochet. Lou thought the idea of a new nose could maybe work to his advantage, so he managed to borrow enough dollars for a plastic surgeon.

The operation in New York was successful and both Dean and Lou were more than pleased with the result, the young singer feeling a bit more confident now that perhaps his future may turn to better things.

"I kind of hoped this surgery was a turning point. I guess it was."

Meanwhile, back in her uneventful life, Betty was suffering in the atmosphere of her parents' home, and becoming very upset when her parents and friends told her she was a fool. That her husband didn't care that much for her was clear; he rarely supported her in a proper manner.

Angela and Guy Crocetti even offered their home for Betty, and upset, frustrated and with financial problems mounting up, she took the decision to move over to Steubenville for a change of atmosphere, moving in with her parents-in-law.

She told Dean to make more effort with her and the children, but he wasn't interested. He had enveloped himself in appearances and had found the attention from female followers to be rewarding. He wasn't faithful to Betty and his gambling never wavered.

In his head, he simply didn't have time to be a husband and a father.

Then he got drafted for military service.

He was stationed at Akron in Ohio in training for fourteen months, and hated every minute of it until the army doctors discovered he had developed a hernia. He did not actually leave the base during his tenure so never saw active service, as such. Instead, he came out rather pleased with his invalidity and went home at last to his family.

Perhaps it was due to a shortage of artists because of America's part in WWII, or just sheer luck, but by 1945 he had put in so many appearances locally and places further afield such as Chicago, New Jersey and the like, that he never brought in less than $250 a week. He peaked at $1000 a week.

Perhaps Lou's faith in him was not unfounded after all.

This was way above anything New York had given him overall, but he was still in debt, with hordes of people chasing him. Family life was not at its best either, letting Betty have money as and when he could spare any to send back home – his situation had improved but the way he lived his life hadn't altered one iota.

Dean wore a camel-hair coat in those days, and it proved to be something of a beacon, certainly as far as one particular person was concerned.

He was leaving the Belmont Plaza one lunchtime and spoke a few words as usual with the doorman. Walking nearby was 19-year old Jerry Lewis.

Jerry, of course, remembered Dean from the Riobamba. Dean didn't even notice Jerry was there at the Plaza, and Jerry never got the chance to say anything.

That camel-hair coat, or rather the man inside it, was the path to Jerry's new world – but neither of them knew it.

On a cold March morning sometime later, Dean and Lou were walking down Broadway. Lou, knowing, of course, most of the talent in the area, spotted singer Sonny King on the other sidewalk. As they crossed Forty-Ninth Street, Lou called out to Sonny, beckoning him over. But Sonny wasn't alone. Lou introduced Dean to the singer, then turned to Sonny's companion.

"Jerry Lewis, meet Dean Martin. Dean, meet Jerry."

4

Dean had thought that Jerry was a bright little kid, but hadn't thought much more about him since their occasional brushes past each other over the last few months. Other than those notes that Jerry had left Dean here and there, neither of them had had time to really talk to each other, and Dean had been somewhat dismissive before: they moved in different circles, and their acts were miles apart.

Sonny King suggested they all get together for a drink one evening.

It was Dean who did most of the talking, spilling out much of his past history for what it was worth, all the while Jerry hanging on to his every word, enthralled by his new-found friend's exploits.

These were strange times: both men were only just starting out and getting to know who they were themselves, let alone exposing their respective talents to the world.

Yet here they were, in Sonny's rooms, performing for each other. Sonny and Lou had both thought each of their acts was good in his own right, although all four of them knew there was one hell of a way to go before any substantial sort of success would be realised.

Jerry had more or less been performing since he was six (his father Danny was in vaudeville), so it was natural for him to have ambitions of becoming a star, but thirteen years later, Joseph Levitch was still struggling to be as internationally famous as Jerry Lewis.

As a kid, Dean had also had big ambitions of getting somewhere and being somebody, but after a routine life of playing around with his school buddies, owning his first bike (even if it was second-hand) and a brief period as a Boy Scout for Steubenville Troop Ten (where he was the troop drummer) he still wondered, even now, what would become of his dreams.

"I liked playing cowboys when I was a kid. I loved playing the drums – but I was never gonna be a Buddy Rich – and I loved to sing. Sure, I'd spin Russ Columbo and Bing Crosby records on my wind-up player and sing along with them but, man, I still wish I could sing like Bing."

Dean found singing an easy way to express himself and Lou still had that faith in him, so much so that he secured a brief recording contract with Diamond Records.

Although Dean's first recorded performance was in Chicago, August 1944, with the Jerry Sears orchestra on a radio show, 'All of Me' became his debut commercial 78rpm single.

"I think we sold about eight copies! I'm sure they put the hole in the side of the disc instead of in the middle!" he later joked, but you could already hear the strength he had as a recording artist. Accompanied by Nat Brandywine and his Orchestra, Dean's tonal approach was pitched lower than his later output, but listening to those early recordings, they have that clearly definable and very recognisable Dean Martin sound.

The original issue of 'All of Me' (recorded July 15th, 1946) is now of course an extremely rare collector's item.

Metro-Goldwyn-Mayer and Columbia Pictures both showed some interest in this new singer, with a view to him appearing in musicals. This genre was a great money-spinner at that time and guaranteed international exposure for the artists once those films had been seen around the world.

But both companies rejected him: it seemed that he did not have the correct phrasing and speed when he read the scripts given him and, in fact, some later reports stated he was almost illiterate and just could about hold a conversation.

Lou managed to book him into the Glass Hat in the Belmont Plaza, where Jerry was appearing on the bill. He was presenting his usual mime act with records and still remained unsuccessful.

Dean and Jerry's paths didn't cross that much during the few weeks Dean was booked there and, once his tenure had finished, he was out of work once more. Meanwhile, Jerry had moved on to the 500 Club in Atlantic City, continuing his act.

But Jerry was unhappy with the faltering start of his career and was desperate to improve.

He'd been corresponding with Dean by postcard and, when Paul 'Skinny' D'Amato (the club's owner, so-named because of his stick-thin silhouette that made even Jerry look overweight) threatened to end Lewis' run, Jerry immediately thought of Dean.

He suggested to Abner J. Greshler (his own agent) if Dean could be booked in there for work, thinking that somehow, they could support each other's solo acts.

Abbey agreed and Dean arrived July 25th, 1946 in Atlantic City.

But Skinny thought Dean was terrible on his own, almost as bad as Jerry was, and suggested they either do something together or they'd be out on the street.

Dean and Jerry went to their dressing room (a nail on the wall!) and tried to think about what could be done.

Jerry had always been highly creative and so it's no surprise that it was he who came up with the initial, albeit crude, idea of Dean simply starting to sing while Jerry would follow and make a 'lot of noise' as he put it.

"Jerry put on this busboy's jacket and out he came. He'd juggle, run around off-stage, throw dishes, drop trays while I sang. We'd just create chaos."

Amongst the still and cautious audiences was Sophie Tucker, a Ukrainian-born American singer/comedian otherwise known by the nickname 'The Last of the Red-Hot Mamas', and upon her laughing out loud, this was the cue for the rest of the public to laugh at this pair of lunatics with their act.

And laugh they did: Jerry went mad turning over customers' empty (and full) plates; switching off all the lights so that the waiters dropped even more trays; squirting soda down the girls' blouses; cutting off the men's ties – and ended up getting most of them to join up together to make a long conga line.

With a look of horror and shock on Skinny's face, everyone loved them and patrons were queueing up right around the block every night, waiting to see this madcap pair everyone was raving about.

Skinny made the pair do their act six times a night, upped their salary to $750 a week and kept them there for six weeks.

Dean and Jerry themselves would even come up with inventive ways to bring more people to see them: Jerry made out to be drowning off shore one afternoon, and Dean rushed to his 'rescue'. With crowds gathered, including the lifeguard, they'd both jump and declare to everyone that they were at the 500 Club that night!

They had blasted themselves on to the scene and it seemed that nothing could stop them.

5

With World War II over, people were looking for some pleasure and difference in their lives and live entertainment was, whilst a luxury, certainly a prime objective.

Martin & Lewis perfectly filled the bill; they arrived just at the right time and were able to realise those dreams for their audiences. But there was a problem: Dean was tied to his contract with Lou Perry for another couple of years yet, so they could not call themselves a team or even a working partnership.

They were in the Havana Madrid on $1,500 a week, split evenly, and following their raging success in Atlantic City, Abbey got them into Latin Casino in Philadelphia. But Dean was billed on the top spot with Jerry as the extra attraction, most likely Lou's doing, something that Abbey was not happy about.

When I asked him what happened with Lou, Dean wouldn't be drawn on the subject but clearly some behind-the-scenes wrangling meant that Abbey Greshler was, before long, in full charge of the act, with a $4,000 pay-off to Lou.

'Martin and Lewis' was born.

All the help and assistance Lou had given Dean in the formative years had kept him from many debtors, but now it was big money coming in and things were going to be so different from now on.

Dean had become a father for the fourth time (their third child, Gail, had been born on April 11th, 1946). Deana had arrived August 27th, 1948 and, although he saw Betty as often as he could, things were still far from pleasant in their family. He was spending almost ninety percent of his time away from home and although the family was better-supplied with money now that Dean was fast approaching the big time, this did not compensate for his lack of devotion.

Work came thick and fast, including radio shows --which gave them an even wider audience --and Dean found that as well as the public liking him for his comedy, he particularly noticed the applause he received when he did his uninterrupted solo songs.

His first love was singing, and from time-to-time, he privately considered whether he would ever make it to a recording studio again. "Those previous early attempts of mine had proved totally useless and I really thought that they were most likely lost in some vault somewhere."

He organised the move for Betty and the children to New York, enabled by a much-improved income (at one time $15,000 a week, the radio contract giving Dean his half-share of the £30,000 Martin and Lewis were earning). Television also beckoned and their debut on Ed Sullivan's 'Toast of The Town' on June 20th, 1948 was followed by their appearance at the Copacabana which sealed their success: two or three lines of people wrapped twice around the block, absolutely desperate to see these two talented and marvellous entertainers with a brilliant new, outrageous approach.

Variety, the trade tabloid, gave them accolades and sometimes gave Dean a better review of his tonsils than they did of the team. Chesterfield-sponsored radio shows ran for ten weeks, and more TV spots followed – including the famed 7pm Sunday night 'Colgate Comedy Hour' and every show caused havoc and jammed telephone switchboards all over the country.

Even in those early days, Abbey was also convinced, just like Lou Perry before him, that Dean could become great on his own, but everyone demanded the double act: they wanted the singer, yes, but they also wanted the comedy act.

With Betty and the children now in a ten-room rented apartment, things were really looking up in many ways; she had become great friends with Jerry and his new wife Patti. The four would frequently spend time together and go out dining Italian.

But while on the road, Dean was not too hesitant in dating any girl his brown eyes noticed wherever and whenever he wanted.

He naturally left a trail of broken hearts in various places, with one instance of a certain Miriam Davelle who had followed him around as far as California. She later committed suicide, although no explanation was ever found suggesting any affair or connection with him at all, other than media gossip.

Nevertheless, Dean's libido never wavered and Jerry, disapproving, would on occasion mention his partner's flirtations to Patti.

Money seemed little object now and he had already moved his parents over to Long Beach in California and wanted to do the same with Betty. He felt that a move to California would be ideal for his career and had never really liked the East, particularly New York.

It was now 1948.

While working at Slapsie Maxie's in Hollywood, both Jerry and Dean began talking to one of the owners, Mack Gray, Dean pointedly mentioning his Diamond recordings. That September, Gray secured him a new recording contract with Capitol.

Martin and Lewis were highly-acclaimed, and considered at the top of their game now, and being based in Hollywood meant they attracted people like Cary Grant, Edward G. Robinson, Bette Davis and Darryl F Zanuck. They also had renowned brothers Dick and Joe Stabile and their orchestra backing them.

But amidst all the glitz and glamour, Dean's marriage was, unsurprisingly, in trouble. His affairs with other women was becoming out of hand, although one in particular had caught his heart. "She'd won the title of 'Queen of the Orange Bowl' and I presented her with a huge bouquet of flowers on that New Year's Eve [1948]. I fell in love with her there and then."

Nineteen-year old Jeanne Biegger was an art teacher at Miami University and Dean spent as much time as he could with her, incredibly avoiding Hollywood gossip columns. But Patti and Jerry knew, and had decided to keep this romance as far from Betty as they could.

Joseph Hazen (business partner to Hal Wallis, who had produced *Casablanca*, *Now, Voyager*, and *The Maltese Falcon* among others) had seen the Martin and Lewis act and signed the pair to a five-year contract for seven films at $100,000 a picture. Further, both Hazen and Wallis agreed to allow them to freelance one picture a year for their own company, York Productions, that Dean and Jerry had set up a few weeks back. This meant they were able to make their own films whenever they wished, agreeing that distribution would be through Paramount Pictures. Such was the faith in this double-act.

Yet Hal Wallis admitted that he had only seen Dean and Jerry live, and not limited by a script. He'd recently bought the rights from CBS Radio to the very successful comedy series 'My Friend Irma' and, after much discussion and screen-tests (nine on Jerry's part, mainly because the original radio stories didn't lend themselves to the physical comedy Jerry did), roles were pencilled in for both stars.

Released in 1949 and directed by George Marshall, who'd cut his teeth on silent movies, *My Friend Irma* tells the story of Irma (Marie Wilson) and Jane (Diana Lynn), two working girls who room together in Mrs O'Reilly's apartment house. Ambitious Jane wants to marry a millionaire and lands a job as a secretary to one, Richard Rhinelander (Don DeFore), who falls for her. Irma loves Al (John Lund), an unemployed dreamer who wants to get rich quick and easy (via Rhinelander). Al meets two talented performers, Steve (Dean) and Seymour (Jerry) and promotes them to Broadway. Meanwhile, Irma, an incessant bungler, tries to help everyone.

Filmed on a budget of $500,000, it made over $3 million. Martin and Lewis' film career had begun in earnest.

But at home, for Dean, things had finally crumbled. He had no hate for Betty but had fallen out of love with her. His infidelity had fuelled that, but he admitted that he'd fallen so hopelessly in love with Jeanne that he was prepared to make the break from his wife forever.

Usual US marriage laws in the 1940s stated that persons had to wait one year for a divorce to become final before any further marriage can take place, but Jeanne and Dean were so impatient that they actually asked Elizabeth if she would mind going to Nevada for a special 'quickie' divorce. After eventual consultation with her lawyer, Betty agreed and left for Las Vegas, the four children in care of Dean's parents.

Angela and Guy were deeply upset by the decision and manner of their youngest son. Their disappointment plain, string-willed Dean had, nevertheless, made up his mind – and that was that, no discussion.

Betty and Dean were divorced August 24th and just over a week later, on September 1st, 1949, Jeanne Biegger legally bound herself to Dean at Herman Hover's Beverly Hills home. Jerry was best man. (Hover was the owner of Giro's, a venue where Dean and Jerry had appeared countless times with great success.)

The newlyweds moved into a large house on the corner of Lomitas and Alpine Drive in Beverly Hills – but there was no honeymoon. Dean's time with his new wife was spent on a mad, rushed tour around the country promoting *My Friend Irma*.

Was this already a case of history repeating itself, with Dean focusing so much time on his career?

Although his first-ever Capitol release, 'The Money Song,' was with Jerry, Dean managed to record a few songs…which one could say more 'escaped' than were released: not exactly gems for him to be enthralled about, but singles that certainly increased his bank balance.

Every little helped, of course, because payments now had to be made regularly to Betty in addition to the payments towards the debts that had occurred in the earlier years of his career.

Now in the millionaire class, Dean and Jerry had a good footing in order to gain more confidence, and while the pair were carrying on their publicity for …*Irma*, Paramount were working on their next film appearance.

Abbey was also pushing hard at NBC Television for them to appear on the network, because although Martin and Lewis were box-office smashes nationwide, broadcasting had not really boosted them nationally and he felt the time was now ripe for them to be presented across all states; the films and records would do their own thing around the world, but this fairly new medium of television reached people in their homes.

True, their debut had caused a stir, but Abbey wanted regular appearances, as many as possible, to promote hard the image of these two talented men.

Paramount moved forward to make *My Friend Irma Goes West* in 1950, with Dean's Capitol contract letting him have most of the songs he would sing in future films issued on that label as a matter of course. This was a good way for Dean to have a double-dose of remuneration, something he was to continue to do for almost his entire film career.

This sequel again starred Marie Wilson, Diana Lynn with John Lund, and listed Martin and Lewis as supporting cast with guest star Corrine Calvet. Hal Walker directed this time, and it followed much of the same storyline as the previous film with the luckless Irma helping those around her. A Hollywood film tycoon signs up Steve and Seymour, but turns out to be a racketeer.

Both films had that scatty comedy approach, where the established stars were somewhat overshadowed by the new comedy team; indeed, you just watched for those first moments when Dean and Jerry appeared on the screen.

Dean and Jerry continued to make various appearances and publicity tours to build up their very popular image even more. Dean always went along with the tremendous amount of practical jokes and antics that his partner Jerry got up to at different times and places. Their regular orchestra leader Dick Stabile was their favourite target and over a short period he had lost eight tuxedos, which were quite literally destroyed during part of the nightclub act. His shoes, he found very often glued to the ceiling in the dressing room. Jerry was the main instigator of these drastic ideas, but Dean was just as bad (or good, depending on the mood of the victim and the situation), such as the instance when they were in an office on Broadway and yelled out the window to the crowds below that they were being murdered. Naturally, the police arrived and had to smash the door down, only to find Dean and Jerry sitting reading magazines.

That was the happy, odd madness of Martin and Lewis, America's favourite pair. No one was safe from their pranks (which all helped with publicity as well, of course) not even the Paramount top executives, even practising jokes on each other.

This attitude, mixed with their presentation, was what made the team tick; it was totally unique. No one could come anywhere near the art and finesse that was Dean and Jerry. It was all a part of a pleasant history that happened in my own lifetime and I am so glad to have been there at the start, watching Dean's fledgling career with adoration.

With Dean now recording such songs as 'I'll Always Love You', 'Rock-A-Bye Your Baby' and others, he was beginning to be noticed by the record-buying public. His initial attempts at Capitol were marred by the musicians' strike in 1948, where he travelled with Jerry to Mexico to lay down the tracks.

But his recordings after that were all recorded at the Capitol Tower in Hollywood and Vine, a magnificent and unique structure on the Californian skyline that looked like a pile of discs on top of each other.

York Productions commenced operations with *At War With the Army* partly financed through Screen Associates, organised by Abbey. Dean and Jerry's natural top billing allowed them more screen time. Released in January 1951, as song-and-dance pals prior to drafting, Puccinelli (Dean) and Korwin (Jerry) clash when they become Sergeant and Private respectively. A slim story but nevertheless one that allowed Dean to showcase his singing talents. Dick Stabile had a part in this film as Pokey, with Hal Walker directing plus Mack David and Jerry Livingston writing the songs. Dean's girlfriend in this little romp was Polly Bergen, who would also make a name for herself later.

The Stooge went into production just prior to *At War With the Army* but stayed on the Paramount shelf for some time. Directed by Norman Taurog, Jerry played Ted, the stooge to Dean's conceited variety singer, Bill, and in a plotline that would repeat itself over most of their pictures together, the two conflicting characters would reconcile at the finale. Polly Bergen would return to accompany them.

And Dean was neglecting Jeanne.

Touring, filming, recording, or playing golf (a pastime he had been introduced to by Lou Perry and which easily countered his hatred of confined spaces, having been stuck in an elevator or two in his time - giving rise to his claustrophobia), Dean left her alone many times in the first phase of their marriage. Further, he had begun to detest parties and meeting people, and had no real friends. Jeanne was also being snubbed by Patti Lewis, who had seen what Betty had gone through.

But Jerry told Patti that Dean was his best friend and that he loved him, so Patti eventually came around to Jerry's way of thinking and relented in her animosity towards Jeanne.

But Dean was so very much a loner. He worked the way he wanted to, but any spare time he did have, he spent watching television at home (or, of course, playing golf). He just didn't want to be involved with any problems that arose with arranging recording dates or his next call time on a film set – he just wanted to know where and when to turn up. Even domestic chores disinterested him.

6

In those days, even the great powerhouse film-makers Metro-Goldwyn-Mayer showed an interest in Dean for their musicals, but he never even got the opportunity for screen tests, the reason being given that 'there are too many other Italian crooners about'.

By 1951, Dean himself was earning around $80,000 a year, but still had to pay out approximately half of that amount to Betty. Troubles surmounted when Dean and Jerry were reminded by the Inland Revenue that they owed five years' back-taxes, which came as a diabolical shock to both partners as they both understood that Abner Greshler had been dealing with their finances and tax payments.

Dean was worse off than Jerry. He'd already filed for bankruptcy in January 1949 and, with his success, all of his previous associates had suddenly re-appeared, suing him for back payments never received, or in relation to contracts that Dean had signed over the last handful of years without bothering to look at the large print, let alone the small wording.

Sam Watkins, Xavier Cugat, Lou Costello and numerous others all had debts owing to them from Dean, some going back to his cigar store days. He had signed, too, individual contracts with three different record companies (prior to Capitol Records) so that he could have a cash advance each time. He would record a few songs (sometimes just two) for one label, then go on to another company and possibly do the same thing again and not bother to keep track of what he had recorded and where. Some of these early efforts have now been lost in the mists of time. And while some have appeared since, Dean himself had no idea what some of the songs were, or where or when he even recorded them.

But these debts had to be paid somehow, some of it jointly by Dean and Jerry, but some of it was 'worked off', as in one case

37

when Dean had delivery of a brand-new Cadillac and it was claimed back; only for the fact that Harold Kopler gave Dean $6,000 on the understanding that he and Jerry play his Chase Club in St. Louis (which they gladly did!).

In the midst of all the many commitments, Jeanne announced that she was pregnant and that the baby would be due later that year. Dean had already arranged that his four children with Betty would move in to his home, to be looked after by Jeanne. He had claimed that his former wife was not capable of looking after their children in a proper and reasonable way, and a fairly strict discipline was in order from Jeanne; she knew she had to be firm with the four children already growing up, and with her first due soon.

Dean, naturally, as was normal for him, left all the details of day-to-day routines to his wife, whilst he carried on with his career.

Dean and Jerry became very concerned with their business affairs. *At War With the Army* had earned them nothing, and any fees from stage appearances and record sales were being swallowed up with debt.

Martin and Lewis came to a decision: they both decided once and for all to be rid of Abner J. Greshler.

No one ever really knew why Abbey had behaved this way to them. Greed, perhaps?

But whatever, there was no need to cause themselves any more worry or concern over this matter. They had been together now for over five years and the work could only be called magnificent for them both, with much more than they could ever hope to accomplish in their lifetimes.

Television was now beginning to attract the pair, too. They had felt previously that the time was not right, but after several talks with NBC, they appeared as guests on various shows, amongst them the famous and renowned Milton Berle Show, plus numerous guest spots elsewhere. They even headlined their own *Martin & Lewis Show*.

But within himself, even after several years working with his very talented partner, Dean wanted out, to be on his own.

He frequently became frustrated and annoyed with Jerry taking much more interest in the behind-the-scenes work that went on when making a film or television show. That was Jerry's ambition--he wanted to get more involved with the production side of their partnership and much time was spent behind the camera, sometimes suggesting major changes in the making of their films with the producer and directors.

"I was hanging around for the next shot but Jerry was there telling everyone else how to do it. Even my parts were getting less and less important than Jerry's."

Arguments came up between the two. Jerry could see Dean's point of view, but he still insisted on being behind the camera, and wanted more time in working behind the scenes as well as being in the picture with his partner.

There was increased annoyance and more frustration from Dean on the set of *That's My Boy*, their fifth film together, in August 1951. With a bad atmosphere on set, the pair argued frequently and rarely saw eye-to-eye with the numerous suggestions that Jerry made.

Sadly, the truth of the matter was that Dean wanted to go solo; he wanted to be able to do his own things when he sang and made films and he could see nothing here that would improve that situation for him personally.

'Today's top-line comedians: funnier than ever!' ran the original press release for the movie, giving no hints of the friction that was gaining momentum. Hal Walker returned for directing duties, guiding Dean and Jerry against the odds to tell the tale of an ace football player (Eddie Mayehoff) who is disappointed with his hopeless son, Junior, played by Jerry. Dean would play the crooning football coach who would turn Junior's life around.

'Their best yet!' played to packed houses all over the States but Dean wasn't feeling it. The press remarked again that he was 'a likeable fella with a fairly pleasant voice' whilst Jerry got rave reviews for his comedy antics.

Nevertheless, at the same time and in contradiction to his own frustrations, he was content to let Jerry do all the arrangements and organisation for them both, while he carried on with his work and playing golf as much as he could: a trait Dean had had in the early part of his career and which he carried on until he retired.

He wanted to plan his future, but let the others carry it out for him, as long as it went the way he wanted it.

The *Martin and Lewis Show* on NBC was doing well, as were their films, but Dean's recording output was not yet making many people sit up and take note. True, as they all said, he did have a likeable and pleasing sound, but that did not see too much of an income from Capitol. Dean, though, was using the expertise and facilities of musicians such as Lou Busch, Paul Weston and Frank DeVol whenever Dick Stabile was not available.

It was the later recordings that were to regularly use Dick's accompaniments for the bulk of Dean's output, more or less until 1959, when Gus Levene and Nelson Riddle were to complete his repertoire for Capitol until he left the label in 1960.

Meanwhile, Jeanne and Dean's first baby, Dean Paul Jr, came along on November 17th, 1951.

At Sea With the Navy (an intended follow-up to *At War With the Army*), was released in 1952 but not before it was retitled *Sailor Beware*. The film itself once again showed the cream of the partnership against the backdrop of the US Navy, with Jerry's character having a peculiar allergy to cosmetics and Dean's suffering from a weak knee. 'Start nineteen-fifty-two the Right Way…the Martin and Lewis Way!' screamed the publicity slogan, and it seemed that indeed the Martin and Lewis machine had no intention of letting up.

Jumping Jacks came off the production schedules next, in July 1952, featuring Robert Strauss again, and Mona Freeman. The movie had Jerry, as Hap Smith, sneaking onto an army base to help his Corporal pal Chick Allen (Dean) provide some entertainment for the troops.

One of the stuntmen on this production needed an expensive operation following an accident, which Dean and Jerry paid for in full, something this pair were to do for many years hence.

Not so hilarious was the Martin household.

With baby Dean Jr, Jeanne was well involved with domestic chores and family organisation. Although the Martins were now in a nice position to be able to afford staff at home to cope with the many and varied situations in running a family home, Jeanne liked to be directly involved with what was going on, the stark opposite to her husband.

Jeanne managed well, even though Dean Snr was still noticeably absent.

The *other* marriage in Dean's life, that of Martin and Lewis, was ever more fractious: Jerry would involve himself deeper and deeper in production while Dean, admittedly working harder than ever too, would simply get out as soon as shooting was finished for the day.

Those arguments that had only happened occasionally, became more frequent, but Dean and Jerry maintained a pleasant facade to the ever-clamouring public: Dean was the handsome man who always got the girl while was Jerry the clown who always seemed to create havoc in whatever he did.

They'd done a mere ten-minute segment in the 1952 Columbia feature *Hollywood At Play* plus a cameo in the Bing Crosby/Bob Hope film *Road To Bali* and many more special appearances, and *The Stooge* was finally released in February 1953.

Jerry was making a handful of recordings, with moderate success, but then his recordings were only in moderate quantities, even when he did the occasional duet with his partner.

Dean, on the other hand, was now beginning to see his recordings sell in large numbers for Capitol. This was exactly what he had always wanted: that he could perhaps make a career of singing at last, his original ambition many years back in Steubenville when he was a teenager.

The record executives knew that they had a popular singer on their books and he recorded many, many songs for them, not all great, but providing Dean with more and more valuable time in the studio, as well having film-acting experience alongside Jerry.

Even in those days, Dean cracked jokes whilst recording and it was always a popular event when word got out that he was at Capitol in Hollywood. He took his work very seriously but, at the same time, put in those light-hearted quips which always made him very popular with the musicians, technicians and anyone else who was lucky enough to have been there in those studios at that time. Some of those instances have since been made available on such commercial releases as the remastered 'A Winter Romance' and the 2012 concept album 'Forever Cool'.

It was this unique and pleasing attitude that made Dean Martin popular with everyone he ever worked with and, while this was prevalent *at* his work, his home life was somewhat different.

A lot of the friction between Dean and Jerry, and the problems that arose as a result, spilled over when he got home to Jeanne. Many times, he took it out on her with arguments and experienced fits of depression, where he would go to a room in the house to be by himself, and would not speak to anyone for hours. At this particular time, Jeanne and Dean separated; she went home to her mother and Dean spent some of this time to try to get something cleared if he could with Jerry. Although they spoke about these problems, and Jerry was upset that his friend had split with his wife, nothing came of their differences. A few days later, husband and wife were both back home, having settled their problems for the time being.

7

On March 3rd, 1954, Dean and Jerry came perilously close to a parting of the ways.

The volcano of tensions that had been angrily bubbling away finally erupted into a crisis at the winter headquarters of the Clyde Beatty circus in Phoenix, Arizona. Here, the top comedy team of their generation had been on a 2-month location shoot for *Three Ring Circus*.

"I was sick and tired of playing stooge to that crazy mixed-up character," Dean said.

Conversely, Jerry said at the time that he was *"...fed up of [Dean's] sensitivity. Everything I do is wrong! Anything that happens that he doesn't like, he blames me. He hates me. He's got a chip on his shoulder."*

For nine days, both men sulked, refusing point-blank to talk to each other until March 12th when a truce conference was set up in the Beverly Hills office of MCA. Tempers were somewhat soothed and a statement was issued that they intended to remain in partnership. Then, when Dean wasn't invited to Jerry's birthday party, whispers started expanding across Hollywood. Experts and critics gave them anywhere from three months to a year before Martin & Lewis would dissolve for good.

I asked Dean if he had felt at the time that the partnership really was washed up.

"Listen, I want to be honest with you. If people would only have left us alone back in those days, then maybe Jerry and I wouldn't have had any trouble. Sure, we had a blow-up in Phoenix and I guess you'd say it was kind of tough but we'd had them before. I hated the trip to London, too. When we did the Palladium. I don't know if it was because of what was going on. Do you know any two people who didn't sometimes have their arguments or fall out? It was like I was married to the kid.

"If Jerry and I had been in the hardware business or running a hamburger-and-root-beer joint on Ventura Boulevard, nobody would have had any interest in our spats. But because we were who we were, I guess it was big news.

"Now you write this part down, Bernard, word for word just like I say it: I felt then that individually, going it alone, we would never be as great as we were together. When we shook hands on our partnership, I said in my heart that it was forever, until death do us part. I really believed that."

And then Dean spoke at great length about Jerry's talent and it was clear to me all these years later that he still saw that spark in him.

"Jerry is more than a wild crazy guy. Like any comedian he can project sadness and pathos. There's nobody living who can play a scene like he does. What I learnt about acting and timing and how to make an audience break up...it's all from being with Jerry. Yeah, sometimes he made a mistake. I guess he probably still does. Hell, I know I do. But I just wanted all these people to leave us alone, to allow us to keep going."

Jerry's feelings towards Dean not long after the truce said much about his relationship with the Italian, saying ...*the closer you are to a person, the deeper the feelings, and if they are hard feelings, they hit twice as hard. If you're emotional like Dino and I are, well, you can't help flipping your lid sometimes. Instead of us settling arguments in private, we yell at each other in public and then everyone says we're gonna bust up – but never in a million years! We're a real partnership: people have the idea I'm the clown and Dino's the straight-man but it's wrong. He has the same amount of jokes that I do, it's just a different style of putting them over. But we're both essential to each other's success.*

Outside of my wonderful wife, Dino is the closest friend I have. When I was young I was a lonely, unhappy kid and didn't have any brothers or sisters or any friends until I met him. Now to me, he's the best man in all the world – that's why our act is good – only because of the friendship between us. You think I'm crazy enough to throw this partnership out of the window?

For years, Dean's recording career had never properly made its mark, then suddenly, with 'That's Amore' from 1953's *The Caddy*, he had a two-million copies seller on his hands (in fact, it became a requisite part of his subsequent live stage acts even though, ironically, Dean became to detest the song).

At once, movie studios and recording executives began to sing a siren call in his ears. *You could be as great as Bing [Crosby] if Jerry wasn't holding you down,* they said. *Get rid of this ball and chain and you'll be playing romantic leads in pictures; you'll have more hits; you'll be your own star. Why let Lewis plan your career for you?*

Ordinarily, these arguably malicious remarks would have fallen on deaf ears. But by the time of the rift, the seeds dropped into fertile soil: in *Three Ring Circus*, Dean's part was so small as to be almost invisible. He came on set to sing a few songs, and that was it. He had virtually no part in the story and for the first two weeks on location he had nothing to do; he saw a local magazine that ran a feature of *Living It Up*, displaying a publicity still of co-star Sheree North between Dean and Jerry – except the editors had cropped Dean out of the photograph. He strolled one afternoon into Jerry's trailer and found professional photographers taking pictures of his partner.

"I thought I was the fifth wheel. If I wasn't important to the act any more, I just wish Jerry had had the guts to let me know. 'Say the word' I used to say to him. I wanted it to be over but dammit, I kept going."

In fairness, the truce did turn things around, albeit temporarily.

Jerry approached Hal Wallis and insisted he would not continue making pictures unless Dean's part was expanded to equal stature with his, a demand Wallis met. Yet Lewis had an almost maniacal compulsion to work, pushing out three movies a year, doing regular television, constant engagements in night clubs and personal appearances as far as Europe. This desire clashed head-on with Dean's easy-going, shrug-of-the-shoulder attitude. He deliberately left all the decisions to Jerry, content to make one movie a year and record some records. This of course meant that whenever Jerry made, in Dean's eyes, a bad decision, Dean found himself forced to go along with it. Therein was the paradox: Dean's continued unhappiness in the situation he was in fuelled by a level of his somewhat *laissez-faire* outlook.

When I examined their relationship myself in 1957, I considered that they'd probably attempt a trial separation. If Dean and Jerry could prove to themselves that they could stand alone in show-business, I doubted that they would ever reunite. But I knew that they were magnetically together in more ways than one and that any break-up would not be easy.

The balance was skewed for the remainder of their pictures together. Yet *Living It Up* and *You're Never Too Young* included ballads that were to become typical of Dean's ultimate style: 'How Do You Speak To An Angel?', 'I Know Your Mother Loves You' and 'Simpatico'.

But in all honesty, and Dean admitted to me the same, everyone went to see *Lewis & Martin*, not *Martin & Lewis*. Who really went just to see Dean sing?

Yet as a set of films, the Martin & Lewis canon had their ups and downs, as do all modern franchise equivalents. They included *Scared Stiff* (channelling Abbott and Costello's *Universal Monsters* comedies), *Money From Home*, *You're Never Too Young*, 19-year old Shirley MacLaine's film debut in *Artists and Models*, *Pardners*, and finally *Hollywood or Bust* in 1956, arguably their finest hour.

"The best thing I ever did was to join up with Jerry," Dean said. "The other great thing was to split from him. That gave me the chance to show the world what I could do by myself."

Dean was my catcher, stated Jerry, *the greatest straight man in all of the history of show-business. His sense of timing is flawless, so infinite and fragile, yet he always looks as if he does nothing at all.*

Such beautiful words and expressions, but nevertheless most sincerely meant by both artists. They had had their time together and had been more than successful; but time told them both that they had to go it alone. When it was finally announced that Martin and Lewis were to split, it shocked the entertainment world.

Drastic meetings were held at Paramount with Hal Wallis and his executives to inform Dean and Jerry that because of contracts binding in law, there was no way the partnership could split.

At this particular juncture, Jerry was willing to negotiate something that would please the board and mainly his partner Dean. However, Dean was not interested; he had had enough of this partnership and was weighing up his singing career (which seemed to be doing fairly well at Capitol). Now that he had spent over ten years in films, radio, and live appearances with Jerry, he finally wanted a solo career and was willing to step out alone. While he was not so sure about this comparatively new medium called television, he felt secure that his voice could maybe carry him on to more lucrative pastures new if he had the chance.

When Dean had previously signed with Jerry for a five-year contract for NBC TV, they did not consider the eventual possibilities - but now it was getting bigger. As important artists in their own right, NBC eventually adjusted Dean and Jerry's contract so that they could appear as solo artists.

But even though he wanted and yearned for the split for so many years, once it had actually happened, Dean felt empty. Yes, he knew deep inside that he could do more in this business but he couldn't deal with conflict and was unsure what he thought he *could* do and what he *wanted* to do.

Quietly, he was convinced that he could make it out on his own as a solo artist but, sadly, everyone else thought differently.

Critics as well as company executives were unconvinced when the split finally occurred that Dean Martin would be any sort of success without Jerry Lewis. He was sick and tired of the whole affair and wanted out, recklessly threatening to walk out of everything, disregarding his legal liabilities.

Jerry was broken up: he had pleaded with his partner and Paramount to get their problems sorted out before they had even started making *Artists and Models,* but the bitter arguments raged back and forth, Dean wanting out at any cost.

He hammered at the situation, so annoyed and depressed now that he just could not be persuaded to listen to all the discussions taking place. At times, he was not even present at Paramount when talks took place about his own future.

Again, he had not looked too closely at the contract when he had signed with Paramount, which had tied him and his partner together far more than perhaps either had realised at the time.

Both men had been in the business for some years now and they wanted changes in their careers that the other simply couldn't accommodate: Jerry was always lining up the cameras, the shots, the positions, sometimes taking over from the producers and directors, taking this extra time to get involved behind the camera.

Many times, Dean had asked Jerry to let him know when he would start work on this picture instead of Dean waiting around, and he would furiously walk off the set, until Jerry was ready.

Their films, however, continued to attract large audiences. I can remember queues outside the Croydon cinemas in South London each time a Martin & Lewis film was showing there in my youth: buildings like the famed Davis Theatre (a beautiful building, sadly, like the way of many, now demolished); the Granada Thornton Heath and the ABC Savoy in Broad Green.

Cinemas throughout the country enjoyed similar success. Dean and Jerry were a good box-office attraction everywhere and the films returned to cinemas time and again.

Meanwhile, Dean's recording career was steadily creating a gentle stir here and there. Songs like 'There's My Lover', 'When You're Smiling', and 'What Could Be More Beautiful' had reasonable sales, and his name was popular among record-buyers everywhere.

His grand success with 'That's Amore' made Dean even more determined, and 'Memories Are Made of This' sealed the decision he was to make.

This increased financial success now helped Dean to clear some of the debts that still hung around: he was getting near the end of those past nightmares and gaining more confidence.

Dean was still paying his former wife Betty $1,000 a month and, declaring that she 'was an unfit mother and not caring for them in a satisfactory way', he now filed a suit against her for the legal custody of their four children. Elizabeth did not contest at all this claim by her former husband and on December 10th, 1957, the courts granted the official custody to Jeanne and Dean.

With all children now residing with him, Jeanne and their three own children, the Martin family needed extra space and he bought a $250,000 home in Mountain Drive, Beverly Hills. This was an English-style mansion containing a tennis court, swimming pool (Dean had always been an excellent swimmer), and hosts of other features for the good life with his wife Jeanne and their children.

With one legal affair dealt with in his personal life, Dean now faced another great upheaval and this, too, was soon to become legal and final.

8

On Monday, June 19th, 1956, Martin & Lewis officially separated.

They still had a few joint commitments to complete, with their final appearance together as a team July 24th of that year. The end of a decade and more, with all of its publicity, promotions and merchandise (including comic strip adventures in books and magazines), was placed in the history of our times.

Dean was out on his own with an uncertain future and one of the first solo appearances was in May 1957, in the 24-hour 'City of Hope' telethon in New York. While he'd decided to sell his interests in York Pictures Corporation and Hal Wallis had eventually settled all of the legal entanglements concerning the Martin & Lewis team, Dean was still committed to remain under contract. This ensured that Wallis could get at least another four films each from the estranged pair, twice the number of pictures had Martin & Lewis actually stayed together.

Dean would eventually make *Career* (1959), *All In A Night's Work* (1961), *Who's Got the Action?* (1962) and *Who's Been Sleeping In My Bed?* (1963) to clear his fixed contract but was free to work with other studios too.

Prolific Hungarian-born film producer Joe Pasternak, who in 1945 had made *Anchors Aweigh* with Frank Sinatra and Gene Kelly, approached Dean with the view of casting him in a new picture that told the story of millionaire playboy Ray Hunter who travels to Rome to acquire a hotel. Although not the most complex of plots, 1957's *Ten Thousand Bedrooms* at least gave Dean his own screen-time and finally a shot at solo stardom, but still no strength in a meaty character part. His career needed a strong and substantial role to prove his point but absolutely nothing was forthcoming.

His recordings for Capitol were not too healthy either, having recorded insubstantial songs like 'Give Me A Sign' and

'Bamboozled'. They sold in reasonable quantities overall, but there were no other golden efforts.

"I didn't know what was going to happen to me. I couldn't imagine myself working in an ordinary job again. I'd come this far." His management was desperately searching for suitable roles but it was proving unceasingly difficult. "It was smothered with ballad singers, why should the world want another Italian?"

Because of his years with Jerry, Dean was already labelled as a light-hearted singer and comedian, nothing special, and with not much else to offer.

That was the general consensus in the late 1950s: Martin & Lewis had broken up, and everyone had assumed that Jerry would succeed over Dean.

It did seem that in those initial months, Jerry was going from strength to strength while Dean was floundering. They had both attended Judy Garland's first live recording at the Cocoanut Grove in the autumn of 1958 but remained on opposite sides of the venue, Dean keeping himself to himself more than ever.

After the lukewarm reception of *Ten Thousand Bedrooms*, everything seemed to be the absolute pits: he had recorded the songs from the film for an EP album by Capitol but sales across the world reflected the film's failure as it went around the cinema circuits.

At the beginning of 1957, Dean had recorded a batch of good solid standards, compiled as 'Pretty Baby', earning him roughly $250,000 and allowing him to clear more debts. Today, it's a great example of early Dean, and quite an enchanting album (in 1996, I approached EMI, suggesting a 'two on one' CD release coupling 'Pretty Baby' with 'This Time I'm Swingin'' and the format instigated similar highly-successful releases for other artists by EMI).

But the vocal stance Dean took on 'Pretty Baby' simply echoed the roles he'd been playing since he started his film career: that of a romantic, light-hearted balladeer.

Consulting with his management, Dean decided not to have the lead role in his next few films (if any ever came along that is, and overall this decision was something that marred his movie career as a whole) but meanwhile, he carried on with live appearances here and there.

While performing at the Twin Coaches in Pittsburgh, Dean took a telephone call from his agent asking if he would like a part in a war film with Montgomery Clift and Marlon Brando.

"Brando and Clift? Man, those guys were *huge*. I said I'd do it for nothing!"

In fact, his salary was considerably less than his two co-stars, yet third billing beneath them meant his $35,000 pay cheque was something he could easily swallow.

Part of the filming would take the crew to France, and Dean had to admit he was not too happy. Travelling was not one of Dean's favourite pastimes and he'd previously had to accept so much moving around with Jerry in the past. But this time there was no Jerry in his ear: this was *his* career and he knew he would have to disregard this fear as best he could. The seven weeks he spent in Paris he despised, but got on well with Brando and Clift. Jeanne stayed with him for part of the time, easing his anxiety.

Directed by Edward Dmytryk in CinemaScope for 20th Century Fox, *Young Lions* was an outstanding war film for 1958, gaining the 'Picturegoer' seal of merit but Dean remarked he 'was the ham between Brando and Cliff', perhaps recalling his earlier roles!

Dean was never a big reader but did complete the original Irwin Shaw novel prior to filming, convincing himself that this was one of the biggest gambles of his career, sharing screen time with two heavyweights of Hollywood.

Yet it paid off handsomely when the acclaim he received for his performance made some critics even remark that he 'outshone Brando and Clift' giving Dean a terrific boost of confidence that he'd never had before and for the first time, he actually sat down and thought about acting seriously.

Bold! Outspoken! Frank! Sinatra!

So proclaimed the advertising slogans for Dean's next film, another military effort and another where he didn't get top-billing. That, of course, went to Frank Sinatra.

They'd met before, crossing paths at various venues around the US but the opportunity to work together had yet to present itself. That took place when Vincente Minnelli was looking for two strong personalities for his adaptation of the best-selling James Jones novel that told the story of an ex-serviceman who returns to his home town, only to trigger a series of tragedies. Cast as Dave Hirsh, the protagonist, Dean would share scenes with Frank who would play Alabama Dillert, a playboy-type drinker and gambler.

But it soon became clear to Minnelli (best known for *Gigi* and *An American In Paris* as well as being Judy Garland's second husband and father to Liza) that Dean would be better suited as Dillert and be stronger at supporting Sinatra than the other way around.

Some Came Running became Dean's third solo film, reuniting him with Shirley MacLaine and shot in CinemaScope, the comparatively new wide-screen look to many films since its inception with the Richard Burton vehicle *The Robe* in 1953.

Dean gave a demanding and full characterisation of a strong part, playing it to perfection (and never removing his hat!), as did Frank, who was pleased to finally be working with Dean. It goes without saying that it was a blossoming friendship for the two men in both their personal and professional lives.

Shortly after the film wrapped, Shirley was dining with Dean and his family at his home when a fishbone caught in her throat. Somewhat in a panic, it was Dean who removed the offending item and today, Shirley still remembers the day when she says he saved her life.

Released in 1959, Dean had superb notices on his performance in *Some Came Running*, with columns reporting that he out-acted most of the cast, cementing his abilities in the critics' eyes.

His recording career was building, too, with hits such as 'Volare' and 'Return to Me' forcing those people with influence to take another hard look at his output and hopefully, help realise his potential.

This was endorsed further when Frank conducted the orchestra on Dean's new album 'Sleep Warm', a lush and dreamy album and a good seller for them both, with Dean's voice in excellent form.

During the hazy summer over a period of three days (29th July/4th and 6th August 1959) Dean recorded a dozen songs at the Capitol studios in stark contrast to the season: a batch of winter and Christmas songs to make up his first-ever collection of seasonal Yuletide music. With fine arrangements by Gus Levene, 'A Winter Romance' was Dean's most successful album at that time and his clout in the industry, coupled with his friendship with Frank, was gaining momentum.

He had also set up his own production company, Deanric, to allow better control over his projects, and his agent, Herman Citron, was now able to pick and choose on behalf of his artist, the most promising selections for his future.

Fellow performers were also noticing what an impact Dean was having: Bing Crosby said that he was *...a charmer and a friend, despite his pranks. I reckon he's wittier off-stage than most professional comics, sings a pretty good song, too.* A compliment indeed from a master of song who had certainly been around!

An actor Dean had greatly admired for many years was John Wayne and, when he was offered the part of Dude, a no-good down and out drunk in *Rio Bravo*, alongside Wayne's Sherriff Chance (not to mention a supporting cast of Angie Dickinson, Ricky Nelson, Walter Brennan, and renowned filmmaker Howard Hawks) he jumped at this golden opportunity.

Hailed as the greatest Western since George Stevens' *Shane*, *Rio Bravo* became an instant classic. Crisp, witty, fast-paced and straight from the shoulder, this glorious drama budgeted at $3million contained all the highest traditions of the Western genre.

It also gave rise to a number of interesting facts and events: Wayne hadn't picked up a rifle since appearing in *Stagecoach* in 1939; Angie Dickinson's legs were voted the prettiest and longest in Hollywood; Ricky Nelson's duet with Dean was wonderfully understated; Walter Brennan drove a nail into one of his shoes so that he jolted himself into the limp he portrayed throughout his scenes, and Wayne gave Nelson the hat he'd worn in Stagecoach.

There's a scene where Dean, as Dude, pours his drink back into the bottle without spilling a drop. Horror maestro John

Carpenter, in an interview in 1994, classified it as being his very favourite film sequence of all time.

With his first solo western, Dean finally got the recognition that he deserved. While John Wayne had always pulled in the crowds for most films he made, for this film in particular, Dean had a much bigger audience. He received very impressive reviews for his part and had thoroughly enjoyed making the film, even managing to sing some songs on screen and giving Ricky Nelson some 'insider' tips on singing (even though Nelson was already a successful singer in his own right, having been in the business since a child with his parents).

With this sort of success and acclaim, Dean was now able to add more strings to his bow: he agreed to appear on stage at the prestigious Sands Hotel, Las Vegas, creating his own unique act and an association with the venue that was to become so very famous for him in years to come.

He had that flair for working very hard and making it look as if he did nothing, but he was determined to gain more and more experience and confidence in all chapters of the business. When he sauntered on stage for the 1959 Academy Awards in his rubber-soled shoes with blue slacks, a pork-pie hat and a dark red shirt, he was effortless in his delivery and quips – but he'd been spotted in the wings learning his lines and timings to the second. He always knew his cues --and those of others-- and was ever the professional.

Dean returned to Paramount for *Career*, a film that was promoted as *the Most Scorching Drama of Young People to Ignite The Screen In Years!* It was a tough drama exposing the behind-the-scenes of show-business: the tricks, the dirt and the deceptions. It was a fascinating story of an incurably dedicated actor played by Anthony Franciosa clashing with a ruthless director (Dean Martin). Shirley MacLaine co-starred and Joseph Anthony directed for producer Hal Wallis.

I love this acting stuff, said Dean at the time. *At last I am getting interesting roles. The one I have here is the most colourful and exciting one I have done...such a change from my past characters.*

Dean recorded the title song for Capitol on 31 August 1959, released as a single titled '(Love Is A) Career'.

Yet, while he was sky-rocketing, it was Jeanne and the children who still suffered. Dean was rarely at home: if he wasn't on set he was on stage or recording. To compound Jeanne's frustration, he was often seen in public with Anne Francis (a New York-born actress with the sci-fi classic *Forbidden Planet* on her résumé) and the subject of divorce was raised.

With tempers at home temporarily subdued, Dean changed management, with Eddie Traubner stepping into the fray.

In 1960, Dean completed his first film for Columbia Pictures. *Who Was That Lady?* was his return to comedy since the final Martin & Lewis picture, *Hollywood Or Bust* four years before. Headlined by Tony Curtis (still no top-billing for Dean), their mutual co-star was Janet Leigh, Curtis' then-wife who had recently performed together with Kirk Douglas in *The Vikings*. While Curtis had been seen in arguably his most memorable role in *Some Like It Hot* in 1959 with Marilyn Monroe, Leigh's next movie after *Who Was That Lady?* would become the one that *she* became most associated with: *Psycho*.

The high-tension drama of Hitchcock's *Psycho*, however, was miles away from *Who Was That Lady?* in which she played Ann Wilson, catching her husband David (Curtis) kissing another woman. In a convoluted series of events in which David, and Dean's character Michael, convince Ann she didn't really see what she saw, Martin and Curtis bounce off each other perfectly, leaving poor Janet flummoxed at their respective characters' every move! It's one of my son's overall favourite movies and his 'go to' Dean Martin film!

Following his success for Vincente Minnelli in *Some Came Running*, the director cast him again as the male lead, this time in an adaptation of *Bells Are Ringing*, a hugely successful Broadway show starring the talented and vivacious Judy Holliday. MGM produced the screen version and Holliday reprised her stage role.

Capitol Records purchased the soundtrack from MGM, including the song 'My Guiding Star' which was made for the film but not included in the final cut. 'Long Before I Knew You' was the other song recorded but not included and it seems to have been lost in the transition of ownership. One of the highlights of the film was the duet between Judy and Dean singing 'Just in Time' and Dean recorded his own solo version of the same song less than ten days later on May 17th, 1960. He added a new batch of songs to his catalogue too, a policy which was to continue to naturally build up his prestige as a singer as well as an actor.

9

Dean seemed much happier of late. Most of his financial debts had been paid off, and he felt assured about his rosy future, now being able to consider what *he* wanted to do next, as opposed to having been *told* what to do for most of his career so far.

"I felt I had this freedom I'd never had before. I always hated being ordered around and having the chance to choose what I wanted was a long time coming," he told me.

His own satisfaction with his role in *Bells Are Ringing* showed throughout his performances in this Arthur Freed production and he loved working with his leading lady, even though her illness held up a lot of the filming. But Dean was patient and only worked when she was ready, and he relished every moment.

For the 'Hello' sequence, the film crew used 350 extras, 50 bit players, 70 taxicabs, 100 cars and 2,000 feet of the MGM lot for filming!

Sadly, it proved to be her last film. Judy succumbed to breast cancer and died five years later in 1965.

"She was a gorgeous girl. It was heaven working with her," Dean said.

On the very day of completion, Dean had to leave immediately for solo appearances at the Sands Hotel and, owing to excessive commitments, he had to refuse a part in the Sophia Loren/Clark Gable production *It Started In Naples*.

Excessive commitments was perhaps an understatement!

Dean had so many offers coming in that his management had a hard time deciding what would be best for him. He himself wanted variety, in his film work particularly, but had no wish to be tied down to one studio. Many were offering incredible sums to get him to sign an exclusive contract, but he refused them all.

Instead, he decided that an assortment of film roles for a variety of studios would suit him better; each company had their own routine and method of film production and, with his own production companies, he could ensure good financial deals and top status with each and every project.

Thus it was that the man progressed; he was very sure of what he wanted and, determined, he now had the finance and the power like he had never had before. Things were looking very good and there was so much more he knew he could achieve. His friendship with Frank had widened his appeal and they were often seen together along with Sammy Davis Jr, Peter Lawford and Joey Bishop. Dean wanted total security and independence for himself and his family.

It was going his way – and the way was his!

With *Bells Are Ringing* less than a month into its journey around the cinema circuits, Dorchester Productions signed him for the Warner Bros film *Ocean's 11*. Dorchester was Frank's company and the story concerned the robbing of five Las Vegas casinos simultaneously at precisely 1 minute 38 seconds past midnight, when everyone was celebrating the New Year.

This was the first gathering of the Rat Pack for a film, the title the media attributed to Frank Sinatra and his friends when they worked and played together. It was a label they never acknowledged or used themselves.

Frank had gathered together Dean, Sammy, Peter, Joey, Angie Dickinson and Richard Conte plus guest stars George Raft, Red Skelton, Cesar Romero, Akim Tamiroff, Henry Silva, Patrice Wymore and Ilka Chase, together with the splendid musical works of Nelson Riddle.

With all of these celebrities, the film could not help being a huge box-office success; it was the epitome of cool, encapsulating the Rat Pack's image. In fact, its success at defining the Rat Pack is still maintained to this very day. In 2001, Warner Bros green-lit the remake, *Ocean's Eleven*, directed by Steven Soderbergh, featuring its own contemporary ensemble cast including George Clooney as Danny Ocean with Brad Pitt, Matt Damon, Don Cheadle, Andy García and Julia Roberts. Two sequels of the remake followed, *Ocean's Twelve* and *Ocean's Thirteen*. A fourth (all-female) variation, *Ocean's 8*, starring Sandra Bullock as Debbie Ocean, the younger sister of Clooney's Danny, was released in 2018.

A regular remark of Dean's became the title of one of his very popular single record releases: 'Ain't That a Kick in The Head!'. Some American radio stations actually banned its release, due to the suggestive lyrics by Sammy Cahn and Jimmy Van Heusen. Dean recorded it on 10th May 1960 especially for inclusion in *Ocean's 11* and was one of thirteen in a session for Capitol. The other tracks formed the superb collection 'This Time I'm Swingin'!', all arranged and conducted by Nelson Riddle.

Dean didn't return to Capitol until mid-December, and with 1961 almost upon him, he was nearing the end of his contract with them. Rumours were strong that he may join his pal Frank on his newly-formed company Reprise.

After a handful of years out on his own now, Dean Martin had certainly proved his capabilities without any doubt.

It was only a few years earlier, that I myself had discovered Dean Martin as an entertainer. During the autumn of 1953, I had gone to my local cinema to see a film entitled 'The Caddy', not ever having heard of Martin & Lewis at all, and not sure what the film would be all about.

Thinking that this was just another average disposable, forgettable comedy, when I heard and saw this Dean Martin fella sing 'You're the Right One' in the film, I can only say I was- for want of a different word - *shocked* - by the sound of his voice.

It just got me. I was just a teenager and this was the first time that any singing voice, male or female, had ever affected me this way!

From that time on, amidst my various activities, I eagerly went to see any Dean Martin film that came along. In those days, with an abundance of cinemas all over the place, it was so easy to catch up on a film or two that you may have missed the first time around – and I always went again and again!

Whether or not any of my girlfriends ever became staunch admirers of Dean's work after being taken to see his films I shall never know, but I paid my dues at the box office and in I went!

So began my almost demented desire to find out more about Dean Martin.

My collection of 10" 78s (and very fragile!) singles were quickly starting to take up more and more space in the cupboard and I began to collect what I could on this actor and singer from America, articles, cuttings, photos…anything.

The man himself, meanwhile, was working harder and harder, and with the numerous offers of film work, plus his appearances, he had made a strong name for himself in show business.

With my continuing interest, I was somewhat surprised to eventually discover that what had been then the world's only Dean Martin appreciation society had closed down some time before.

After some thoughts and considerations, I made up my mind at some point in 1959 to contact Dean for permission to set up one myself.

Although my dear parents thought I had perhaps cracked up with such a crazy and useless idea, I did write to Dean.

Over a period of around eighteen months, across what must have been about ten letters merely and politely asking for his permission, I received absolutely no response at all.

Without actually saying 'we told you so!', my parents were now convinced that I had finally gone mad and had wasted my time by sending all these letters.

In December 1960, I received a letter dated the 14th, signed by a Mrs Lois F Greene, secretary to Dean Martin. It was a small letterhead, with no address embossed on it – but at an angle in black italicised print in the top left corner, was the single name 'Dino'.

In the letter, she addressed me as Mr Thorpe and apologised for the delay in answering my letter sent in October to Mr Dean Martin. She continued by saying that Mr Martin had been preparing for a new picture *and* recording, so had been difficult to reach. She said that the day before she wrote the letter, he had some free time and she was able to get his 'most pleased consent' of my plan of a fan club in Great Britain. She trusted that she would be hearing from me for any aid that she could give me from her side.

I was stunned!

Less than a week later, another letter arrived, on the same clear and simple letterhead.

Except this time, the typed (albeit brief) letter dated 21st December 1960 began *Dear Bernard...* It referenced the previous letter and said that personal authorisation for such a project was given. Regular contact, the letter said, would be welcomed. The letter was hand-signed...

Dino.

I was twenty-two years old and Dean Martin had personally given me his permission to set up what I called initially, Dino's Fan Club, but Dean soon requested the revision to the International Dean Martin Club (Dean didn't like the term 'fan club' and asked me to avoid using the phrase).

I commenced our operations straight away, writing to Capitol in Hollywood and London, and to every film company both here and America. I asked his management for as much publicity material as they were willing to send me. I expected this to be a few photos and not much else, but within weeks, along came batches of varying (signed) photos and boxes of his then-latest vinyl LP 'This Time I'm Swingin''. Dino's secretary Lois Green was so very helpful in arranging regular supplies and we were able to quickly advertise the album's availability from us which helped to attract subscriptions. Dino had also signed a few copies of that as well which we were able to give away as competition prizes. Not long after, copies of the soundtrack to 'Bells Are Ringing' arrived and we were able to sell these prior to their official UK released in October (they had already hit the US shelves in July).Everyone was forthcoming with so much information and I was overwhelmed with the support, especially given the fact that appreciation societies were relatively rare and occasionally given bad press because of the unprofessional approaches that sometimes came hand in hand with 'fans' managing such groups.

Warner Bros wrote to us, too, asking if we would find some advertising material useful for their new motion picture Ocean's 11. Useful was something of an understatement! This was Dean's big film for 1960 and Warner Bros. were amazing at supporting us supporting them - as if a giant such as Warner Bros. needed us anyway!

It was these initial dealings with my new Hollywood contacts that showed me the entertainment business wasn't always closed doors and hierarchical boardrooms. I do wonder if the fact that I was representing Dean Martin lent some weight to us receiving such attention. He himself was highly respected in the industry and wielded a lot of influence.

We issued our very first newsletter in November 1960 [reproduced elsewhere in this volume, Ed.]. It was, admittedly, a very basic one-sheet typed bulletin and we followed with similar issues for Christmas, then, for 1961, May, August and December. Our first specially printed issues, headed 'A Letter from Dino' commenced monthly from January 1962, complete with an authorised photo of Dean, as the club's Honorary President, at the top of the first page. In those early days, that was as about as 'illustrated' as we could get for our newsletters.

Yet I knew from the off that we had to be respectful and professional in all our dealings.

We were, after all, representing Dean Martin.

Representing Dean Martin!

Even now after all these years and after everything we did for Dean, that still sounds surreal!

With our initial membership fee at four shillings (equivalent to 48p then or approximately £6.00 today), we were off!

In a matter of a few years, Dean Martin had proven himself in great demand - exactly the opposite of the critics' predictions after his split with Jerry. He had ensured that he would not tie himself down to one studio.

"It gave me complete freedom to portray different characters, as well as working with all those people through whom I could gain experience. I knew I would never be a great actor. I just wanted to be a good actor."

Demand for Dean was great and, after wrapping *All In A Night's Work* for Paramount (again with Shirley MacLaine, and the first solo film in which he received top billing), he did a cameo for Columbia Pictures' epic production *Pepe,* starring the comedian Cantinflas. It told the simple story of a kind-hearted ranch-hand who, because of his love for a horse, found himself going on an adventure in the outside world where his path kept crossing with show-business personalities.

The promotional work for *All in a Night's Work* included Dean's recording of the title theme. As part of the four-picture deal with Hal Wallis, the producer had decided that this part was made for Dean as a playboy and working with Shirley again was just a dream for him. Paramount delayed the start of this film because they required Dean for it and no one else and at this time, he had already arranged enough work to clear him for the next three years - and demand for his talent was increasing all the time.

Joseph Anthony, who had directed Dean in *Career,* occupied the director's chair for this comedy, but this was the first time he'd tackled this genre. Comedy was new to him, but he found working with Dean to be rewarding, appreciating his star's natural and laid-back approach.

My wife Irene and I attended the film's UK gala premiere (on Paramount's invitation) on Thursday 11th May 1961 at the Plaza Theatre, Piccadilly Circus, London. It would be the first of many such opportunities my association with Dean would provide.

My family and friends, however, still considered me foolish to bother with this work for Dean, for some American celebrity who did not really need me, nor would ever take any notice at all or make contact. But the whole experience was so different and nothing like I honestly expected.

It was one evening in the summer of 1961, I think it was June, when our home telephone rang. I answered, wondering who would be calling at such a relatively late hour.

"Hello?" I said, hearing a couple of clicks and a pause. Then:

"Hey, Bernard," a voice said, with the emphasis on the 'ard'. "Dino."

I nearly fell over.

He asked me how I was, how my family was, how the club was. I have always prided myself in the fact I rarely become tongue-tied but this call, completely out of the blue, knocked me for six. But I swallowed my overwhelming sense of excitement and chatted with Dean as if it was the most natural thing in the world. As I told him what the club was doing, he responded positively and said that he was hoping to make a picture with Lana [Turner] at some point and he hoped I'd like it. I said we'd seen *All in A Night's Work* and he replied, saying he'd been happy with this film and recalled the incident when mayonnaise was applied to his face to encourage the dog, Jasper, to lick him and make a fuss of him on camera!

As the conversation ended (it could only have been five or ten minutes), he said I could call if I ever needed anything. I thanked him. He never responded but just said goodbye.

When I had the idea to set up a club for him, I don't think I really, truly expected anything more than a couple of letters, if that.

But I'd just spoken to Dean Martin.

10

I wondered if he'd made the call himself to 'check me out' so to speak, to see if I was really determined to make this work. I'd like to think I'd impressed him because his office sent more and more updates on his work and words of encouragement in what we were doing.

But our society was just finding its feet. We'd had a bad start with membership and, even though we were advertising as much as was financially possible, things did not take off too well until 1962.

There was a very gradual intake of members – painfully slow if I'm honest – but we kept our determination to establish the organisation for Dean, and, with his support, and photographs and various other items that we regularly received from his office, things were slowly but surely trundling along!

Meanwhile, Dean was earning approximately $300,000 a picture, $50,000 a week in cabaret, similar for television appearances and on top of all that, other payments from his company stocks and shares plus his royalties and payments from Capitol Records.

Everyone was asking for him, so demand was now outstripping the number of days in a year for Dean. The fact that he still found time to contact us amazed me.

Meanwhile he was harbouring a secret passion to own his own Italian restaurant and had noticed the Alpine Lodge bistro up for sale in Las Vegas. He went into co-ownership with the then-owners and renamed it Dino's Lodge, complete with his name and image above the door. The front entrance soon featured on the popular weekly television series *77 Sunset Strip*, boosting both public and celebrity interest. An instrumental jazz LP, 'An Evening at Dino's Lodge', was released some months later.

He returned to MGM to star with Susan Hayward in the gritty drama *Ada*, an examination of the deep machinations of behind-the-scenes politics. The film company had acquired the screenplay rights of the Wirt Williams novel 'Ada Dallas', and Dean had one of his strongest dramatic parts to date in governor Bo Gillis. Location shooting took place in the US Government offices in Sacramento and Dean went there for interior and exterior shoots. This was the very first time that a motion picture company had actually filmed inside the government building.

Even though Ada was far from light-hearted, Dean still managed to include a song 'May the Lord Bless you Real Good', which did not appear out of context of the story.

He pushed his character very hard in this story and director Daniel Mann said of Dean in this film *...he is one of the most easiest and prepared professionals I have ever had the pleasure of directing.*

The Rat Pack reunited on film for *Sergeants 3* (you'll notice that all the Rat Pack movies have numbers in the titles and that those numbers don't appear as words... *Ocean's 11*, *Robin and the 7 Hoods* and so on...) and with our membership now steadily increasing, the months of frustration wondering what the future would hold for the club finally paid off as we began to show signs of success.

Dean's recordings were still providing him with substantial sales, with songs such as 'Sparkelin' Eyes', 'Giuggiola' and 'Somebody Loves You', with the inclusion this year of one of his most successful and lush collection of songs on 'Dino – Italian Love Songs'.

This was exactly what the album title implied: Dean singing Italian love songs. This, his penultimate album for Capitol, came with sleeve notes announcing that this was just what his admirers had wanted all along! He'd spent three days in September recording those dozen beautiful renditions of songs, some of which I can even remember my Italian Grandmother singing to me (or to herself) when I was a child!

I classify this album as my very firm favourite from Capitol – the inexplicable genius and orchestrations of Gus Levene, together with Dean's voice, which was nothing other than perfect when he recorded these songs; all in all, an amazing combination of music and voice which remains unsurpassed. The album was released in February 1962 and entered the American charts the following May, staying there for a period of sixteen weeks. For this production, Dean had re-recorded two of his hit songs, 'On An Evening In Roma' and 'Return To Me', giving them a bigger, more sophisticated sound with elevated presentation values.

This was the definitive Italian collection for Dean, which he never surpassed in his entire recording career, although he would continue to include the occasional Italian style song in his repertoire.

Spread over the course of three days in December (18th, 19th and 20th), Dean entered the Capitol Tower for what would be his final set of songs for that record company.

He had been with them since the autumn of 1948, with a surprising list of just over 300 titles for the period. As is the case with all artists, some songs were very good, some he would rather not remember, and some were big hits, making the compilation a *very* varied selection of songs of all moods and rhythm for a man who had long since proved he could sing like the rest of them.

"I can sing just about everything quite good, perhaps not the greatest voice, but I do my best and you cannot say much else after that. I've had a good time doing that, which is nice."

With his contract now ending, he spent these three sessions recording another gorgeous set of popular and beautiful songs, this time set to *cha* rhythms, arranged by the master Nelson Riddle, whose orchestra played superbly. Dean again did his unique best, his own inimitable phrasing well-suited to the arrangements for this set.

'Cha De Amor' was released in America in March the following year with the UK release the November after.

Dean had already felt a couple of years back that he needed a change of situation with his vocal work, and had been considering offers with some of the record companies since then. Considering several options and financial deals, the place he ended up seemed an inevitable one: Frank had created Reprise Records.

In late 1961, Dean told us he was signing with Frank's label and requested that Frank, Sammy, Peter and Joey be honorary members. He told us too about his family and asked about ours, saying that Jeanne, his daughter Claudia, and his parents had all spent time in hospital, but luckily, they were all back home and feeling a lot better. He had been quite concerned at the health problems they had all been through.

Dean said he was pleased we were working hard for him. Even with our not having been in operation for two years yet, we already had members overseas and things were generally looking favourable. He mentioned a London visit to film his cameo with Frank for *Road to Hong Kong* and hoped to meet, adding that he hated flying but accepted when he had to do it for his work. Ultimately, he apologised that the meeting didn't happen due to his family commitments in Germany.

He did say, however, that he'd been at the Savoy Hotel in London for two days, where one of the guests was Hollywood restaurateur Mike Romanoff. He'd managed to pull off some practical jokes with Romanoff by cutting his expensive cigarettes into pieces and his ties into shreds!

Sinatra's Reprise, 'to play and play again', had signed up a myriad of artists with a unique feature: each and every artist had the advantage of actually owning outright their recorded works and masters. Each artist therefore had the prerogative of releasing their work as and when they wished (or not at all if they so desired) merely loaning out the actual tapes to a company that would do all of the distribution and selling to the public.

This was unheard of in the record industry, for all artists on all labels had no say or any rights in what happened to their recordings - but at Reprise this legal innovation came into being and at precisely 3.30pm on the afternoon of Tuesday 13th January 1962, Dean signed his name to a thirteen-year contract.

But even Dean himself was yet to realise just how illustrious and successful his new era would become with this label; it did not occur to him at that time the phenomenal achievements he would experience in those thirteen years.

Exactly one month to the day after his signature appeared on his contract, he recorded five songs: his very first was entitled 'Senza Fine', written by Paoli and Wilder, being the love theme from *Flight of the Phoenix*, with orchestration by the fine musicianship of Neal Hefti (later of *Batman* fame). The remainder of songs, also with Hefti, at this session were 'Just Close Your Eyes', Baby-0', 'Dame Su Amor' and 'Tik-A-Tee,Tik-A-Tay' (this latter song was to become his first regular issue, announcing in the press *Dean Martin's On Reprise!!)*

They were released as singles, although 'Senza Fine' seemed to lose itself somewhere for a while and was not issued as a regular single for either the American or United Kingdom markets.

For the future, Dean's management would carefully work out the release schedules for both singles and albums: he would record batches of songs at a time and all would be chosen for albums of songs, with singles being used for the usual heavy promotion within the industry.

With his initial five songs, even then he threw in a smattering of the Italian style ballads – but he changed his theme entirely for his second studio visit when he taped a dozen songs all in one day, on February 26th. He'd decided to record an album of French-inspired style songs, gathering them all together and with the impeccable talents again of Neal Hefti, Dean really embraced this theme, even remarking at the end of a song … *there's some good stuff around here, Frank!*

'French Style' was a good selection of songs for his first Reprise album release and in my own personal opinion, I always thought that this was one of his finest albums for his new company, but, strangely, it did not do very well and was not one of his best-selling releases. I have wondered why ever since, and have considered whether or not it was down to the public's reception of the album's cover image – where a not-entirely serious Dean had adopted a beret and a cigarette-holder! (There had always been a conflict for the public with Dean the actor/comedian and Dean the serious singer – it was as if people couldn't marry the two.)

Very few of the companions and staff at this time realised that he was suffering from arthritis in his spine, a painful and aggravating condition. He told no one about his problems and suffered in silence, taking medication recommended by his close friend Mack Gray. His life was so very busy now and he felt he had no time to complain or bother too much about his health at the age of 45. This was a habit that he was to keep throughout his life: he detested any medical issues or hospitals and would leave things to the last minute before he would do something about it.

It seems many of us have a phobia and in Dean's case, this was his - plus his other worries of travelling in elevators or on an aeroplane.

After two years of existence, the International Dean Martin Club published its first complete film list, detailing to date all the information of Dean's films. This was issued to all of our members, along with the regular monthly newsletter.

Slowly but surely, we were gaining more members, and we were able to supply a selection of photographs of Dean, which his office had provided for our use.

At Dino's Lodge, however, there was trouble.

Even though it regularly attracted icons such as Judy Garland (but not Dean himself), his partners had been found mismanaging the business and Dean sued, receiving damages, but his demands to remove his name and image from the fascia were rejected. He was able to bring in his brother Bill to manage things, and he did so until the venue eventually closed as business dried up.

His film career now garnered the attention of Hollywood royalty.

Marilyn Monroe asked for him (and no one else) to be her leading man in her next picture with 20th Century Fox, who then made him an offer of $300,000. *Something's Got to Give* was based on the film *My Favorite Wife* which was in turn based on the poem 'Enoch Arden' by Alfred, Lord Tennyson. Fox were eager to recoup their losses for *Cleopatra* and they saw the joint billing of Monroe and Martin to be the way towards it.

Dean liked Marilyn, and she greatly admired Dean's looks, his singing and his manner. She was the top actress of her time, well known for her temperament, but nevertheless in great demand for her work.

She had that wonderful status of being known, like Dean, by her first name only, so it was a match made in heaven.

Dean's advisers did warn him that she was renowned for various temperamental tantrums and complications, but he was personally flattered that she'd asked him, even though the script, he felt, wasn't what he wanted to do.

"I felt like I was going backwards but how could you say no to her?"

As production commenced, so did the problems.

Marilyn continually arrived late or sometimes not at all, causing nightmares for the film executives. The budget was expanding by the hour for every one she lost them, and eventually the studio issued a suit of $500,000 against her for breach of contract, announcing that she had been taken off the film to be replaced by Lee Remick.

While she was still adored by fans worldwide and in their millions, her exquisite charm was wearing thin for the studios.

The very next morning, Dean himself announced he would not be making this film.

Fox had no choice but to close down production, and attempted to sue Dean for every cent that had been spent so far on the movie (only a few feet had been shot so far) plus an extra $1million thrown in for 'exemplary damages'. With the demand of over $3,339,000 on his head, Dean counter-sued for $6,900,000, citing 'fraud, oppression and malice'. He stated, too, that he had no objection to the talents of Miss Remick, but his contract stated otherwise.

It was, he stated, Marilyn or no one.

Several weeks later, Fox agreed to continue production with both original stars but no sooner had the cameras started to roll again that Marilyn was in hospital suffering a miscarriage.

She then descended into a severe and uncontrollable depression and never returned to the set. The production was finally cancelled on 11th June 1962 and on 5th August that same year, Marilyn was found dead at her home.

Something's Got to Give was never completed and Dean and Fox settled out of court. Fox did however overhaul the entire production and remounted it as *Move Over, Darling* with Doris Day and James Garner in 1963. The footage of the original version was released in 1990 as part of the one-hour documentary *Marilyn: Something's Got to Give* then re-edited again in 2001 for *Marilyn: The Final Days*.

11

Dean now went straight on to his next film *Who's Got the Action?* for Paramount, another comedy, this time about a gambling husband whose wife (played by the beautiful Lana Turner) was sick and tired of his losing money on the horses.

As part of his agreement, Dean again would record the title song for a single, amongst other tracks that took on multiple genres, including Latin and Country. With fine arrangements by such talent as Don Costa, Gus Levene and Neal Hefti, he slowly moved back into the charts.

His popularity in Europe was growing (as our club membership could attest to) and there was a (now long since defunct) radio station called Radio Luxembourg that was using Dean's recording of 'One More Time' as a theme to one of its regular features where listeners wrote in about their most hated record – and I'm pleased to say that none of Dean's ever featured!

We also had a feature on the club in the magazine 'Cherie' in 1963 and we held our own top ten record poll: members wrote in with their top ten Dean Martin songs and the favourite chosen above all others in this instance was 'How Do You Speak To An Angel?'.

The tape cassette format was introduced in the United Kingdom this year and UK label Pye Records stated that they would not be issuing stereophonic versions of Dean's albums unless his sales improved.

EMI Records' mail-order company, World Records, asked us to compile a special album for them for release sometime in 1964 and this was to comprise songs taken from previous Capitol releases, and songs chosen by us for their UK customers.

As far as British television was concerned, we did not see much of Dean's work, although BBC TV screened 'Laughter USA' which included some vintage Martin and Lewis segments.

Among many others shows and appearances, Dean had been the guest with Martha Raye on the Bob Hope Show for NBC TV on 14th April 1963, and had taken Jeanne to see Frank in concert at the Flamingo, Las Vegas. He also hosted a Dick Powell Theatre production and was the first competitor for the Frank Sinatra Annual Golf Tournament for November 7th, keeping him very active with his work and the occasional --if not indeed rare-- private function.

The Frank, Dean, and Sammy trio had found their act by now and were pulling in huge audiences in towns like Chicago, and, of course, their adopted home, Las Vegas.

Sammy and I met briefly in London and he talked with such verve about his working relationship and friendship with Dean, saying he was a perfect gentleman and a complete prankster, and said he did very little but laugh when he was in Dean's company. From photos of him and Dean together, and where they are with Frank, you can clearly see this relationship.

Two further films were now scheduled for Dean, *Boeing* with Frank, and *I Love Louisa*, but shortly after this announcement, Dean was admitted to hospital suffering from exhaustion, not surprising when you looked at his working schedule covering the next four years!

Returning home a few days later to rest and recuperate, confirmation came (which Dean was expecting) that Frank had sold out his complete ownership of Reprise for it to merge with Warner Brothers Records (meanwhile, many miles across the globe, it was noted that Dean's version of Johnny Cash's 'I Walk the Line' had reached number three in September...in South Africa).

If you take a careful look at the film *Come Blow Your Horn*, you will see a dishevelled tramp wander past as he is presented with a piece of steak by Frank Sinatra. Only on the screen for a few seconds, Dean makes the cameo appearance here that only he can – even in that fleeting moment, as he goes past the camera, you know it's him.

Dean then made a dramatic change in his character roles, choosing to play the part of Julian Berniers alongside Wendy

Hiller and Geraldine Page in Lillian Hellman's original story *Toys in the Attic* for United Artists. This disturbing story was presented on the screen in an excellent version of the play, the first written by Hellman in almost a decade. Dean's brutal portrayal shocked quite a number of critics: they simply weren't used to seeing him tackle such an extreme role.

He reverted to type for *Who's Been Sleeping in My Bed?* with the delectable Elizabeth Montgomery. This film now marked the completion of the original Martin & Lewis contract that producer Hal B. Wallis adjusted when the two stars parted company back in 1956, so there was no longer any obligation to revert to Paramount.

He switched to Warner Brothers for his next film effort, again with Frank Sinatra, teaming with Bond girl Ursula Andress and Anita Ekberg for the Robert Aldrich-directed western comedy *4 For Texas*. Produced by the SAM Company [Sinatra, Aldrich, Martin], the film was to originally have cast Dean with Gina Lollobrigida, but, as she was unavailable, the title was changed from *Two for Texas* to its familiar title and the subsequent four actors with equal billing.

Opposed as he was to too much travelling outside of California, Dean had declined to go to Broadway for the grand opening night of *Toys in the Attic* at the Hudson Theatre, but asked me to attend, which I duly did.

With Dean Martin's star rising ever higher, he was cultivating the relaxed, drunk image more than ever but at the same time working much harder and diversifying into many roles in his film work. His recordings too were moving towards more sophisticated attitudes all round, with carefully planned issues and promotion.

What little time he did have for relaxation, he would sit at home and watch television or perhaps rest in a steam bath for an hour or so before his next commitment, playing as much golf as he could possibly fit in between.

He was now part owner of the Sands Hotel in Vegas, with his own production companies and real estate businesses: he had become partners with Laurence Harvey and Frank Sinatra for a restaurant, the Bistro, and he was a major shareholder in RCA and many more investments that gave him an excellent income, not including his payments and royalties from his films and recordings.

The original Reprise offices had gone now and were incorporated within those of Warner Brothers at Warner Boulevard. But the label was still attracting some of the biggest names in the recording world, as well as licensing material from abroad.

Although by mid-1963, Dean had had four albums and a gathering of singles issued, there was not much headway towards chart positions related to sales. He continued to sell in reasonable quantities, though, as each release became available in stores around the world.

He hosted the original show *The Hollywood Palace* on Saturday 7th March 1964, which gave him more coverage on the small screen; he began to consider making more of a presence there but was conscious that over-exposure would be a detriment.

He was invited to the famous Grauman's Chinese Theatre on 21st March to make his handprints on the sidewalk outside and with his crazy humour he made sure his shoe prints were there as well!

Dean continued to increase his workload all the time, regardless of his health (he continued to have his arthritic problems and occasional intestinal infections.)

Nevertheless, he loved to stay up late and sleep late when he could and, of course, watch television, finding inspiration in commercial breaks and soaking up ideas that he could use himself. He played golf and tennis, had always been a good boxer, swimmer and tennis player, and although he was a past master at *portraying* relaxation, spare time was becoming a rare commodity.

This was just one of the reasons Dean gave out such an air of laziness. He worked hard, maybe even harder than the average artist, but as he worked, he made his act look easy because of the way he did it. He'd come to a film set prepared and ready, sailing through it while cracking a few jokes -- wherever he was, and whoever he was with. The end result was a unique, professional entertainer, with a charming and relaxed persona presented to the public.

Although his personal life with his wife and children was in a reasonable situation now, he was still seen on numerous occasions with a woman on his arm.

This seemed to contradict with his stance that he had no time for complications, yet by encouraging extra-marital dalliances, he incurred exactly that.

From a working viewpoint, all his affairs, no pun intended, were dealt with by his management. He performed what was asked of him, and expected everyone to accept that fact and leave him to do his own thing as and when he wished.

He was quite often found difficult and aloof by many as a result but this was only at the first instance: once you had accepted his mannerisms and general attitude to his own life, he was found to be likeable and effervescent in his approach.

Dean had always been a loner – not lonely, that is something entirely different – and few people who were associated with him, either in his career or his private life, were able to get through to him. Through to the man inside, what he thought, what he felt. Only a small handful of people, primarily those in his own family, found the way into his domain of thoughts and deeds.

"I know I'm arrogant and argumentative. I've pushed people and businesses to get what I wanted. In this business, there's no way you can sit back and wait for that something to happen. You have to push hard for what you want."

With continued appearances at the Sands Hotel, he also stood in for Nat 'King' Cole when the famous singer became ill at Christmas.

Meanwhile, we had completed the compilation for the World Record Club: the song list was finalised, as were the sleeve design and notes. I chose the title 'Let's Be Friendly', a song included on the album, and it was released 15th June 1964, eight days after Dean's 47th birthday.

Coverage for this album included an interview with Dean – conducted by me and issued by the record company. EMI did us proud with some splendid publicity for the release as well as for our organisation. This was our very first album release that we had had the chance to work on and, unbeknownst to us at that time, we were to have many more opportunities to do so.

Dean had also recorded quite a number of varied songs with Reprise, working with his pianist and arranger Ken Lane, who had agreed with Dean at the singer's home all but one of twelve tracks required for a new album.

Going through numerous manuscripts, Ken came across one that he and Irving Taylor had written in the 40s entitled 'Everybody Loves Somebody'. Playing a few bars on the piano, Jeanne immediately remembered the tune as one of her favourites from a few years back. Frank himself had recorded it for Columbia on 4th December 1947 but had not had any particular success with it. Dean remarked that, following Ken's piano rendition, it was 'quite nice' and that if Jeanne liked it, it was good enough for him!

'Dream with Dean – The Intimate Dean Martin' was released in the US on 4th August, with the UK release following a month later. It was one of Dean's most sophisticated albums, and unusual for the fact there was not the normal full orchestral backing, but just four top musicians, namely Irv Cottier on drums, Ken Lane at the piano. Barney Kessel was on guitar, and Red Mitchell on bass. Together, they created Dean's very first Gold album, reaching 15 in the American charts on 29th August and remaining in the charts for 31 weeks.

It came in the wake of *What a Way To Go!* (originally titled *I Love Louisa*), a 20th Century Fox release with a stellar cast that included Shirley MacLaine, Robert Mitchum, Paul Newman, Gene Kelly, Bob Cummings and Dick Van Dyke.

He had also filmed two segments for a travel extravaganza special showing some of the world's top nightspots. Dean was seen relaxing poolside at his home then taking a drive as two of his hit songs 'Return To Me' and 'On An Evening In Roma' played in the background. Its title depended upon which country you saw the film; as it had three: *Songs of the World*, *World by Night*, and the suggestive *38-24-36*.

More studio time followed and Dean was now – finally-- considered a best-selling artist, which led to the idea of teaming up with Bing Crosby to record 'Bing, Dino and Dixie'. Reprise even scheduled a catalogue number (RS6127) and designed the cover for the Dixie-land style album but sadly, the artists were never together for long enough to record at the same time, so the whole project was scrapped.

Just over a month later, with Dean having to specially record his songs for the soundtrack of the film *Robin and the 7 Hoods*, he included amongst them an up-tempo version of 'Everybody Loves Somebody' at the suggestion of his record producer Jimmy Bowen. Jimmy liked the melody and was convinced it could be a big hit if they were to and give it a sing-a-long approach, something in the music industry which was beginning to prove popular. His singles sales were moderate at this stage but with this, Dean hit the jackpot. The hit version went to number 1 in America and gave him his first Gold single for Reprise, the press calling him 'Beatle-buster Martin!' for knocking the British pop combo off the top spot, a feat that no one else seemed to be able to do. Reprise had a winner on their hands and released a new album 'Everybody Loves Somebody – The Hit Version' securing another Gold album.

Frank, Dean and Sammy had an intriguing idea to record some songs calling themselves the Bumblers, but nothing came of it.

In 1964, we issued the first edition of the discography, also choosing the front cover photograph for an album to be released later in the year entitled 'The Door is Still Open to My Heart'. Dean had contacted me directly inviting me to his home (he had been in London for a mere three days this year shopping!) but around a week later, work commitments meant he had to cancel.

Rumours of Dean and Frank coming to England for concerts were unfounded and didn't form any part of the workload that had been scheduled for the next five years ahead.

One again, though, his personal life could not be said to be as mapped out: Jeanne had no social life and complained most bitterly about her lack of time with her famous husband.

His children saw even less of him and only heard him on the radio. It was off to school or college when their father had maybe only come home an hour or two earlier, going straight to bed. He very rarely saw them or shared breakfast with any of them, even his wife.

With his monogrammed clothes laying around some of the rooms, they knew when he was home (he was not the tidiest of people, very often leaving clothes around.)

When he wasn't working (a rare occurrence), he and Jeanne would be in bed by 11.30pm, but he would stay awake to watch late films until the early hours.

He had always had the habit of eating fast (one of the reasons he had developed an ulcer), and suffered indigestion frequently. Numerous times over the years, Jeanne would try anything to slow him down. He would eat the average meal twice as fast as she or anyone else did which always concerned her.

With his massive popularity in the recording scene, Capitol sought various ways of making money by re-issuing numerous songs from their large back catalogue of his recordings with them. They were reluctant to choose unusual or little-heard items, instead they tended to issue 'best of' compilations which, admittedly, did sell in large quantities, although they did not in any form reach the giddy heights of Dean's Reprise material.

His tremendous successes in the US meant numerous compilations were appearing on licensed releases on the Tower and Pickwick labels. However, in 1965, EMI had created a brand-new budget label called Music For Pleasure, in collaboration with Paul Hamlyn Limited, and the very first UK album to be issued was MFP1001 'The Dean Sings', a solid collection of his singles, some quite unusual. But just to confuse everyone, this collection was exactly the same as the former 'Dean Sings Again' album via World Records, but for a different cover.

The label itself was to become one of the most successful budget series ever, enabling the availability of mostly re-issued material from hundreds of artists across many labels. It continues its success today, backed by the efficiency and years of experience of EMI Records.

Meanwhile, our society remained popular and busy, and we increased the annual subscription to ten shillings from 1st February 1965. Membership was steadily increasing year-by-year now, and we were becoming more popular as we increased our international advertising.

Frank and Dean led the parade for the late trumpeter Conrad Gozzo this year, with Dean being voted the '23rd Best World Singer' by UK pop newspaper New Musical Express and Dave Dennis from the 'pirate' radio station Radio London, chose '(Remember Me) I'm The One Who Loves You' as his 'Pick of The Week' for two weeks from 14th June. These little snippets into the public's awareness of him showed he was within their consciousness.

As one mere example of Dean's record sales, his single 'The Door is Still Open To my Heart' sold over 400,000 copies, remaining in the American charts for eleven weeks and reaching number six - with even a UK chart entry at a more leisurely 42! With Dean's eventual release of another album, 'Houston', he was made an honorary citizen of that city in Texas.

We were privileged enough to attend the recording sessions for 'Houston', a wonderful insight into a typical working day for Dean. He was always so relaxed and effortless, not one for demanding take after take.

During the late sixties and into the seventies, there was a significant boost of material around from Dean: Both Reprise and Capitol were coming out with numerous releases – all to whet the appetite of the record-buying public. 'The Lush Years', 'Dean Martin Deluxe', 'Dean Martin Hits Again' and 'Young and Foolish' were just a handful of the many releases on the market at this time, although the bulk of these were issued for the American market.

But, as everyone was now well aware, it was not just Dean's records that were blasting his name to the top all around the world. He also had his films, cabaret, and guest spots everywhere.

NBC TV kept on at him to attempt a friendly persuasion to launch his own television show but he simply wasn't interested.

As a way to stave off their advances, he demanded certain conditions, some so unusual and out of line that he genuinely believed no executive in their right mind would accept them.

"I told them that if we were gonna do this, then *I'd* own the shows. And if I didn't want to sing in any of them, they weren't gonna make me." Dean had a wry smile on his face as he told me this, the outcome of his demands of course well known. "I said I'd be at the studio for one day a week and I'd suggest the guests. I never imagined they'd go for it!"

But go for it they did.

Even Dean himself had failed to recognise the magnitude of his status in this business, or see how far he had progressed. Neither did he realise just how much his associates respected his achievements so far.

12

With a contracted fee of over $34,000,000, the *Dean Martin Television Show* first aired at 10pm on Thursday 16th September 1965.

Dean seemed happy, although he appeared to wander around the show on screen as if he had never been on television before, with jokes like: *I got picked up the other night on suspicion of drunk driving. The cop asked me to walk a white line. I said not unless you put a net under it*, and parodies of songs: *In your Easter bonnet, with all the frills upon it, you'd look a bit peculiar in the men's room, my dear*, or: *Return to me…I've a sink full of dishes*, and *Take me in your arms…I'll never make it to the car*. That was the sort of thing that Dean told his audiences he'd do: he'd play with the material he'd been singing for years, would ad-lib, crack endless jokes and occasionally fail to finish a song.

His guest stars were giants in the industry: John Wayne, Orson Welles, Bob Newhart, Frank Sinatra, Sammy Davis Jr, Dom de Luise, Jimmy Stewart, Foster Brooks, Tony Bennett -- to name but a few. They, along with Dean, readily parodied themselves, sometimes in outrageous wigs and even in drag. Dean also showcased newcomers such as the effervescent and beautiful Goldie Hawn and welcomed British stars like Petula Clark, Marty Feldman, Stanley Holloway and Peter Sellers. The roll-call went on and on and was, quite simply, impressive.

With a regular series and weekly TV exposure, his record sales increased and he garnered more recognition than his films could achieve.

When asked a few weeks later what he would do if NBC did not renew his first season, he replied by saying that he'd made up his mind for regular television and would go to ABC or CBS or, if no networks wanted him he'd stick to his recordings, his cabaret and movies.

"After all, that's what I'd done already, made sure that I'd have several strings to my bow, you know, not relying on just one thing in this business. I don't think you can do that if you *really* want to be successful in this game. Diversification is the name of it and I like to think that I tried all chapters of this and did the best I could."

The best that Dean Martin *did* do was bring in the television audiences in their millions – and he did so with the public loving his devil-may-care attitude. Every show topped the Nielsen ratings, and there was never any doubt that NBC would renew his show for future series.

Into the second year, he and producer Greg Garrison formed their own company to produce the shows, with a staggering (for the time) weekly budget of $200,000. Dean himself was receiving $50,000 a show, plus massive investments from his shares in RCA, NBC's parent company.

Dean's rota for taping his segments for each show was always the same: the guest stars and crew would rehearse their parts (usually with Greg standing in for Dean) to get everything timed and set. Dean, of course, used to learn his lines by having three tapes made at the studio: one for home; one for golf; a third for wherever else he may be. He possibly spent more time than his guests in learning his lines, rehearsing whenever he had the chance, and then walking onto the set on the Saturday to have his own contributions filmed and finished, ready for the completed shows to be transmitted the following Thursday.

So many people thought he was a miracle man, coming in to the television studios in the morning and knowing all his lines and where to stand, sit or film the next take without having been with them all week.

"I found learning my lines pretty easy to do from having to learn the words of songs, so my TV show was no different."

Dean kept his actual studio rehearsals to a minimum. While he knew the script verbatim, he insisted on cue cards at all times when he filmed and made sure that the audience *knew* he was using them. It was all part of the act.

Part of his job meant he had to socialise.

And he *hated* socialising.

Being at home or in his hotel room with a TV and a glass of milk was how this superstar enjoyed himself.

Dean was rarely found at Hollywood functions, although when the necessity arose, and where it may have been beneficial to his career, along he went.

Jeanne became somewhat used to the idea of having to socialise by herself. Her husband was all too often away with his work and if he was with Frank, Sammy, Shirley and the clan, she knew it may be some time before she would see him at home again. As Dean himself said ...*where else can you go out and do a day's work, have lots of fun with the girls and the guys and get well paid for it? You tell me where else anyone can do that!*

With this appealing atmosphere, anyone could see what Dean Martin meant, especially when his professional and relaxed approach showed up so well on screen, particularly in films like 1963's *Robin and the 7 Hoods*, sadly the last film the Rat Pack made together and, in fact, the last musical for Bing Crosby.

A somewhat quieter but stronger story came next for Dean when he signed with Billy Wilder for the film version of Anna Bonacci's stage comedy *Dazzling Hour*. Released in February 1965 as *Kiss Me, Stupid*, he starred as cabaret singer Dino opposite Kim Novak as the wonderfully-monikered Polly the Pistol. Peter Sellers was signed as Orville J Spooner but because of the talented British comedian's increasingly bad health with his heart, he had to be replaced by Ray Walston.

This was a shame, as I had personally followed Peter's career from his early days with Spike Milligan and Harry Secombe in the BBC Radio series *The Goons*. Dean had done likewise and they did eventually work together on an episode of Dean's TV show.

The songs for *Kiss Me, Stupid* were supplied by George and Ira Gershwin, one of them entitled 'Sophia' which Dean recorded for Reprise but was never generally released to tie in with the film. The music was scored by renowned classical conductor Andre Previn.

This was classified as an 'X' film for its day, because of the suggestive and sexual scenes.

Dean's status had really moved to higher spheres: he still owned property and estates that would make a book on their own in their paper capacity; investments he had made (and not including his career) were now making him a very wealthy man. This enabled him to easily part with $20,000 to celebrate his parents' 50th wedding anniversary and lavishly furnish his rambling $600,000 mansion in Beverly Hills – although at this time only four out of his seven children were actually living there (Deana, Gina, Ricci and Dean Jr).

All of his children had always been devoted to him and some years later I was fortunate enough to talk with Deana, who lavished such honest and loving praise about her father that it was hard to be unmoved.

He would willingly offer to write notes to his children's teachers, excusing them for their homework if they wished, although they hardly ever took him up on his offers!

On one occasion when Craig had failed his woodwork examinations, his sisters told him that Dad would be very annoyed – but when Dad saw the reports, he just simply said … *well, he ain't gonna be a carpenter!*

It was usually Jeanne who controlled the children's discipline and organised the home routine. She was a lady that preferred to be the wife and mother as opposed to partaking in the glitz and glamour of Dean's world, although she would have liked to have taken part in just *some* of his socialising. She was a stickler for impeccable manners, teaching all seven children to be polite at all times, and how they should behave inside and outside of the family circle. When asked to pass the bread at the dining table, she would expect just that, but sometimes Dean himself would be liable to throw a slice or two on to their plates just for the kick of it all.

That was Dean's way, which does not mean he had no interest in family manners. To the contrary, he was strict, but believed that they should all go on their own way and decide what they would like to do, with his guidance and advice, for what it is worth (he added).

He was happy that they were all content with their various careers and lives and, without any singing lessons, their father proved to them and everyone else in the world that you *can* make it by sheer hard work, a lot of luck and, in Dean's particular case, a natural flair for entertaining (and with over forty million people watching his weekly television show, who could argue with that?).

He always did want to entertain, but he also wanted it to look easy, so he worked extremely hard at looking laid back and relaxed and, of course, he became a global success in everything he cared to do.

If there was a rare day in which he was not working, he would be off to the golf course, as he liked to play a few rounds before the dew went and before too many people arrived; but if his mind took him off that idea, then he would sometimes lay in bed until nearly lunchtime!

Then, of course, there was Dean Martin's mammoth capacity for drinking.

A complete myth.

There was only ever apple juice in that glass tumbler.

It was a prop, nothing more.

His drunk image was just that, an image manufactured by the man himself in the early days of his career, simply because he noticed audiences loved the stance. He became synonymous with booze and encouraged it. Even some of his peers believed he was drunk, he was *that* good at it. Yet at the same time, I believe it became something of a burden for him: people expected him to be drunk so he simply had to keep up the act.

"If people see me as a drunk, let them," he told me. "I sure couldn't hit the right notes if I was as stoned as they say I am. I could never do a good show like that."

The Dean you saw on chat shows or being interviewed wasn't the Dean at home. The times we spoke on the telephone, he had none of his stage drawl. His act was his act, his private life away from the cameras and the microphones was one where he could relax.

But relaxing wasn't easy: his success at work was not matched by his personal life. He had reached such a pinnacle of work and engagements that he spent less and less time with Jeanne. She understood the drive in him, but at the same time would have liked to see more of him at home and not have him so distant, in both mileage and emotion.

Tensions built up again, but he had no desire to go to any functions with Jeanne and, as a result, she became very upset so they parted again. But like last time, this was a brief separation: Dean agreed to cut back on some work and things were patched up between them. Although they both agreed that the money was more than nice, it seemed Dean was working himself just a little too much and Jeanne did think that he could afford to cut back on some of his commitments. As a result, the film *Community Property* with Margaret Rutherford, Ann-Margret and Frank Sinatra was never made, neither was the previously mentioned *Boeing, Boeing*.

He continued his recording sessions for Reprise, however, with such wonderful songs and albums like 'Dean Martin Hits Again' (originally to be titled 'You're Nobody 'til Somebody Loves You') 'Red Roses for A Blue Lady' and the classic 'Welcome To My World', a song he used frequently in his TV shows.

But although Dean did reduce his workload, he continued his cabaret and other appearances, including a guest spot in the western series *Rawhide*.

He was also approached to see if he would consider a series of films in which he would play a character called Matt Helm, the hero of the successful super-spy novels by Donald Hamilton.

The Sons of Katie Elder for Paramount came next, though, a very strong western in which he again starred with John Wayne, together with Earl Holliman and Michael Anderson Junior. Filmed in Durango, Mexico, the film was originally going to be called *Durango*. The Durango Country Club golf course entertained Dean in between shoots, and he actually got his first hole in one! Dean even cooked a pasta meal for the director and cast on the set, but forgot to add vegetables to his heavily spiced dish of spaghetti and fetuccini. As a result, local doctor Pedro Peres was called in because they all had excessive stomach pains!

A further collaboration with Frank (and Deborah Kerr) led him to film the comedy *Marriage on the Rocks*, with Cesar Romero, (future Joker to Adam West's unique *Batman*), and soon-to-be *Star Trek* icon DeForest Kelley). Frank's own daughter (and Dean's god-daughter) Nancy featured in the cast but it seemed to me that most of the actors seemed uneasy in this venture. Perhaps that was just the way I saw it, but something didn't gel, although it did have moderate success at the box office.

13

Dean's recording manager Jimmy Bowen had arrived in London in early 1965 with his fiancée Keely Smith, and I spent a couple of days with them whilst she recorded some wonderful songs at the Pye studios under the expert direction of Tony Hatch. Jimmy he said he enjoyed working in the UK, finding the approach by British technicians to be far more relaxed but nevertheless as professional and dedicated as any other studio.

"The atmosphere is less charged," he told me. "You guys get the job done." I asked him, too, about working with Dean. "Oh, he's a laid back guy. You know that. One take more or less and it's there."

On any further recordings from Dean, Jimmy said, "It would be great to get new material down, but he seems reluctant to commit himself to any more recordings."

Unaware of the fact at the time, it was while I was with Keely that she told me that she was the 'little voice' on the record that Dean had made (called 'A Little Voice'). She remarked how easy and lovely he was to work with and that she would have loved to have recorded some songs with him.

I was also advised whilst at Keely's recordings that future Dean Martin albums in the UK would now be in Stereo as well as Mono. This was excellent news as this indicated his British sales were increasing much more!

Dean had been interviewed for the National Guard sessions, a series of fifteen minute shows for American radio to help promote the National Guard; light-hearted chat interspersed with some of his popular recordings.

He also did a three-week season at the Sands Hotel and turned down another film, (*Luv*) that had been provisionally scheduled for the autumn.

With Dean's record releases, nothing else could describe his success in this field other than stupendous! 'Dream With Dean', 'Everybody Loves Somebody', 'The Door Is Still Open To My Heart', 'Dean Martin Hits Again',' (Remember Me) I'm The One Who Loves You', 'Houston' and 'Somewhere There's A Someone' had given Dean *seven* Gold Albums (for a million sales each) in succession up to October 1965, a feat no other artist had achieved, and an event that also happened in the midst of a semi-explosion in the music business where there were such changes in style.

Dean took all of this in his stride. He was astounded at the conveyor-belt of hits he was having, but at the same time he recognised that it *was* success and ensured that he recorded songs that were very typical of the times.

In the period of two years from June 1964 through to mid-1966 he sold in excess of 3,415,000 singles, plus a staggering collection of over 2,899,000 albums, making him the hottest artist on Reprise.

With his deal now completed for a series of six Matt Helm films, co-produced by his own company Meadway-Claude, work began on *The Silencers*, based on the novels 'The Silencers' and 'Death of A Citizen'.

Intended as America's answer to James Bond, the Matt Helm films were just as removed from the Hamilton novels as the Bond films were from the Ian Fleming works. They even 'out-gadgeted' the ridiculous inventions from Q Branch.

This was Dean at his relaxed, caricatured best. He played the part to perfection and every film in the series bordered on comedy with a moderate amount of danger, thin plots, bikini-clad girls and lots of action. Dean even sang parodies of his songs in the films where he could.

He recorded a special set of songs for Reprise for *The Silencers*, also including some powerful instrumental tracks on the same album, released in America on 8th March 1966.

Such was the success of *The Silencers*, a full range of Louis Marx and Crescent toys were made available to tie in with the film. Locations were filmed in the Columbia ranch and street area which was rebuilt to look like a residential New Mexico town, complete with a Bel Air Hotel and swimming pools. The fast automobile chases took place at Santa Fe, New Mexico, and Phoenix, Arizona. In the course of filming, five stuntmen were hurt: one of them, Tom Henessey, had three front teeth knocked out and had his head heavily bruised by Dean during a fight scene.

Interestingly, the out-and-out comedy spy series of *Austin Powers* decades later seems to owe more to Dean's secret agent than EON's more successful take on James Bond.

In the closing weeks of this year, Reprise in America decided to have what they called a 'Dean Martin Month' (it was actually a two-month period) when they issued two new albums, '*The Dean Martin Television Show*,' and 'The Dean Martin Christmas Album,' with a massive publicity campaign commencing 1st November and lasting until New Year's Eve.

His first picture for Universal was the comedy Western *Texas Across the River* with Alain Delon and fellow Rat-Packer Joey Bishop.

Next came the second Matt Helm movie, *Murderer's Row*, and we attended a special private showing at the 20th Century-Fox Private Theatre, 31, Soho Square London on Wednesday 25th January 1967, prior to the film opening in the UK, and we brushed shoulders with the cast and crew (but not, of course, Dino!). Matt Helm's Slaygirls were in attendance, too. It was a great start to 1967.

Several locations were used for this film, among them the picturesque Isle of Wight. Dean had invited me to come to the shoot, to watch him film and to spend some time with him afterwards. It had intended to be an all-expenses paid event for me, with hotel accommodation and something like 3 weeks' worth of filming for the star. Dean cancelled not long after the invite, citing increasing workloads, but I took up Columbia's kind offer and watched the UK filming anyway. All the scenes filmed in and around the hovercrafts were with a body double. You don't need to look too hard to see, in the finished film, that it's not Dean! The Isle of Wight hovercraft that was used was re-named 'Matt Helm One' after the filming.

A sort of family affair, Dean's son Dean Jr appeared with Desi Arnaz Junior and Billy Hinsche, all three making the pop trio Dino, Desi and Billy, who were enjoying reasonable success in the music market themselves at this time.

With the co-operation of Dean and Pye Records (who were the licensees for all Reprise product in the United Kingdom at that time) we had issued a special one-sided single of Dean talking prior to his song 'I'm Not the Marrying Kind' which we presented to all guests at the private showing.

The following month, in February, we supported Pye Records with their Dean Martin Week from Monday the 13th then collaborated with them for a 45rpm one-sided single issue of 'I'm Not the Marrying Kind', complete with an introduction from the man himself and the catalogue number 'DMA1' (this number too reflected our recent change of name: we were now the Dean Martin Association). The release was limited and is now a very rare item, so rare that even the DMA doesn't own a copy - and if anyone out there does, please contact us through our website!

Meanwhile, Dean was voted 'Music Man of the Year' by the Academy of Country and Western Music in Los Angeles, but the award was collected on his behalf by his daughters Claudia and Deana on 6th March. And talking of daughters, my own was born just two days before! Dean congratulated my wife and me, and in June even sent over the same brand of doll that he had been photographed holding on the front of his 'Happiness Is…'LP. Carole still owns the doll to this day and remains proud that Dean gave it to her as a present.

Pye now began to issue cassette tapes, and Dean's first album re-appeared in this new format as ZCK4-44022.

We issued an interview with Dean via our newsletter for July and this created quite some excitement with the members (he had agreed to answer a series of set questions from me over the telephone).

With Reprise, Dean was now talking of recording an album of songs in the Hawaiian style, but nothing further came of this project. Prior to this in 1966, Dean had proposed a religious type collection that was even assigned a catalogue number and title (RB6189 Old Time Religion). Again, nothing had come of it – but was an intriguing concept.

At a charity concert in Los Angeles, Dean donated $350 to hear Bobby Darin sing and one of Europe's offshore 'pirate' radio stations, Britain Radio, featured us during September, which again boosted our status somewhat. Also, the teen magazine 'Diana' gave us a large feature, giving details of our club and our aims for the future.

As part of a deal he had made with Universal Pictures, Dean made another film for them entitled *Rough Night In Jericho*, teaming himself with the beautiful and well-known Jean Simmons and an up and coming actor called George Peppard who was beginning to make a good name for himself. Peppard would find fame ultimately as the cigar-chomping, wise-cracking Colonel John 'Hannibal' Smith in Stephen J Cannell's 80s action series *The A-Team*.

As Alex Flood, this was the very first time that Dean actually 'died' in character on film, as this was something he had always balked at before. His part was described as 'very heavy' and he gave an excellent performance as the antagonist, treating Simmons' character with such poison.

Nancy Sinatra was finding her own way in the industry, and her hit single, 'These Boots Are Made for Walkin,' has since gone down in history. Dean guest-starred in her TV special *Movin' with Nancy* in 1967, fitting in his recorded sequences in between his own shows and Reprise studio bookings. One such song could almost have been the theme to his acted persona, although this was generally by the public and not him: 'Little Ole Wine Drinker, Me' was more of a hit in Europe than it was in America when it was released in June of this year.

Incidentally, the song that Dean had had re-mixed for Nancy to sing in his original recording of 'Things' reached number one in Sweden that same July, and remained in the chart for five weeks, having never been issued as a single either in America or the UK.

Capitol Records USA released their first-ever boxed set in October, and it was aptly named 'The Dean Martin Deluxe Set,' containing three albums of songs all previously available.

A worry for him, though, was his mother Angela, who had become seriously ill. Her love of charity work had to be cut back and Dean ensured the finest treatment money could buy would come her way. She and Guy Crocetti had been living in a beautiful home Dean had bought them in Westwood and while Guy had been suffering with pancreas trouble for some time, he was able to enjoy his retirement with Dean's support: the strong Italian upbringing shone through and he could never be accused of forsaking them for anything. He continually asked them what they wanted and they would only have to say and it was done.

Both his mother and father would attend some of his stage performances from time to time, but now, with Angela ill, Guy longer had the heart to do anything.

After spending some happy years at Westwood, it was decided that his parents should move nearer to Dean and reside at Doheny Drive.

Whilst working at the Sands over the Christmas period, Gail had assured her father that Grandmother was in reasonable health and that she did not really need any more gifts, even though she knew that her son just loved giving his parents endless items.

Whilst staying at his hotel in Nevada, Dean received the fateful message that his Mother had died in the early hours of Christmas morning. He raced back to his home devastated, but with unique dignity, he laid her to rest at the family plot in the Westwood Memorial Park.

14

Amongst all the glitz, glamour, and false existence in the world of show-business, it was very easy to forget that Dean Martin, the total entertainer, could not have kept up the pace of his work if he had been true to his stage persona: these long-standing stories of excessive drink had never been true. Years of dark and ominous tales are really to be laughed about, mostly found in tabloids looking for a story or a hook to grab the media's attention.

Contrary to those 'drink' jokes that would be spread around (a lot of them by Dean himself) he would drink healthily and ensured that he took daily exercise even without any of the fancy equipment he could have purchased. One always smiles when thinking of Dean drinking milk! While he adored being the entertainer he was, at the same time he wanted to keep away from the outside world and not allow anyone to see the true man (although he always said that what you see on the television screen was his real self).

Jeanne said many times that she never really knew her husband, even after all those years they were together, but it was particularly intentional for Dean to do this. Brought up to believe it was somewhat unmanly to show emotion, to shake hands with people was generally not his style – he would sooner place his hands on your shoulder as an expression of affection.

If he was disinterested in a social gathering or similar atmosphere, he was known to sit away from everyone, pretending to be drunk, tired, or both. No matter what he felt inside, good or bad, it was a rare chance for Dean to show emotion to anyone.

Yet for all his exercise, he continued to suffer with arthritis in his spine, and with stomach problems and anxiety.

He had now completed his third Matt Helm production *The Ambushers*, this time with Senta Berger, Janice Rule and

Beverley Adams, scoring yet again another smash across the world, although a little short off the mark from the first.

The film went before the cameras on April 24th in Mexico, with Hollywood work all completed in 44 days, two days ahead of schedule. The two previous pictures had given Dean a gross profit of $25million (a fact relayed to him whilst he was filming).

He was looking at a further film with Columbia (*How To Save A Marriage...and Ruin Your Life*) as well as signing on for a production with James Stewart, together with an unprecedented $34 million for a three year deal with NBC for his television shows. That amount of money proved the status of Dean Martin now: he could do no wrong in his career, and it was also because of his tremendous popularity that the association was getting so busy.

Throughout these months, he had raced ahead with his Matt Helm productions as well as *How to Save a Marriage...* (originally to be called *Band of Gold*) with Stella Stevens and Eli Wallach, and returned to the Western genre in style with Racquel Welch and James Stewart in *Bandolero!* for 20th Century Fox (accompanied by a wonderful and expressive score by the genius that was Jerry Goldsmith). Another dramatic Western followed alongside the great Robert Mitchum for Paramount's *Five Card Stud*. For this production, Dean agreed to record the main title as a Reprise single release, going in to the studios 23rd July 1968 to lay down only this one song.

He was working practically non-stop, which was, admittedly, due to demand, but he was unhappy with his health and was still, naturally, devastated by his mother's death.

He sought an outlet for his problems by finding solace outside the marriage and rumours once more spread around town that he was to divorce Jeanne. The tabloids ran stories that he had thought nothing of his parents, and these vicious and wholly unfounded stories caused him much upset. He was in a nervous state and it was a great tribute to his inner-self that he could actually show his talent to the public and yet be so strung-up inside, not sure of perhaps which way to turn.

He worried about his father even more after losing his mother, and, after a marriage lasting more than 53 years, Guy passed away 8 months later. He died of heartbreak: he could not cope with life without his beloved Angela and, although Dean tried to do everything for him, it seemed absolutely nothing worked. He was finished, and died a sad and broken man, his only consolation perhaps being that Dean had really made it in the world, a famous and household name.

Guy was buried with his devoted wife on 1st September in the Westwood Memorial Park in the family mausoleum, having spent the last few weeks of his life in a nursing home.

Dean, of course, working at this fast pace, seemed to take just about everything in his stride: but inside, he was complex and felt so screwed up, so unsettled. His career was practically perfect but he couldn't cope with the loss of both parents and then, on 20th October the same year, his brother Bill died from brain cancer. Bill had worked for Dean as manager of his brother's York Productions for a while (as well as being in charge of Dean's Lodge, of course).

Although each personal tragedy affected Dean greatly, he portrayed the swinger and drinker persona with ultimate ease, publicly dating numerous women but strangely, keeping most of everything else in his private life away from the world.

Again, he attended more recording sessions, having completed all songs for the 'Gentle On My Mind' album prior to his 'Five Card Stud' taping, whilst Reprise issued the first volume of his greatest hits in May this year, followed by volume two the following August. It was also decided to re-issue some of his hits on 'Back-To-Back' singles and they appeared around the same time as the release of 'Gentle On My Mind' on 17th December 1968 (although the UK had to wait until the following February).

Dean's original deal with Columbia was for six Matt Helm super-spy films. He'd completed *The Wrecking Crew* (working title *The House Of Seven Joys*) with Elke Sommer, Sharon Tate, and that esteemed British actor Nigel Green, but broke his contract when he refused to do any more (via Meadway-Claude Productions).

Having started production on 3rd June 1968, *The Wrecking Crew* was eventually completed the following November, amidst complications and delays. Producer Irving Allen then began preparations for the next Matt Helm entry. But *The Ravagers* never saw the light of day, and Matt Helm's movie future was decided. I thought this was a pity as these films showed the relaxed and casual Dean Martin, with a total laugh at spy films in general, with the added bonus of Bond-esque action and girls by the dozen! (Columbia still retained the rights, however, and went in to produce a one-season TV series, *Matt Helm*, that debuted on ABC in September 1975. Dean of course didn't reprise his role: it instead went to Anthony Franciosa (who had previously co-starred with Dean in *Career*).) There were rumours in the mid-noughties that either Amblin or Dreamworks had secured the rights to the Don Hamilton books but nothing ever came of it and, to date, Mr Helm remains a spy who is definitely out in the cold (although the Hamilton novels have since been republished by Titan Books).

The BBC had negotiated with Dean's management for a series of his renowned television shows to be screened in the UK. Although the four they showed (9th and 30th October, 27th November, and 26th December) were superb, the BBC advised us in early 1969 that they wouldn't be showing any more under the deal as they had had very little audience engagement at all.

I found this very disappointing: he *was* liked here, but, I felt, always underrated, and it seemed this type of variety show did not appeal to our market like it did in the US.

But his popularity was still considerable and the club gained many more members and acclaim as a result of the shows being aired over here.

When Dean sent me copies of his new album 'Gentle On My Mind' in November, I naturally played this collection of songs and was quite taken aback at his astounding version of John Hartford's song used for the title. In my opinion, it was a far superior version by Dean than I had ever heard by any artist previously, and I was absolutely convinced it would make a single here and sell very well.

Naturally, the unique way that record companies behave, I was told that I was biased in my opinions and attitude towards

Dean in general. But I had this very strong feeling in my heart that if this song could be released as a single here, it would get into the UK charts.

But Pye weren't budging (to be honest, why would they?) yet I still felt strongly about it. I was told numerous times that Dean Martin was mainly an album seller, a comment I did find strange when I thought of the many singles that had become big sellers, even though they did, admittedly, all make chart entries.

It took many weeks of negotiation and persuasion with Pye records in London who, in turn, had to consult with Dean's office before I won my battle on this suggestion. I was not concerned with the b-side of the single. It was the fact that I was 100% sure that 'Gentle On My Mind' could and would make it as a single.

Finally, they announced that the single would be issued 24th January 1969 and, without writing several pages just on this subject, with the work and excitement that this caused, the record actually reached number 2 in the UK charts March 1st and stayed there for two weeks! Moving down after a fortnight, it stayed in the charts for a total of 23 weeks, including a meagre re-entry in August at number 49. I tried my hardest to get Dean to appear here as a promotional tool, but he could find no time in his very busy schedule. Whether he would have *actually* come over had he got the time is something we'll never know.

The BBC's weekly music show *Top Of The Pops* usually had the artists perform live in the studio (albeit miming on some occasions to whatever chart single they were pushing) but with Dean they showed various photographs on screen whilst the record was playing and sales (plus our membership) gained a tremendous boost for this year, with our being almost unable to cope with the sacks of mail we were getting.

Conversely, I had also forecast that 'Gentle On My Mind' wouldn't fare well as a single in America and, unsurprisingly, it did not gain any chart entries, achieving only reasonable sales.

Pye themselves suggested a follow-up single after the success of this issue, but I believed there would be no point in anything like this, as it would not produce any results.

My premonitions seemed to be proven right yet again, because although they did release a single ('By the Time I Get to Phoenix' coupled with 'Things') on 23rd May, it didn't do well at all.

Dean called me when news reached him of his success in the UK with 'Gentle On My Mind', saying too how very grateful he was for our continued work and support of his career. In all the years I worked on behalf of Dean, it never felt once like a job. It was a pleasure from day one to the day I stepped back and handed the reins over to my son, Elliot.

With the UK success of this single, it seemed to make certain people sit and take notice of my remarks that Dean did make hit singles and could do it here as well as America. On Monday 2nd September, the inimitable presenter Desmond Carrington included a 15-minute segment on Dean on his BBC Radio 2 programme *Roundabout*, giving Dean more UK exposure.

The music publication *Melody Maker* announced that 'Gentle On My Mind' was the most played song; the club had its first society meeting Sunday 19th October 19th and the US-trade paper *Billboard* gave a special tribute to Dean. Meanwhile in the US, Capitol issued 'The Best of Dean Martin' plus 'Dean Martin's Greatest!' (different compilations of 'The Best Of Dean Martin, Volumes 1 and 2' appeared in the UK).

After almost a year's gap in recording now, Dean taped ten songs for his new release album and the title song (Merle Haggard's 'I Take A Lot of Pride In What I Am') appeared as his new single in 22nd July, reaching only number 75 in the American charts, although it did wander around the chart positions for four weeks! He had recorded all the songs for this album over two days (11th and 12th June) and a second single lifted from this set of songs did not chart at all.

Back in Nevada, Dean took a 10% stake in the Riviera Hotel and agreed to appear there on an exclusive basis. This was a new chapter for him, allowing him to go on stage when he wanted to, and by now, his fortunes were unalloyed: as well as the Riviera shares, he also had numerous other assets. These included investments in the LA Rams, and real estate assets (he owned several homes and apartments as well as being the largest individual landowner in Ventura County). He also owned a handful of production companies, and property businesses, and a large batch of RCA holdings, with numerous other investments and deals always circulating. He also held total controlling interests in his television shows, and several films, as well as complete ownership of every song recorded for the Reprise and Warner Brothers labels.

None of this money or fame could save Dean's marriage to Jeanne. His affairs with younger women (all averaging around 20 years old, he was 52) were making the news, especially when he was seen regularly with Gail Renshaw. Rumours of a break-up with his wife abounded, and when asked what she thought was going on, Jeanne commented ...*I do not know what he is up to. He cannot seem to make up his mind what age group he is interested in.* But several weeks later, the day before he made his appearance at the Riviera Hotel's 14th anniversary on 11 December 1969, he finally filed for divorce.

15

Gail's the girl for me, Dean reportedly said. *Jeanne might get the ranch, you know, I could never find it anyway!*

His quips belied his real feelings.

He was starry-eyed over the beauty queen, the Virginia-born Miss World USA titleholder and runner up in 1969's Miss World competition. They'd first met backstage at the Riviera in late November 1969 when she asked him to pose with her for a photo. They dined at the Riv's exclusive gourmet restaurant Delmonico between shows and had a nightcap in Dino's Den, an intimate cocktail lounge off the casino area, following his midnight performances. After a photo was released whilst they were having a meal together, the media in general just could not wait to hear the sound of wedding bells, hungry for something new about Dean and his love life.

But after all the coverage and publicity, the engagement lasted just over four months and it was officially announced that there would be no marriage.

Dean's appearances at the Riviera continued unabated. *It's New Year's Eve every night when he's in town*, said Marty Klein, the Versailles Room maitre d'.

A typical day for the him when he played the Riviera included a 10am breakfast with golfing partners Tony Frabbiele and Don Cherry, tee off at 11am sharp (he was an eight-cap handicap golfer who gave his best high note for a sub-par round), breaking for 1pm lunch at the clubhouse and a return to the hotel at 4pm for a rubdown and a nap. He'd prepare three hours later for the dinner show and go on stage for 10pm at the Delmonico, followed by a midnight show in the Versailles Room. 2am the next morning often meant a gathering in Dino's Den where a couple of impromptu songs with pianist Alice Darr would occasionally take place as well as a story-swapping session with celebrity pals who dropped in from other hotels for a late drink. Then finally, at 3am, it was bedtime in the luxurious Dean Martin Suite.

No wonder his ulcers never got a break.

Looks like I can forget eating Italian sausage for another year, he was heard to groan.

One evening, American football quarterback Joe Namath dropped by the Den, having seen Dean's midnight show. He'd been struggling with his new career as an actor and asked Dean for some tips.

Dean suggested Joe just relax and try to act natural.

Relax? came Namath's reply. *I'm so relaxed I can't stand up. I drink five quick Scotches before I go before the damn camera, but I still feel like the whole of Kansas City line is comin' straight at me.*

Dean's response? *It must be your brand of Scotch.*

In June 1970, Dean was seen at the Delmonico in the company of another woman, 24-year old Catherine Mae Hawn. He seemed more at ease with his new partner and took her on to numerous local functions and eating houses, remarking on one occasion to a reporter that he would have to leave earlier than usual to 'burp [his] girl'.

In the midst of all the coverage he was getting about his love life, his work continued at a fast pace. He signed with Universal Pictures to star alongside the great Burt Lancaster in *Airport*, the film version of Arthur Hailey's best-selling novel of the same name, and looked forward to having a strong part again, with the added bonus of being able to work with a fine actor like Burt.

He was right. His role as the Boeing 707 pilot Vernon Demerest was a very dramatic one. Producer Ross Hunter had seen the potential in casting Dean. "When I first saw and read those proofs," said Hunter, "I immediately saw one man in my mind's eye: Dean Martin. I knew he would just *have* to play the jetliner pilot who has to cope with a maniacal bomb-carrying passenger who wants to blow the plane up in mid-air. I distinctly remembered Dean's dramatic role in *Some Came Running* and, once I had signed him, I cast the rest of the film from there."

Dean agreed to do this part before he had even read the script, and it became one of his favourite roles.

"Dean was a great actor," continued Ross. "People just didn't give him credit for being as good as he really was. They saw him in that Matt Helm picture and others like it, but he was a very serious and professional man. He knew everyone's lines and everyone else's part as well as his own. He was anxious to rehearse in his own way and get everything right. I telephoned him at home one night: I'd just seen the scene when he gets the case with the bomb in it from Van Heflin [who played Guerrero, the suicidal maniac] and he did it with so much authority and dignity, I just felt compelled to thank him and congratulate him for his expertise."

An astonishing tribute to Dean, considering the weight of the rest of the cast in this gripping thriller, which included Lancaster, George Kennedy, Barry Nelson, Jean Seberg, Helen Hayes, Jacqueline Bisset, and many more. Locations at St. Paul Minneapolis airport were proving problematic, with temperatures at 45 degrees below zero at times.

Box office receipts proved the film a resounding success. It had cost over $12 million and had good returns all around the world, spawning a series of airplane disaster movies (culminating in possibly the best tribute of all, *Airplane!*).

My wife and I attended the Royal Charity Premiere at the Odeon Leicester Square in London on Wednesday 22nd April at 8.15pm in the presence of their Royal Highnesses, the Duke and Duchess of Kent.

Dean, of course, didn't go.

Those of us who have followed the life and career of Dean Martin, know that if he had never been a singer he could have made it as a straight actor. But then singing is a form of acting anyway: the way that each song is expressed is a total and unique action of phrasing for each individual. Listen to the voices and styling of, for example, Sinatra, Madonna, Nat 'King' Cole, Dusty Springfield, Michael Jackson, Rod Stewart, Barbra Streisand, Bruno Mars...just a handful of examples over the decades, but each artist has their own unique way of song interpretation.

Dean himself always had that certain style and manner all of his own right from the beginning. His acting, too, was different.

He was practically an expert on making it look so easy. Even in comedy he made it look so casual.

I'd go so far as to say that he was underrated as a comedy performer, adding that he was possibly one of the world's greatest and funniest comedians, although people who perhaps have not witnessed all of Dean's talents might say 'but he's only a singer and an actor, surely not a comedian'.

Even after he split with Jerry, he continued to put his finely-tuned comedy to good use in various forms as he progressed through his career.

There's a great scene in the 2008 picture *Transporter 3*, where Jason Statham's character Frank Martin (and it only just occurred to me writing this, of the marrying of Sinatra's first name with Dean's surname!) is fishing with his friend, Inspector Tarconi (François Berléand). Tarconi talks about the highly developed French sense of humour, to which Frank Martin responds:

"With respect, the French think Jerry Lewis was a genius."

"Well, he *was* a genius," says Tarconi.

"No, *Dean* was the genius."

"No, Dean just stood there with a drink and a cigarette."

"My point exactly," Statham's character continues. "Anybody can fall down and get a laugh but how many can do it standing still with a drink and a cigarette?"

Writers Luc Besson and Robert Mark Kamen clearly knew what they were talking about!

To attend a Dean Martin recording session was a chance to see not only a singer doing great things with a song, but to witness his comedy antics with the musicians and staff as he recorded six or eight songs in one session, perhaps to return the next day to complete another handful for a new album. But there was always the smile and the ability to make the whole room fall about in fits of laughter. The few sessions I was fortunate enough to attend, I remember the joy the technicians and I experienced as we all sat listening and watching the man himself.

It was while completing *Airport* that Dean realised he was now among the elite handful of entertainers in the world who could demand big money for anything they cared to do.

He had reached the top of his profession.

When making films, Dean always disliked the delays involved with the production. He hated waiting to be called for his next scene, so he tried to avoid this by pushing for his scenes to be in the can as swiftly as possible. On one occasion, he completed a film well before the completion schedule, which naturally pleased the studio execs.

By this time in his life, Dean Martin had done most things he had wanted to achieve in showbusiness and he was beginning to gradually slow down the pace of his career, reducing his television appearances as well as his visits to the recording studios. With the completion of *Airport*, he was only to make another five films for the cinema.

This was through choice rather than a dwindling popularity. Dean felt pleased with his accomplishments in the past thirty years; he did the best work he could and found satisfaction in his career at all levels.

Asked once why he never tried Broadway or the dramatic stage in general, he replied in a way that sums him up entirely, but is somewhat ironic: "I just did not want to repetitiously speak the same old lines night after night. Besides, anyone that gets to Broadway usually looks to making it to Hollywood. Well, I did it from Hollywood first and had the luck to be successful from there, so that was satisfying for me. No, I don't knock the stage, it is just that I have never particularly liked the theatre anyway."

The irony I mention is in reference to his stage act. Listen to his segments on the live Rat Pack shows at the Sands in the early 1960s: he usually starts with the same gags and the same songs. Jump to his last concert appearances in the 1980s and he hasn't changed his act, save for a few contemporary lines here and there and a different song or two.

Career-wise, Dean could not have been in a better position, but his personal life was in utter turmoil. Legal complications were starting to appear as his lawyer went through his estate and investments with his accountants and management in preparation for the split after 24 years with Jeanne. Now his hands were tied in his personal situation, but everything had to be legally transacted and it was a matter of time before things were finalised.

His sound recordings continued to appear both on Capitol and Reprise, with such items as 'Tracks Of My Tears', 'Come On Down', 'Cheatin' On Me' and 'Let's Be Friendly' now seen in the record stores, along with a spectacular boxed album set of records and cassettes containing five dozen songs from the Capitol era.

Work continued in earnest for the club as I completed this set for EMI's mail order division World Records.

The sixty songs I chose for this project gave a wonderful insight into Dean's Capitol career, and I had full say in which songs were chosen, as well as the design and sleeve notes. The release was planned for January 1970.

We also assisted the BBC in a 45 minute tribute to Dean for Radio 2, transmitted 2nd June, linking with the club's tenth anniversary.

As a surprise, Dean invited me to visit him at his home in Beverly Hills. It was only a couple of days, but my wife and I were treated like honoured guests. When he mentioned that he had 'ordered' Frank to come see me, I didn't quite believe this was all happening! But sadly, Frank's commitments elsewhere meant he was unable to be there. Dean spoke of purchasing a new Spanish style ranch, suggesting we come back one day and ride with him. He also said he was beginning to think of retirement as he wanted to spend some time with his horses and generally ease up on most things. *After all, I'm 30 now*, he was prone to say when anyone asked him if he was serious about giving it all up. When I asked him about his Reprise contract, he confirmed he'd renewed it up until 1975.

That wonderful Marty Robbins composition 'My Woman, My Woman, My Wife' became the title (and single release) of Dean's brand new album for August, with a batch of country songs recorded in Hollywood on 27th and 28th May, again under the expert supervision and production of Jimmy Bowen.

Dean continued to demonstrate his prowess and knack for songs by recording them in just a couple of days – an achievement not many artists managed, but the end result was perfection, although this album only managed to struggle to number 97 on 12th September, remaining in the same chart for twelve weeks.

He had backed away from recording with a full quota of musicians: these days he would mostly put his voice on tape with just a small group and Ken Lane, with the orchestral backing mixed in later. And that was the way Dean wanted it.

His television shows were still peaking and had entered syndication too, meaning Dean was on virtually every week of the year. He did not like repeating his part in a show – at the most he would act his role twice, as he wanted spontaneity with each song, each joke, each sketch: he worked best that way. Large white cue cards were in front of Dean all the time he was working but he never needed them. It was part of his act, joking he couldn't see or read the writing or the spelling. He'd wander or stagger in front of the cameras and audience holding a glass half-filled with apple juice, and sing a song, some of the time not actually completing the words or, if he did, replacing them with his own amusing parody.

"I just have never understood when people say that acting or singing is hard work. Learn your lines and sing the words and that's it, it's easy. Try standing on your damn feet all day dealing black-jack and see what the difference is. Now *that* comes hard! If you cannot be bothered to go to see a film, then the artists' work is lost to you, but on television, there is no effort, you can sit back and just watch that screen and the programme is there with you."

Now, of course, there are any number of Dean's movies on satellite or streaming channels, as online uploads or on DVD, so the medium of television has meant his statement is of its time. Being the advocate of TV viewing as he was, I wonder what he would have made of the saturation we now all have of the small screen?

Unfortunately, as the new decade continued, his health was against him. His ulcer was causing a lot of discomfort, but although he was strongly advised to enter hospital, he twice refused, saying he didn't have the time. Unable to overcome the pain while in San Francisco, he finally relented and had surgery for the chronic condition.

During the course of 1970, the UK arm of Warner Brothers created a new label called Valiant. This was to be a budget label representing various artists whose material would be re-issued at a lower price than the original (not unlike EMI's Music For Pleasure).

A handful of albums appeared from other artists (these are now very rare indeed), and such a release was planned from Dean's back catalogue. Dean took umbrage with this, objecting to material he owned being re-released at a cheaper price. Although a catalogue number was allocated for Dean's issue (VS145), it was never released, and strangely, the other albums that had been released by fellow artists were quickly withdrawn.

One of the places Dean had never visited was the fine continent of Australia. He had never had any particular desire to visit, but was asked if he would appear in a series of live concerts. As expected, he refused, citing his workload was too much for such a tour. The point in fact was that his aversion to travelling stopped him saying yes, even if he had the time. So, sadly, Australia was denied that talent but his TV and film work was readily repeated across the continent. We had numerous members in Australia at this time and our membership was growing steadily. We opened our own small office in Beverly Hills, giving us local facilities to Dean's office, and had another DMA meeting on 15th November in London, while the man himself was gathering finance for charities. A Joe E. Lewis tribute raised $75,000, his appearance for the Roger Baldwin Foundation for American Civil Liberties Union accrued $200,000, and in an on-stage appearance at the Riviera hotel, Frank Sinatra joined Dean in a surprise walk-on.

As 1971 came into being, the entertainer 'par excellence' (as one magazine referred to Dean) recorded more songs for release, forming his new album 'For The Good Times,' an apt title considering his present success. Having taped these ten songs 29th and 30th September 1970, with the release for February this year, he only recorded a further 18 for Reprise for the whole of the year, sure signs that he had slowed down his song output.

16

In his next few years with Reprise, Dean was to record even less, his popularity in the charts now waning. He had spent his time working much harder than most of his peers, and was still half-threatening to retire.

I'll do that around 1975 I guess, Dean had said, *then I can sit around all day and do nothing but watch television! But no! I gotta get up in the morning and do* something!

More and more album compilations appeared from the Capitol stable to compete with Dean's output on Reprise. I suggested to EMI an album of songs Dean had recorded with other artists in his Capitol days (such as Nat 'King' Cole, Margaret Whiting and Peggy Lee), and while they never even acknowledged my ideas, shortly afterwards, an album did appear with similar content entitled 'Nat, Dean and Friends'...so I put it down to a remarkable coincidence.

The club was given a big feature in 'Woman' magazine but our newsletter distribution was somewhat suspended early this year due to a 47-day postal strike in the UK. When the strike ended, we combined two issues for our members.

After a long break between films, there were almost two years before *Something Big* was to appear, in which Dean struck a deal with 20th Century Fox for yet another western saga, this time bringing him to work with Brian Keith and (former) Bond girl Honor Blackman.

Filmed entirely on location in Durango, Mexico, this was 108 minutes of very 'vigorous' action (according to the publicity manual!) and Dean was quoted as saying that *...this is a great fun film.*

Advertising slogans stated that 'everybody wants to do something big once in his life', but unfortunately this was not one of Dean's big box-office smashes, although it gained larger audiences across America than in any other country. Nevertheless, it gave Dean another chance to play the villain, a part remote from his previous role as the dashing airline pilot. Although there was a song composed by Burt Bacharach and Hal David for the title theme, it was performed not by Dean but by Mark Lindsay, lead singer of Paul Revere and the Raiders.

After filming had wrapped, he visited Hawaii and was quite taken by the islands and their people, even taking time out to watch Jack Lord film an episode of the hit police drama *Hawaii Five-O*.

"I was pretty impressed," he told me later on. "Jack was a good guy. Really professional. We hit it off and he suggested I should do a guest spot."

Dean of course never did appear in the series but he did ask me to make Jack Lord an honorary club member. We duly did so but never ever heard from Mr Lord!

From Dean's recording sessions at the end of September, it was not until 12th April that he recorded again, this time only three songs, with another gap until mid-November for a batch of ten more, for an album with the most unimaginative title ever for Dean: 'Dino'!

The album included Dean's second version of Baker Knight's 'The Right Kind of Woman' (his original version was recorded with the other two songs in April, none of which have ever been issued in any format, at the time of writing this).

With meandering record sales, the album struggled to chart in the US in 1972 - and was in point of fact the last of his albums to ever chart, even as abysmally as only reaching 117. A stand-out track was the Kris Kristofferson-penned 'Kiss the World Goodbye' but, for me, it was the Belvins' 'Guess Who' that cried out to be released as a single. But the aforementioned lack of album sales meant Reprise wouldn't entertain the idea, a reluctance I understood but I did unsuccessfully argue the notion that a single may have boosted album popularity.

Meanwhile in Europe, Warner Brothers issued a series of double albums entitled 'The Most Beautiful Songs of...', with 23 songs by Dean, using low-grade packaging (a bright orange cover with a smaller version of the photograph used on Dean's Christmas album). But it was altogether a grand compilation, even including Dean's duet with Nancy Sinatra on 'Things'.

Still romancing Cathy Hawn, Dean made a surprise visit to London on 11th May (just for shopping, he told us) and returned home on the 16th, having stayed at the Park Lane Hotel and managing to escape the prying ears and eyes of the media.

Trundling along with our newsletters, we changed our format slightly and reduced our page size from the original A4.

Health wise, Dean was suffering from ulcers again, and the arthritis in his back made him dependant on pain killers. His recent vasectomy had given him enough hospital time to be getting on with, he complained.

After a year-long row relating to non-payments from *Airport*, this was finally settled and his dues were cleared: he claimed and received his 10% of the profits after film costs were all paid. Dean always considered this one of the 'most interesting' films he'd made so it was a shame that the remuneration difficulties somewhat marred his experience.

During 1972, he was unhappy with the arrangements at the Riviera, whose management insisted he perform two shows per night for each night he was to appear. As they were set on him doing this, tempers flared, disagreements arose and Dean walked out. He simply didn't *want* to do two shows a night. Whilst things were settled amicably, he did not appear there very often during the remainder of his contract.

Additionally, his accountants and lawyers were gradually clearing his problems relating to his impending divorce from Jeanne.

Within the society, we were always looking for ways to promote Dean as much as we could and, after many negotiations, the BBC actually showed an episode from Dean's NBC series on 21st April starring Tony Bennett and Zero Mostel. Our meetings this year were successful and these were held 30th January, 26th March and 13th August. I guess you could compare these to the modern day fan conventions, albeit on a much smaller scale. We had guest speakers, showings of very rare footage (remember, this was pre-internet!), panels, and memorabilia stalls. A typical meeting lasted from around lunchtime to 10.30pm and we welcomed fans from around the world. On one occasion, we were delighted when Dean recorded an audio greeting for us to play to our guests, saying (as per his usual sign-off on his TV shows), '...keep those letters and cards comin' in'.

After much persuasion, BBC Radio 2 had a 'Dean Martin Week' from Monday 31st July and this proved a tremendous boost to our society and, of course, to Dean's record sales. Meanwhile, a format change was made to his regular television shows and producer Greg Garrison suggested some alterations , mainly toning down the scantily-clad girls and sexual remarks in general. Times were changing and the US did not want this suggestive type of comedy any more.

With numerous ongoing negotiations concerning Dean's affairs, it was agreed between Jeanne and Dean themselves that to offload some Inland Revenue problems, they would sell their ranch to the state to avoid paying too much tax. They appeared amicable and eventually, a divorce was granted to them on 12th December 12th: they had been married for 23 years. Dean spent this Christmas at the ranch before it was sold off.

Now he was out on his own.

After so many years married to Jeanne, he had chosen to leave her –for good this time – no going back after a few days or weeks like he had done many times before. Although he was now involved with Cathy, his mind went back a while and he thought of those times when he had been alone once before, when the million-dollar partnership with Jerry had finished.

They had both felt then that things had to come to an end; he'd left his partner over 20 years ago now and struck out on his own for a different and (he hoped) more successful future.

And now he was alone again, even if for different reasons, yet the feelings were the same. All those years of familiarity with his beautiful Jeanne, his children growing up - and he had broken away from all that of his own choice. Whether he regretted it, only he knew, but there was a fondness and love for Jeanne that I don't think ever truly went away, even though he seemed infatuated with Cathy.

His solitude, his privacy, his desire to not let anyone in, meant very few people understood him or realised how this jarred with his stage act or working persona: he was such a pleasure to work with and be with, but there was no way the average person could penetrate that outer shell. He remained for all of his life a man that kept himself at a distance, only letting you in if *he* wanted to...yet he would give his all to you on stage in front of untold numbers of people.

He had made his mind up to marry Cathy and now in the coming year he knew there were many things in his personal life to be re-assessed and thought out. Problems he hated, but now he had put himself in this position, giving thought to the many complications divorce and marriage bring to all of us. Jeanne was given both their Californian homes (Beverly Hills and Palm Springs) with contents from both, and with the biggest alimony settlement at that time of $6.5 million. She also received a couple of sleek cars, portions of his stocks and shares, and proceeds from various other assets. Dean was very amicable in his settlement with Jeanne: he wanted to ensure that she would never be in need of anything for the rest of her life.

From my personal impressions about Cathy and Dean, there was a strong feeling that this would not be successful...something told me that this would not be right and that it would not be a case of 'third time lucky'. However, I made no comment to him regarding their forthcoming marriage.

Jeanne and his family could not understand what he was doing: he had everything he had always wanted, a tremendous career and home life with seven lovely children and a loving, beautiful, attentive wife. But no more.

With all of the legal tangles and complications taking their time to be ironed out, Dean was content to sit back and wait for all this to be concluded...after all, that was what he was paying heavy fees for professional people to do!

But Cathy was impatient and unwilling to wait. She walked out, telling Dean she was fed up waiting for him to decide on a wedding date. But the date was finally arranged and, amid the typical Hollywood glamour, the wedding took place on 25th

April 1973 at the Beverly Hills Hotel in a room specially converted to a Catholic chapel. Sasha (Cathy's six-year old daughter) was chief bridesmaid and Frank was Dean's best man. The bride wore a peach French Chiffon gown made of satin with lilies placed in her hair. We weren't allowed to take photos but it was certainly a lavish affair. Dean acknowledged my wife and me being there and we definitely never expected any further exchanges, but were overjoyed when he brought over Frank Sinatra to say hello! Mr Sinatra, much to my surprise, knew who we were, what we did, and didn't seem at all fazed that we were even there! I felt somewhat humbled that Dean would have even mentioned us to him.

Cathy and Dean bought a house in Bel-Air and she was soon to have it completely re-styled just to her liking. Dean had taken a break from cabaret for a while but returned to his stage with vigour, yet had no desire for continuous film-making now, and no roles came along for him that he had any inclination to follow. He was losing interest and those roles didn't grab him like they had done a few years back when he admitted to enjoying making the most of them. Dean was not a person to bother watching many of his rushes (the filmed sequences were approved before the final edit) and was mostly inclined to leave that to his people to check over for him. If it was not possible for him to return home when he had finished his day's filming, he would have his own trailer to reside in with all his facilities and comforts awaiting that next call.

His daughter Deana suggested this year that he should write his autobiography, but he stubbornly refused, having no wish for a publication of this nature. Knowing full well that over the years there had been so many untruths and exaggerated stories and fantasies written about him, he felt that it would make not a jot of difference if he *did* write his life story. I couldn't see that he would have had the patience to sit down and write one anyway, but it nevertheless would have been quite something to have read about his life from his own unique and rarely heard point of view.

Meanwhile, he had asked me to change the name of the club, and so, at Dean's behest, we became the Dean Martin Association on Monday 2nd April 1973. We remained the only official world organisation on his behalf, gaining new members all the time and continuing to promote and publicise Dean to the best of our ability. We received positive promotion when we were given a three-page feature (written by me) for the November edition of the magazine 'Listen Easy'.

After all these years, we have become very well-known and quite the advocate of Dean, offering information and assistance to any member of the public or organisation that contacted us, as well as the occasional record album or single that was issued at our suggestion. This was more work than perhaps could have been imagined but it was all very much worth it!

Some of the more spectacular pleasantries of the job were attending those illustrious film premieres, meeting numerous stars, and getting to know the many people who starred and worked with Dean.

And once more, that word *retirement* reared up again, not only from his own lips but in the press. His record sales were diminishing and his box-office returns at the cinema weren't great.

17

In between all the work that Dean was still relatively happy to do, he was still suffering from his ulcers and relented at last, admitting to Cedars Of Lebanon Hospital in early July for treatment. He had to overcome his dreaded fear of all things medical and it seemed he would sooner rely on his addiction to Percodan than seek medical attention.

His face was becoming quite bloated and he was not looking like the handsome Dean the world knew. I could always understand his numerous remarks in the early 70s about retiring (even amidst all the joking) but he had committed himself to a lot more work at this time, so, luckily for his admirers, there was no chance he would be leaving the business for a long time yet. He continued his shows but they did not have the same appeal as before, and ratings were sliding. Variety shows in general were losing favour: public taste was changing and, like so many things, this genre unfortunately seemed to be losing face, with or without Dean Martin. Its days were numbered.

At the very end of December 1972, Dean had taped a dozen songs in the studio, ten of which made up the album 'Sittin' On Top of the World' for release 29th May. Photographs for this album were taken by his son Ricci. Again, this album didn't chart, even though there were familiar compositions such as 'Smile', 'I Wonder Who's Kissing Her Now' and 'Ramblin' Rose'. Dean recorded another five songs on 25th July, coming back on the 26th for three more. On 10th August, he taped 'I'll Hold out My Hand' but this was not included on the 14th December album 'You're The Best Thing That Ever Happened to Me'. To date, the missing song has never been issued anywhere. EMI Records in the UK managed to release a 'Very Best of' compilation for the Yuletide season on Capitol, which remained a steady seller for a good few years.

Dean managed only one film in 1973 and he went to Universal Pictures for producer/director George Seaton (Seaton was the screenwriter and director of *Airport*, so Dean was in familiar territory for this one). The Western *Showdown* co-starred Hollywood legend Rock Hudson, and Dean gave a strong and dramatic performance in his favourite genre. It sold to packed houses upon release in the US even though it did not get many favourable comments by the critics (comments that Dean never listened to anyway). Henry Kissinger had visited the film set and was very taken with Dean's professionalism and unconventionally laid-back approach.

Although Dean was pleased with the story, circumstances seemed compelled to doom the outcome: he had insisted on only working on this particular film for twelve weeks at $25,000 a week because of other commitments, but production was held up for weeks when Hudson suffered a near-fatal accident during filming. With no disrespect to his co-star's injuries, Dean was fuming: he was desperate to get this production in the can as fast as possible - but it wasn't to be. Then, to make matters worse for Dean himself, his beloved horse Tops (with whom he had starred in every one of his solo Westerns) died under him. Dean, in a rage and very upset, walked off the set (later giving his 15-year-old horse a funeral). Universal informed him that unless he returned, they would slap a $6million suit on him. But again, like he had done several times before with any legal threats or demands, all was settled amicably between his management and the studio.

Thus *Showdown* was finally finished after such problematic circumstances, leaving a very disenchanted Dean Martin, whose waning interest in films was worse than ever.

I suppose no one could blame him. After almost thirty years, Dean could financially afford to sit back on his television and cinema history and reap the rewards of an even longer illustrious recording career.

I asked him about this particular period in his life, mentioning to him that he seemed to have dropped the 'I'm going to retire soon' comments.

"I always have a reason for getting out of bed each morning, otherwise you just die, y'know? You have to have something."

At the end of 1973, Cary Grant attended the Gala opening of MGM's brand new brilliant Grand Hotel, which featured Dean Martin as the first billed entertainer to appear. As someone remarked later, when Frank Sinatra is in town the hotels are full, but when Dean Martin plays Las Vegas, he fills the town.

This was certainly true when Dean performed in the Celebrity Room, a part of the $100 million fantasy complex that only Metro-Goldwyn-Mayer could ever dream of. The 2,100 rooms and 376 suites were just part of Nevada's latest and most spectacular building, towering into the Las Vegas skyline.

Dean, now one of the world's richest and most popular all-round entertainers, was part of all this when he signed a deal with MGM for a package consisting of five films plus exclusive cabaret appearances.

Health problems loomed again and he continued to suffer the usual stomach and back pains, once again relying on his addiction to counter the agony. Furthermore, Cathy was becoming extravagant, spending so much of Dean's finances that he was becoming concerned. Several times, he picked her up on her lavish spending, always ending with bad arguments. True, he was not exactly short of money, but he did not like to see anyone wasting it, particularly if it was his. He had always kept himself in a huge range of clothes when he was younger, but he found in his later years he did not need so much and therefore had only a minimum wardrobe, so he did not understand why Cathy wanted to purchase so many clothes. She would purchase a dress in perhaps twenty different colours. This seemed to be the thing to do as far as she was concerned, when she had gone from earning a handful of bucks a week to becoming the wife of one of Hollywood's richest men.

Perhaps it was the age gap, too, that meant they never saw eye to eye on this. And, in a repeat of both his previous marriages, she was unhappy at home. Why? Because if Dean wasn't out performing, he was at home watching TV. He would frequently sit at home watching the small screen for hours whilst his young wife would be wearing a dress costing around $2,000 or more, with nowhere to go.

Dean wasn't happy. He was unsettled, but was not telling a soul about it. He'd suffered from depression before and it was something that was rearing up again. Coupled with his addiction to painkillers as well as the conditions he hoped they'd resolve, it was clear that something had to give.

So what did he do? Increase his Vegas appearances, of course, allowing Dean to hide behind Dean.

His television shows were not the same as before, and no matter how devoted an admirer you were, everyone admitted that they needed something...so again Greg Garrison worked out a new formula. From the *Dean Martin Television Show* it went to the (essentially clip-driven) *Dean Martin Comedy Hour*, to be later regenerated as the *Dean Martin Celebrity Roasts*. In essence, no matter what the format, it kept Dean on TV.

He had made so many shows for television, even before his 1965 series began, and had always been a regular guest on other shows, so there had been plenty of coverage for plenty of years. I have talked of the unprecedented success of it all and even Dean himself was surprised his shows had lasted so long: top of the US ratings every time, thousands of letters all requesting replies from Dean that neither he nor his office could honour. They did send some our way but we didn't have the capacity to respond, and we had to tell his office it was a support arm we couldn't continue. On one particular show, he jokingly asked the viewers to send in their piano lids...and dozens turned up days later at NBC. He found this extremely funny but was advised by the studio that perhaps it would *not* be a good idea to repeat such requests !

With the *Celebrity Roasts*, these shows would generally be an hour of friendly insults and remarks made by a gathering of star guests to the man or woman of the hour, hosted by Dean, who would add his remarks about his guest before handing over to that same celebrity to finish the show. This was filmed within the MGM Grand Hotel and again became popular for Dean (he could film his show and appear in cabaret on $170,000 a stint for a minimum of six weeks per year – and he had his own private apartment there, too).

His first wife Betty had received $2,400 a month from Dean since 1949 which had now ceased, the amount hardly noticeable to him the way his present wife was spending money!

In the headlines was the *other* Dean, his son, who had been arrested for being in possession of firearms. He'd collected some as a hobby and the authorities released him soon after when he produced a genuine arms certificate, stating he was a collector.

Meanwhile, his father now started work on the first film under his deal with MGM entitled *Mister Ricco*, in which he played a lawyer defending an accused killer involved in a spate of police murders. This was a strong character role - but Dean's heart was not in it. He could not concentrate on his lines, his depression swamping his waking thoughts. Yet he completed what was actually a good film, together with a good storyline, but he announced that he would do no more films for MGM, once again breaking a deal. It was a pattern that had followed him for his entire career.

MGM didn't promote the film with much publicity and it fell by the wayside to become an interesting yet largely forgotten entry to the early 70s police/action movie genre. It was never going to be a *Dirty Harry*, or a *French Connection* or a *Death Wish* but it *is* of that ilk -- and sorely underrated.

Rumours appeared here and there that a possible concert tour with Sammy and Frank was in the offing but nothing came of this; the three artists were involved in commitments that would not enable them to get together at the same time.

So much of the camaraderie and remarks made in the *Celebrity Roasts* and on stage were very much in-jokes, old pals acting out a comedy. A lot of the gags were lost on the viewers; one perhaps had to be part of the clique to appreciate the comedy. Dean kept some sort of order in all of this mayhem, and again his shows were going up in the ratings. This was something that he was now used to hearing but not necessarily expecting, especially in these trying times with so many younger entertainers coming up fast behind.

However, he complained that there were just too many 'drunk' jokes about himself in the scripts, so these were eased off gradually. The audiences filled the area in front of the celebrities (usually to packed capacity), all adding atmosphere to the shows. Certain scenes were filmed back in the studio with the same props, re-arranged for better continuity, and finally edited to present the show ready for transmission.

With Dean's latest album issued quite some time back, there was now a distinct lack of recorded material for those admirers of the mellow Martin sound, who naturally felt starved of their favourite singer's renditions , even though his sales had diminished of late. In between breaks from his television and cabaret work, he managed to go into the recording studio at the end of November to lay down ten tracks including 'It's Magic' and 'Love Thy Neighbour'. With these, he had finally come to record his last-ever songs for release on the Reprise label.

Although his contract was not officially expired until 1975, Dean had recorded enough songs to fulfil his commitments under that contract and of course rumours started that he would soon re-sign with another record company. A strong contender at the time was thought to be RCA, as he held quite a considerable stake in that company. But these ten songs he recorded were shelved and not released within the normal time-span – no issue date was arranged by either side.

If it *had* been possible for him to retire in 1975, as he had jokingly threatened many times, he would have had no financial worries or concerns. But retirement was out of the question for him --at least for a year or two. He had contracted himself for further cabaret and television work if nothing else.

18

It had now been two years since a new album had been released, and Dean's collectors and admirers were becoming impatient at the lack of products. There was no way that Dean Martin was going to have the commitment he had previously had with any chapter of his career - he just did not want or need such fierce output now and to all sensible admirers of his work, they had to be reasonable and realise that he was an entertainer whose ratings pull or sales figures were becoming less headlining.

The DMA entered its 15th year of representing Dean's career, and I began work in assisting EMI Records for a Capitol album for the summer season with the theme of memories. In conjunction with Kodak, we made a selection of songs by Dean to reflect this, with the public invited to send in their memories, with records and photographic equipment as prizes. The album tracks were now finalised between Capitol and me, with the front cover a collage of small pictures surrounding a larger central photograph of Dean, with the inevitable title, 'Memories Are Made of This'. An unusual twenty-track compilation (most were half that length), the album was issued on 9th July 1975 and became the BBC Radio 2 'Album of the Week' for 22nd July.

We had an international poll amongst our members this year in which we asked them which was their favourite character part that Dean had played in a film so far. When we eventually sorted the answers, we were somewhat surprised when it turned out to be the part of Dude in *Rio Bravo*. In my personal opinion, with the popularity of his spy films, I would have thought the top choice would have been Matt Helm - but it reflected the choice of the public and just goes to show that we all see Dean in different ways!

With such a variety of characters throughout his films, Dean time and time again showed the public that he was not just a fine singer but he also made a damn good actor and comedian. As Joey Bishop once said of Dean, *what a pity he is such a fine singer…he is also the greatest comedian ever!*

Perhaps Dean's talent with comedy is not at the forefront of his repertoire because he portrayed the best of his funny lines and sketches in his own television shows over the years, and they never had the worldwide distribution that they warranted. I always thought that this was a terrible pity, because it was Dean himself who did not allow his shows to have blanket coverage around the world. It was only in America that we had these weekly showings; the rest of the world had to have erratic, broken scheduling. When we played these shows at our meetings, I was surprised that some people didn't appreciate his song parodies. When I mentioned this to him, he quite rightly said, "Bernard, if they wanna listen to me sing properly, tell them to go buy my records!"

With so many years working for Dean, I suppose I had the envious position of perhaps being part of Dean's 'team'. I typically kept a low profile in the representation of Dean and his life and career, but at the same time always ensured that we served the man and his members with as much professionalism and sincerity as possible.

Over the period of those last eighteen months we had issued various items of merchandise such as t-shirts, sweatshirts, pens and the like, plus authorised posters which all sold very well. We had withdrawn our membership cards to cut down on costs, and ran another poll asking them for their favourite Reprise song to date (the result… 'Gentle On My Mind'). Meanwhile, Dean carried on with his appearances on television and in his Vegas shows, and also attended the Linda and Paul McCartney party aboard the Queen Mary liner at Long Beach, heading the 'conga' with Cher followed by Tony Curtis, Bob Dylan and many others!

Late this year I was asked by Reprise to co-produce the very first compilation album of Dean's songs specifically for the UK market, so I began work on song selection and sleeve design for this innovative release scheduled for release later in 1976.

Initial instructions had come from Dean's office for me to manage this project, as he had insisted in his contract that his product would never be re-issued on the Reprise label as a budget item, so therefore this album, even though it was a compilation of all songs previously available, had to be normal price. The album was to comprise twenty songs, leaving scope for a second similar album possibly for release in late 1977. I commenced work on this project in the new year which gave me ample time among my numerous other commitments for Dean to finalise the album overall.

In his personal life, Cathy and Dean continued their relationship as husband and wife, but the problems were building up and they seemed to be at odds all the time. There did not seem to be any improvement between them and they were both now feeling very unsettled and unsure. Dean had yet another operation for an ulcer and, after recuperation, he resumed work at the MGM Grand, carrying on with his favourite occupation in his business, his cabaret shows.

It was sort of 'homely' to relax and watch him, and I relished the chance to witness him perform whenever I was able. He could stand on that stage, presenting his jokes and songs in the inimitable atmosphere of the Celebrity Room, being fully at ease with his audience, letting them all become a part of his world, even if it was for less than an hour most of the time.

But with his personal life again in turmoil, things were a little bleak to say the least: continuous differences of opinion and his wife's extravagances meant the marriage was no longer salvageable and Cathy moved out of their home in late June, leaving her husband once again in a confused and depressed state. He had thought that perhaps with a little more perseverance on both sides they could have made it, but it obviously was not to be. Once again (but this time after only three years) he was to go through the trauma of divorce. There were people around him who could have warned him where things were headed but, in any case, they both knew that this situation just could not go on.

Even living on the other side of the world from Dean, I had sensed from the very beginning that something was not quite right for him when he decided to marry Catherine Hawn. Something went through my mind in April 1973 when he made this decision, but it was not for me to comment or make remarks about this. It is difficult to explain, but I did not feel as if this union would last. Perhaps because I had come to know Dean a little more than the average person, his calls to me were rarely about his public life and he often chatted about family and home. (By sheer chance, it seemed my feelings were right and they eventually divorced in February 1977. Settlements between them were quickly dealt with and completed. But the media had a different take: whilst staying at Mort Viner's home, Dean was inspecting some guns and one accidentally went off, injuring him in the hand and needing twenty stitches at the hospital. With his current wave of depression, a couple of newspapers exploited the false notion that he had attempted suicide.)

Dean had always been the target for negative press, fuelled by his 'drunk' stage persona. When he was pulled over by the police for dangerous driving, he was of course considered to be drunk. But the truth of the matter was that he had taken an excess of pain-killers which caused him to drive erratically. As the man himself had said many, many times, *if I drank as much as I say I do and as many people think I do, then I would not have even been alive after forty years of age, would I?*

No matter what his personal or public affairs were at any time, the public adored him and even though there was a shortage of live concerts and films now, together with the lack of new recordings, they still loved this man.

Since those times with Jerry Lewis, Dean had made sure that the work was continuous. Sometimes things were hard, but he had that passionate determination, maybe because of his Italian heritage, to work hard and play hard and be rewarded with acclaim and success. He had always dreamed of success, particularly as a singer, but he wanted to be able to tackle most areas of showbusiness and be as good as he could be overall.

Even *he* had to admit now that he was a phenomenal success in the true sense of the word.

Even though they had only seen each other on less than a handful of occasions, Jerry Lewis and Dean Martin never really got together. Their careers never crossed paths again, and Dean was never the sort of man to chase after anyone; he liked his own company and did not feel the need to be with anyone, male or female, at any time. He was content being around himself and doing nothing, unless his work called. Then, he would throw himself into that project wholeheartedly and without doubt.

But although Dean and Jerry had not worked together since their break-up, both entertainers were doing an incredible amount of solo work. If they had seen each other, it was merely a passing glance, and Dean did not acknowledge any notes or messages that Jerry left (something Jerry did even before they knew each other). Over 20 years had gone since by they were the world's biggest team, and perhaps the hugely talented Jerry had not quite made it to the same dizzy heights as his former partner - but he was not doing too badly!

Jerry loved the technical aspect of film-making and was a wonderful comic. I had the good fortune to meet him just once in the 70s and he spoke lovingly of Dean, and I found him to be a warm, character, if a little spiky and mischievous. He continued to make films and appeared in cabaret numerous times (and had a terrific resurgence of popularity with his show *Damn Yankees* in 1995). However, he became an advocate of the telethon and he had a yearly Muscular Dystrophy charity show, raising millions of dollars for this crippling disease. But it was his show for 1976 that was to give him the shock of his life!

On 5th September, he had commenced his latest television marathon-seen by so many millions of people right across America. This was a live televised event, this time taking place at the Sahara Hotel, Las Vegas, and Jerry was hoping to exceed over $20 million, beating previous years by far. He had managed to procure the services of no less than one Francis Albert Sinatra and, after an elaborate introduction, Frank walked on and performed a couple of songs, livening up the proceedings somewhat.

When he finished these songs, he mentioned to Jerry that he had a friend who he'd brought along who may help to attain more money for his cause. He pointed off to his right and the camera panned in to see Dean saunter on, totally unannounced and unfazed by the uproarious applause of the audience, to hug Jerry for the first time in two decades.

I thought it was about time, didn't you? Frank said, as the two continued to embrace, both of them lost for words, if only for a few seconds. But it was not too long before Jerry asked Dean if he was working.

Sure, at the Megam, now and again.

Megam! Jerry repeated, knowing full well that Dean meant the MGM Grand. Remembering this was live television, you could see Jerry well up but Dean, ever the closed off person, held back his emotions. Dean told me years later that he did struggle to keep it straight.

"Seeing the kid again? Yeah, it was a blast and I had to pretend to stay stoned so as to not let it out."

He was a past master at this, never showing emotion if he could help it. Nevertheless, he soon showed everyone that he was the great entertainer, as he took over the show. Frank had given them each a microphone, where the former partners chatted briefly before Dean joined Frank in what he called a 'meldy' of songs. This certainly made the money pour in: the impact of such three unique entertainers on stage together was big enough, but the historical event of Martin and Lewis appearing together like that was absolutely enthralling for viewers, production staff and anyone else involved. Frank had actually managed to keep it totally quiet that Dean was even in the building and it surprised more than the public when Dean walked on. As was usual, Dean screwed up his lyrics, made jokes and pretended he couldn't see the cue cards and kept getting closer to the cameras.

The entire event was something that could never happen – but it did and only the great Frank Sinatra that could have organised it.

After this Martin and Lewis reunion, there was much rumour within the industry that perhaps they may work together again, even in a film, and director David Puttnam tried to contact both artists for such a proposal, but nothing ever materialised from either men.

A little while after this event, Jerry sent a message to Dean's management asking if they could get together, even if only for a meeting for old time's sake. He eventually received a somewhat vague comment saying perhaps it would be nice to see each other again, but after a few attempts at a further reunion, Jerry had no response from Dean nor his management at all; no one on Dean's side ever got around to even suggesting a meeting of any sort and so it never came to fruition.

This was a part of Dean Martin that few people could understand: he rarely thought of organising something himself and regularly left such things to his staff. This left many people frustrated, as they would often receive no response at all. This wasn't really rudeness, it was something that he just didn't deal with. It took me a while to get used to this, to not take any silence personally but to accept that was simply his way.

That frustration spilled out into the correspondence the DMA received. We received so many letters daily, some requesting more than the normal from Dean, sometimes money – lots of it – and some asking for things that were just not possible, such as personal home visits by Dean. We responded to these alarming and bewildering requests professionally and courteously and had little or no comeback. We did have a few fans who came to our UK offices genuinely expecting Dean to be there. When my team told them that Mr Martin was a) in Hollywood and b) didn't accept personal visits anyway, they seemed rather annoyed and almost didn't believe what we were saying!

But we dealt with all aspects of fandom as best we could, hoping to enlighten the enquirer about the amazing talent that was Dean. I sincerely hope that we assisted Dean in his own personal life and his career since we were established in 1960 and that we certainly continue to do so as long as possible. The DMA will always exist, perhaps not as it used to, to honour and promote the name and artistry of Dean.

19

With the numerous projects that we had undertaken up to 1976, we knew we were furthering Dean's career when our latest efforts with his first compilation album for Reprise became very successful. As well as song selection, I also had the privilege of designing the complete front and rear sleeves. I chose a blue background, mainly because it was Dean's favourite colour, with the title in yellow and orange. It was my intention to make this album stand out in the record store racks, because after all, that is what sleeve design is all about...something that catches the eye amongst all of the other issues.

There was some disagreement between me and Reprise in London, as they wanted to call the album 'Little Old Wine Drinker, Dean', but I found this offensive, pushing further the continued negative and wrong opinion that Dean was nothing but a drunk. The title I decided on, I left with them for discussion, leaving it in their hands to see if they could suggest something more suitable (which they did not!). Meanwhile, I submitted my complete project, the full choice of twenty songs and the sleeve design and title included, over to Dean for his approval.

He called me after a short while, confirming his acceptance of it all and telling me he was very pleased with my tremendous efforts involved with this special release. His office followed this up in writing to both me and Reprise in London. Later, however, the London office disagreed with three or four of the songs I had chosen and decided to replace them with some of their own suggestions. Being very concerned with this, I could see that if this happened it would soon become *their* project, not mine. I informed the London office of my concerns, advising them that I did not agree and would consider informing Mr Martin, mentioning his own approval of the project as was.

Further time elapsed and eventually I was informed by Reprise that they had been instructed by Dean's office that my original song choices must stand. Having settled that problem, the album was prepared and set for release on 27th August 1976, but then later amended to 28th October (which I was very pleased with, as it was nearer the Christmas selling season).

Now pushing my luck, I suggested a national television advertising campaign, but Reprise UK did not consider this viable. But after many weeks of determination, I did persuade them to test-advertise in the local Tyne Tees television area. They were unconvinced by my passionate claims that this album would go Gold, and they were wary of my complete faith in Dean Martin's sales appeal, even if it was for the Christmas selling period. I was strongly informed that if this album did not sell in reasonable quantities to cover their considerable TV advertising costs they would pull out of all mass advertising and treat the album as an ordinary release. Regardless, I was convinced the executives at Reprise here thought I should have been locked away at my almost demented (their word!) faith in this album. I was *that sure* that Dean's name on the cover would sell the records by the box-load! They still didn't believe me and I still wonder what was said in their board meetings at the time about the lunatic in South London who seemed convinced this American singer could still sell records!

They did ask (perhaps just to humour me?) for my prediction about which position the album would reach in the charts. I stuck my neck right out and stated it would reach number 2 in the UK by the end of the year. Amidst stifled chuckling, they were mystified about why I did not say number 1. Considering the time of the year, I reasoned, there was nearly always a seasonal album that found itself at the top of the charts, which meant there was never a *true* number 1 in late December most years, a fact that I thought such executives should be well aware of if they were worth their salt! Once again I was considered eccentric with this outrageous forecast and I did begin to wonder if I'd finally overstepped the mark!

133

Naturally, the DMA worked very hard at promoting this release with the special Christmas edition of the newsletter enclosing a copy of the actual record sleeve (LP not included!) to every one of our members across the globe, as well as a full colour quad-size poster of Dean.

'Twenty Original Hits' became Dean's very first Gold album in the UK and – wait for it – *reached number 2 in the charts!* The album remained *in* the British charts for five weeks and was a proud moment for me and the DMA – a fine reward for all those months and months of work and sleepless nights on this project for Dean. Maybe the only slight disappointment was that Reprise in California tried to arrange with Dean's office for me to go to Nevada to give the Gold disc to Dean myself, but after some attempts at this, nothing came of it (the idea was for me to walk on stage in the middle of his act in Vegas and present it to him!). Instead, it was posted to his office by Reprise in January 1977 and hung in the hallway of his home. I often wonder what became of it after his death.

I visited many parts of the United Kingdom as part of the promotion, which included radio interviews on various BBC stations, and I met many members on the way. I hope that my personal efforts helped to make it go Gold!

20

With his third marriage on the rocks, Dean was in no mood for anything. He'd scrapped any possible films that may have been in the pipeline, and his depression fuelled his lethargy. His dependency on painkillers also spiralled his mood into a terrible slump.

Was this the price of fame?

Many before him and many after have gained top stardom and then fallen, but Dean, through some sense of strength, kept his position as a well-respected and highly regarded individual, even if that didn't include Cathy. Those three short years of marriage were a repeat of his past and one wonders if he had been aware of the patterns and perhaps attributed them to himself.

Yet with depression (let alone his ulcers and arthritis) almost crippling his health, no member of the public would ever see past the stage persona.

By mere coincidence, in the midst of Dean's problems, I too suffered a great loss when my dear father, Henry, died on 26th October 1976, five days before my son's fifth birthday. Amidst all the excitement of 'Twenty Original Hits', this tragic event for my family dulled the happiness at the project into which I had put so much of my time. There is a great chunk of your life that goes when you lose your parents, but life and all that entails *has* to go on and I was thankful that he had had a great and wonderful life. He is forever in my thoughts.

The *Celebrity Roasts* continued on NBC (Dean was the recipient of his own roasting earlier in the year), along with a special clip show of them, hosted by Don Rickles. Meanwhile, Dean, throughout the year, managed to pull himself on to the stage for his cabaret appearances. He also recorded the first of his seasonal *Christmas in California* specials.

19th November saw the divorce from Cathy complete and, although they divided the property in half, she did not come away with anything like the settlement Jeanne had been given previously. She only received $2,000 a month for just three years, with Cathy's daughter Sasha (from her previous marriage) receiving only $250 a month until she was eighteen or got married, whichever was the earlier. Dean also agreed to pay her school fees but cancelled the adoption order.

The future for Dean Martin, the 'total entertainer' as he was so rightly called many times, looked strange: he was not shy in letting people know he was not too bothered with films or recordings now, although he continued with his cabaret and a reasonable number of specials and guest spots for television. Although his net worth was now in its millions (at one time it was thought he had accrued around 34 of them, if anyone could be bothered to count --and Dean was the last to worry about such matters) his status did not concern him too much. He hated unnecessary wastage with money, but at the same time he used it to soften his life and enable a carefree existence. That was what he paid his management for, he considered, and they surpassed themselves in keeping him away from the drudge of routine operations and decisions, allowing him to concentrate on facing his public.

Yet that reliance on those around him meant he had little idea what was going on behind the scenes. Trust, it seemed, was something he bestowed easily to those in control of his finances.

Everyone in showbusiness, in fact in any walk of life, has their share of good times and bad, and Dean experienced more than his fair share of both. But a very fortunate situation takes place when you get to a certain degree of prestige within the business: if you are at the top and you are able to stay there, then talent, hard work and luck must go hand in hand.

Dean was highly respected by everyone (in and out of his business) but even after all these years and even his own death, I must say that today, I believe Dean Martin is extremely under-rated in parts of the world – and the UK is unfortunately one of them.

Certainly, he played to packed houses in his London concerts in the 80s, to great acclaim, and always attracted long queues at cinemas. He sold large quantities of records, too, but there are so many people who still insist that he was just a drunk who took little care or pride in what he did.

To them, all I say is this: just look at his achievements over the years. That usually makes them lose their words, especially when I quote facts and figures, as most people do not even realise just how much work he had done! Nevertheless, I know some people walked away from me thinking I had just exaggerated his achievements and went on too much about him. But Dean *had* that charm and consistency and has managed to secure an immortal niche in the world of entertainment for ever. I can imagine many readers thinking that I perhaps praise Dean too much…but why not? Has he not given so many millions of us so much pleasure?

I don't deny he had many faults, like most of us have, and perhaps I am blinkered because of my association with him, but (and I alluded to this in my introduction) I don't want to linger on his bad points. This recollection is a *celebration* and *appreciation* of Dean, of all that he achieved, and the legacy he left us with.

Dad is always so gentle and understanding, his daughter Deana was quoted as saying. *[He] makes us all feel so important. He always has time for us and I think that that is the nicest thing that can happen to me particularly, but for the rest of us as well. Some of us have often wondered if we will ever find a man to measure up to him. We know why he has been so successful in his career. It's because of his manner and attitude to people. It* does *help, you know.*

And heaven forbid I ever even begin to *consider* I was anywhere *near* as close to him as his children were. *Of course I wasn't.* It would be ridiculous for me to even think I was! Yet I understood what Deana said and, in my own small way, I like to think that in my professional life, he was the nicest thing to happen to me as well and the respect I have for his family is immense.

It had been two years since Dean had been in a recording studio, and continuing disagreements with Warner/Reprise meant that several songs he'd recorded remained unissued. After months of discussion, nothing seemed to be resolved and Dean opted to take them to court for around $1.5million. They remarked that his recent record sales were too low to warrant any new further issues on the Reprise label and so they had no interest in releasing anything further. Dean on the other hand stated that they had not given him a reasonable opportunity to release his recordings!

Meanwhile, Reprise UK had asked me to prepare a second album compilation in follow-up to their surprise success 'Twenty Original Hits'. But now with the arguments raging between Reprise in the US and Dean, the project was scrapped entirely and the album that I had produced became the first and last compilation for Dean on that particular label. That said, I didn't think a second volume would have sold as much as the first, but nevertheless, it was a shame we didn't get the chance to find out.

After many months of arguing, the problems were settled out of court between Dean and Warner/Reprise, stating that just one more album would be issued on that label to clear all legal contracts between them. So, with the split from Cathy and the split from Reprise, it seemed there was more uncertainty regarding the public's expectations. Yes, he continued with his beloved cabaret but it seemed unlikely there would be any new material forthcoming in the way of recordings. Dean's career, it seemed, had peaked, and couldn't climb any further.

He had moved over to Laguna Beach since the divorce and was leading a bachelor life again, being seen in several of the classy clubs and restaurants - with a new woman on his arm every time, it seemed. The media reported later that 'he was madly in love' with Peggy Crosby and that a wedding would take place soon but neither Peggy nor Dean made any comments about such remarks. Admittedly, he had been seen with Peggy on a number of occasions since his divorce, but nothing was ever forthcoming and they eventually parted as good friends. Ever on the hunt for more gossip, the tabloids also ran with the rumour that he was to re-marry Jeanne, but neither side commented on such news: they had always been good friends, even since that divorce, and it did not seem likely that they would get together again in that way. Yet Dean continually stated that he loved Jeanne and when true love is there, does anything really ever dampen it? Even a divorce? Perhaps I'm just an old romantic!

For a man now reported to be worth around $90 million (amusing how the media bump up the worth of entertainers each time!), Dean was now working with more live concerts outside of Nevada, appearing in New Jersey in late May 1977 for five days, Washington for a day and then arriving in Chicago on his birthday for four days on stage there – all with his friend Frank Sinatra.

Frank had on a few occasions tried to persuade Dean to go to London for a series of shows, but even *he* was unable to get him there! And if Frank couldn't do it, no one could!

Dean attended a sad event in August this year when he went with Tom Jones to the funeral on the 17th of Elvis Presley, the King's death triggering one of the biggest and spectacular affairs ever in show-business. Millions of people all over the world went into meltdown, mourning for days as soon as the news broke of the demise of this superb man who had been given countless accolades in his amazing career – ones that would continue long after. It was a sad loss to the entertainment industry and, in my opinion, a totally unnecessary death at such a young age. He had everything to live for but the richness of his life took a toll on him mentally and physically.

The DMA held a special meeting for June, and we had a reasonable attendance, giving prominence (naturally!) to 'Twenty Original Hits' and Dean's 60th birthday. It proved to be our biggest gathering to date, with something like 1,000 people in attendance. We used to hold our meetings in a hotel (long since demolished) in South London, and this was one of the more enjoyable aspects of the DMA.

Meanwhile, Dean had renewed his contract with NBC for a further two years and, along with his various live appearances, returned to another season with the MGM Grand in Las Vegas.

In the UK, there's an annual tradition called the Royal Variety Performance. It's a show that attracts and showcases the top talent of the time. Held at the illustrious London Palladium, stars around the world are invited by Royal Command and 1977's was to be something extra special - because Her Majesty Queen Elizabeth was celebrating her Silver Jubilee Year. But more importantly for us (!), I had been informed to a great surprise by Dean's office that he, along with Bing Crosby, had been provisionally pencilled in for top billing.

Dean arranged his hotel booking for ten days in London, allowing for rehearsals and time for a look around this city (something he had never had the time or opportunity for, but something he had always longed to do). He called me to ask for my availability as he intended to visit our offices while he was here. I'd just appointed a personal secretary, Jayne Kempsey, and I think she nearly fainted when I told her!

Bing had been on holiday in Spain, however, when a great tragedy occurred. He had collapsed on a golf course (Crosby's favourite pastime), dying almost immediately from a heart attack.

With the Royal Variety Performance already scheduled for transmission on 4th December and, as usual, given great publicity in the UK press, the organisers were obviously shocked by this news. To make matters even worse, Dean's management announced that because of a heavy workload and the sudden death of Bing, he would not be appearing. This annoyed the producers and the Royal House: this was just *too much* to turn down a Royal invitation, but Dean had made his decision and it wasn't going to be changed.

Even in the wake of Bing's sad death, Dean continued his workload, and Christmas In California was broadcast on NBC with Crystal Gale co-starring.

Continuing his bachelor life, Phyllis Davis (then the star of Vega$ with Robert Urich) was his latest flame and, unlike his other dalliances, he became very protective of her: one time when she was asked to pose topless, Dean insisted that she kept her breasts well covered, a request she honoured for him during their relationship.

Meanwhile, back in our world at the DMA, we considered arranging a trip to see Dean on stage at the MGM, but costs proved prohibitive for bulk bookings so Jayne had to sadly abandon the plan. However, our membership still continued to rise steadily, even though many had not taken kindly to Dean's cancellation at the Royal Variety Performance.

Even though he was not making films or recordings, support for his career via the DMA progressed without question through 1978 and we were now well established. It was pleasing after all these years to be able to see Dean's association was successful and, with the marvellous support of the man himself plus those many members we had all over the world, we were even more determined to work harder to keep the name of Dean Martin at the very forefront of great international entertainment.

With the agreement settled between Dean and Reprise, songs were finally being selected for a new album to be released this year and, contrary to the continuing media speculation, Jeanne and Dean were not planning to re-marry - but they *were* seen a lot together and when Dean held a special 21st birthday party for his daughter Gina, Jeanne was present too, the family spending the entire weekend at the Palm Springs home of Frank Sinatra.

Dean's television appearances had a resurgence: he guest-starred in 'Angels In Vegas', a two-part episode of the phenomenally successful series *Charlie's Angels*, in which he seemed well at ease playing a character called Frank Howell in and amongst the atmosphere and crap tables of Las Vegas. He was very happy and sociable whilst filming with Kate Jackson, Jaclyn Smith and Cheryl Ladd and, by all accounts, had most of the cast in fits with his jokes and antics on and off set.

He recorded a second *Christmas In California*, too, and agreed on a final selection for 'Once In a While', a new Reprise album. These were 1974 vocal recordings by Dean in Hollywood but backed with 1978 orchestra and singers taped in Nashville. This release finally closed the deal he'd made with Reprise, which now cleared him of any further work on that label. As part of the agreement, sadly, our 'Twenty Original Hits' was now deleted here, along with most of the other albums in the catalogue. From then on, all the original master tapes were (and still are) held in bond at Warner Brothers, but with Dean (and now his estate) still holding the outright ownership of the recordings.

Other record companies did not seem to be interested in signing him, and Dean himself was not interested in recording any more songs in any case. He occasionally remarked that he would ease up on his work (and yes, even retire!) but his work schedule this year seemed to tell the exact opposite story. MGM had supplied him with a four-bedroom house within easy reach of the Grand, and he now increased his cabaret dates throughout this year and into 1979.

21

A very surprising out-of-the-blue and welcome invitation came from EMI Records in very early 1979, when they asked me to choose sixteen of *my* very favourite songs that Dean had recorded for Capitol over the years. A somewhat daunting task, I may say, because so many of them were my real favourite songs, absolute classics in my opinion, and to try to select just sixteen of my favourites seemed just about impossible. But given the chance for another compilation album, I began work on this with great pleasure. Presumably there was confidence in me that I could put together another good solid selection!

There was a paper shortage in the UK at this time which meant restrictions on magazines and newspapers (it seemed the record industry was not directly affected too much, with the number of issues appearing from all the companies) but we still managed to distribute our monthly newsletters, as we had reasonable paper stocks ourselves, owing to forward thinking by Jayne!

Contacting BBC Radio, we asked them if they would be prepared to feature Dean this year somewhere around his birthday and link this with the new album I had just completed. We eventually persuaded them and had a 'Dean Martin Day' on Radio 2 on 1st March - but why they chose that day and not one nearer Dean's birthday in June remained a mystery. They were able to feature one or two songs from the new album, but being as it was not actually released then, it acted as something of a preview, which helped with eventual sales, of course.

But the BBC nevertheless produced a great presentation, with many programmes during the course of the day playing Dean's songs. Numerous enquiries at the BBC further boosted the DMA's membership, too. I did try and convince Dean to record a greeting for the BBC but, while he was appreciative of the dedicated day, his response was a resounding *no*.

The new EMI album finally appeared in the stores Monday 8th June, the nearest we could get to celebrating Dean's birthday, and I sent him copies for his own collection. I had remarked several times to Capitol that so many of the songs they had recorded with Dean were really his 'classic' recordings and so I thought that an ideal title for such a collection had to be 'The Classic Dino,' with which everyone at EMI agreed. The disc became a best seller (for a compilation) and remained in the EMI catalogue for over eleven years, a record in itself for such a release.

The DMA was featured in a two-column spread in the local newspaper 'The Croydon Advertiser,' letting their readers know that we had one of the most famous and successful clubs of this nature in the world at the time, and for an equally famous and successful man. Executives at the newspaper offices were surprised that such an organisation was still going strong after almost twenty years, and that it was somewhat unusual for such a big American entertainer to have his headquarters in South London.

We had such marvellous and loving support from Dean and his office and so many times he helped us with the things we needed for promotion. It was always so very exciting when a delivery arrived from his address in California. And those late evenings when our house 'phone rang and he was there on the end of it? ...truly amazing.

I felt very privileged and humble.

As a singer, Dean racked up over 13 million sales with his Reprise releases between 1964 and 1976, an achievement then-unequalled by any artists of his calibre. He could now look back on this unique period in his recording career with pride, with a fabulous library of songs across multiple singles and albums. We must remember that in those days, an artist had to actually sell a million copies before a Gold award was given - and Dean had received plenty.

The 51st Oscars ceremony this year was presented in part by Dean with Racquel Welch, and he looked well as he walked on stage, pretending to stammer with nerves and awe as he stood next to his beautiful co-host.

Nowadays, his famed weekly television shows were in syndication and a further guest role appeared, this time in the episode 'Dean Martin and the Moonshiners' for the short-lived Claude Akins police comedy series *The Misadventures of Sheriff Lobo*. He also did a special at the San Diego Animal Park and a guest spot in *Vega$*, then filmed his third Christmas special.

NBC put together *The Best of Dean* as a two-hour special collected from his TV shows – but it oddly leaned more towards the comedy angle. I would have thought at least a handful of songs in this production would have been more the 'best' of Dean as we knew him. Nevertheless, it was great to see his antics once more.

So ended another busy year for Dean. His health was not what it once was, and his eternal battles against his back and his ulcers never let up. It hardly seemed he would consider retirement, even though in the midst of all this activity he still muttered that he would stop altogether soon! As well as seeing Jeanne quite regularly, he was still dating various women around town and seemed quite content in leading this type of life for the time being. He said little to anyone about how he really felt, but continued with his usual devil-may-care approach to his work and appearances. His commitments still warranted so many events for some time ahead; concerts and television were his mainstay now and he had no desire for film-making any more, no matter what he was offered. The media continued their aggressive assault on his love life, informing each and every one that he was 'due to marry Jeanne soon', but again, neither of them made any comments on this continual barrage of nonsense.

Our boxed album set from World Records was now reduced to four albums instead of the original six, but also with each album now in its own picture sleeve.

Dean requested another five copies of 'The Classic Dino' album from me, and these were sent direct to his home.

As 1980 appeared, Dean had made appearances in the Shirley MacLaine TV special 'Every Little Movement,' and although he was his usual pleasant and amusing self on screen, he was showing signs of strain. Nevertheless, it was another chance to see him on television, transmitted in May of that year.

I contacted Mack Gray, concerned that Dean was looking unwell again. Mack was a wonderful gentleman who had been with Dean for most of his solo career, and who had done great things for him. He had guided him through his singing career and became a close confidante, helping Dean with so many decisions that he had to make. Mack assured me that Dean was listening to his doctors and told me not to worry or let our members be concerned. We used to have regular communications from Mack, giving us so much intimate and confidential information and we always used this with great discretion, Mack knowing full well he could trust us with such insights into Dean's life and career.

On 21st November 1980, a great disaster struck Las Vegas. Fire raged through the MGM Grand, a 26-story luxury resort with more than 2,000 hotel rooms. It started in the Deli restaurant and claimed the lives of 84 people, leaving an additional 650 injured and massive parts of the building devastated. At the time of the fire, approximately 5,000 people were in the hotel and casino. The rebuilding and redecorating was to take several months before it could re-open to the public again. There was a considerable loss of revenue to the company and Dean was shocked by the tragic event and was later invited to inspect some of the damage caused by this terrible tragedy.

Otherwise, he had ended the year with a visit to NBC for another Christmas special. This time it was studio-bound with guests including Beverley Sills and Mel Tillis. While he was his usual upbeat self on camera, he once more looked tired and weary.

Continuing with his various television spots and other concerts, Dean had flatly refused any film roles but it was to be ex-stuntman Hal Needham who actually persuaded him to come back in 1981 for a reasonable part in an ensemble cast for the story of a cross-country car race - and Dean came through this comedy with flying colours, together with his friends and co-stars Dom Deluise and Sammy Davis Jr. Burt Reynolds headlined, followed by Farrah Fawcett, Jack Elam and the wonderful Roger Moore in a brilliant pastiche of his Bond persona (even getting to drive the model of Aston Martin made famous by Sean Connery in 1964's *Goldfinger*). Produced by Albert S. Ruddy for Golden Communications, *The Cannonball Run* was directed by Needham and distributed by 20th Century Fox.

The DMA was working steadily now: not much of Dean Martin was heard or seen (particularly in the UK) but with *The Cannonball Run*, I foresaw and hoped for a renewed interest. The film was attracting a generous box-office across America, eventually grossing over $150million.

Dean had contacted me earlier this year for a copy of Joan Collins' autobiography and ten more copies of 'The Classic Dino.' I avoided asking him what he was doing with them all, but he expressed the immense pleasure he'd felt when he first listened to the album. He did not mention why he wanted a copy of the Joan Collins book.

As Dean was no longer under any commitment to record any songs, it came as quite a surprise when he suddenly asked me to send him a list of around 25 that I could suggest for him to record. I chose a collection of 30 that I thought would be nice for consideration: mostly those he had never recorded before plus a handful that I thought would be an idea for re-recording in a different style. Some weeks later he did acknowledge my suggestions, remarking that some of the songs I had listed he thought were perfect. But strangely enough, after all of this, nothing ever happened. It would have been very nice for a brand new album to have those songs (or at least some of them) recorded. I asked him if he was considering signing, and who with, but he wouldn't be drawn on the subject.

Because of continuing health problems, he did not accept Bob Hope's invitation to attend his golf tournament this year and his cabaret appearances were now becoming less frequent, but he did take part in a ball game at 3am at the Absecons

Memorial Field with Frank Sinatra. This took place after an August show at the Resorts International Hotel, and I was invited to watch (but not, I'm glad to say, to take part!). The game raised lots of money for charity, with the teams called 'Ole Red Eyes' and 'Ole Blue Eyes', and it does not take much to work out who captained what team!

But both pairs of eyes were very bright in this match, in which both great entertainers were very active and enjoyable to watch. It was a late night and they were still playing well into the dawn. I don't think I stirred from my bed at the Resorts until it was time to check out! It was an excellent change of pace for Dean and he felt exhilarated and happy that he had taken part in such a game.

A couple of days later, I flew home and Dean was back in Nevada for a five night bash at his favourite venue, the lavish and spectacular MGM Grand, playing to packed audiences in his inimitable style. He said to me he felt renewed and I hoped this meant a return to form for him...and possibly the recording studio?

Although celebrating our 20th anniversary this year, we had bad attendances at some meetings, so Jayne and I were considering dropping the events. Hiring expenses were rising all the time for such meetings, but even though membership was steady and new members joined us regularly, meetings were sadly no longer viable.

Sales of 'The Classic Dino' were increasing and although signs of Dean himself seemed to be reducing, the DMA continued its efforts to promote him and were very grateful that we had so many members all over the world who consistently supported Dean and his society.

But Dean's health was not as good as it had been a year ago and he was really showing signs of strain. His painkillers bloated him again, and in a rare television interview, his voice was weak and certainly did not sound anything like the famous mellow and pleasant vocal chords that the world had come to know and love. He looked very exhausted and paused quite often when he spoke, something that was sad to see. Looking at Dean Martin as he was in his numerous clips and then returning to the man being interviewed, you could see such a stark contrast. He was at low par and, to make matters far worse, his depression sunk even lower, being totally devastated about the death of the wonderful Mack Gray, aged 75, on 17th January 1981.

Together with his health subsidence and his state of mind over Mack's death, he turned down Frank's offer to appear at Ronald Reagan's Inaugural Concert, but instead remained a member of the audience.

Frank was one of the very few who partly understood his plight and whilst he was disappointed, he accepted that his friend did not want to support him on stage at this glittering event. Dean had never taken any interest in politics but would always work for a cause if he generally agreed with the candidate, although this time he did not have the heart and energy to carry out this request. He went down with influenza and bronchitis shortly afterwards and had to rest at home.

Quite regularly, repeats of his television shows were seen in syndication – which thankfully maintained his household name, but with his health in such a state, many were asking us what was to become of him. What would he do next?

Yeah, you must take life a little easier...after all I'm forty now, he laughed, *and I ain't gonna be forty again!*

Talks were going on for a possible *Cannonball Run* sequel and Dean had said it may be worth considering. On the small screen, he guest-starred on the Paul Anka Cerebral Palsy Telethon with one of his own specials, and made additional appearances with Bob Newhart and Dom de Luise. NBC also presented more clip-oriented material (*Dean Martin Comedy Classics*) and various compilation albums appeared across America --the usual Capitol material, nothing exclusive or of particular note .

Reprise UK took another chance with the re-issue on 10th July of the 'Gentle On My Mind' single, but unfortunately this did not repeat its previous success, when I had suggested the original release from the album of the same name. Because of the closing agreement Dean had with Warner/Reprise, this was to be the last Reprise release ever to appear in the United Kingdom.

1st July had seen the glorious re-opening of the MGM Grand, hosted by Cary Grant, with the actor stating graciously that it had been Dean Martin who had been the biggest attraction at this hotel, indeed in Nevada, for many years, and that he hoped he would continue to be for a long time to come.

But luck was not with Dean.

When he resumed his stage appearances, his health was guiding his actions: some hecklers shouted at him and critics remarked that it was a disgrace to expect people to actually pay to see him in person doing practically nothing. A lot of celebrities were in the audience and were somewhat surprised to see that Dean was using up more time talking and telling jokes than he was actually singing. It was sorely noticeable that he was not in the best of health, and he did continue his season there, but would occasionally cut short his show. This meant he would sometimes only be on stage for around 35 minutes, unlike the times he had been known to continue for well over an hour.

With the man himself easing back on his career, the DMA was receiving letters asking why we bothered continuing. I personally responded, confirming I would always keep the organisation going, for Dean and his admirers world-wide. What reason would we have to close, just because Dean's career was slowing down? I think I made my point successfully, because we did not receive any more such correspondence.

To make matters worse, Dean had been caught with a gun in his trouser belt. Explaining that it was merely his son's water pistol, the authorities strongly advised against carrying such an article, especially considering the recent murder of John Lennon. Dean, however, foolishly ignored their advice and was later fined $200 for being in the unlawful possession of firearms, as he had continued to carry the gun in his car. He said he needed protection when he went out, but he did admit he was guilty and paid his fine without any further comment. The only amusing end to this saga was the fact that the judge had said that it was nice meeting him!

Two personalities died this year: George Jessel (83) and Norman Taurog (82), the latter having produced several Martin and Lewis films. So many people who had known Dean, or been in some way associated with him were coming to the end of their lives - a thought that made him slump into a worse depression. He was exhausted, in pain, and in a bleak frame of mind that concerned his family greatly. He was rushed to hospital and they operated on his ulcer, the media being informed that it had been nothing but a severe gastric upset. Upon release, he announced that he had cancelled all future commitments, accepting his doctors' advice that he must take stock of himself and cease consuming non-prescription drugs. He went into seclusion and screened himself from all enquirers. Jeanne had visited him at Cedars Sinai Hospital whilst he was there for his operation. With what seemed like a bad decline in Dean Martin's health, out came the media with exaggerated reports that he was very ill, or possibly dying, with only weeks to live, something his doctor had warned him would happen if he did not take better care of himself immediately. Dean realised just how bad things were, but to put the record straight, he did make an official announcement to clear up the numerous reports.

We received many heart-warming get-well messages, which we passed on to his office.

However, he took a long break and recovered enough to make a Christmas special again, this time with Buck Owens. On this show, one could see he did look better, although still strained.

The operation had taken its toll.

Even though he had rested, Dean's health still caused many a problem. Showing extreme signs of stress and strain, he was admitted to hospital for eight days' rest, under strict instruction to rest properly. The mixture of drugs and drink he was regularly consuming was becoming toxic, not just for his health, but for his reputation: Dean had been drinking more now than at any time in his life. With all the stories of his drunken days being mere fiction, it seemed that now he was letting those rumours become facts by downing alcohol and, even worse, taking it with drugs - something he had never done before.

Being so stubborn, it took a lot for Dean to heed his doctor's advice but this time he did, and rested again before he resumed any kind of work.

A return to his cabaret shows in Vegas was difficult. On one particular occasion he walked off stage, clearly struggling, but returning a few minutes later while his band played on. But he was not the same focused and driven entertainer he once was. He was hesitant in his songs and seemed to be somewhere else, leaning a lot on the piano and speaking sometimes so low that he was inaudible.

On his way home from a show, Dean was arrested for irresponsible driving in Beverly Hills. Now that was glorious news for the media: they jumped on this hot information! To think that Dean Martin of all people had been arrested for drinking and driving was all they had ever hoped for! For countless years they had all thought of him as a heavy drinker and now this incident gave them their chance to gloat and spread the word everywhere they possibly could. This sealed it for them: Dean Martin *was* a drunk!

Only he wasn't.

When he was tested, it was found that he had very dangerous levels of Percodan in his blood. Dean had gone back on the medical advice he was given. Again, he was admitted to hospital and given just six months to live if he didn't change his lifestyle.

For such a stubborn man living with an addiction, this was a difficult situation to be in, but he knew that if he did not do as advised, it would be over. But if he did survive, the thought of never being able to perform again terrified him.

I usually contacted his office if there was any urgent news I needed to clarify, but this time I contacted his family directly. Within a few days, Jeanne came back and said Dean was very poorly but listening (at last, she added) to the things he was being told. I felt saddened that he had come to this. It was not the way to end such a magnificent career where he was loved by millions. It seemed that he had given up.

Nothing inspired him anymore, and there was nothing else to experience. He had done it all and he was a changed man.

But perhaps knowing this man a little more than some, I felt sure he would not end up like that. I did not imagine he would *really* give up and had faith that he would eventually be back.

I could only hope my thoughts would be right.

22

Less than a month later, a letter from Dean allayed my fears. He thanked me for my concerns and for contacting Jeanne; I was so thrilled to hear from him. His general attitude seemed to be much brighter than reported, and it was so nice that he had taken the time to get in touch with me when he had so much more to concern him. This led me to hope that he was indeed gaining strength and taking heed of medical advice.

Dean said he was watching more television than ever now and was reading, too. He'd never been an avid reader, but said he had to admit it was a welcome change. He was making sure he took his medication, getting plenty of rest, and taking things easy. It sounded like he had spent his time reaping the benefits of the advice he was given.

His break from work had done the trick and when Bob Hope invited him to appear on his November 1982 tribute to Peter Sellers (Peter had died July 1980), Dean jumped at the chance of making a live appearance on television again – his first for many months.

He looked so well when he walked on. Bob had already mentioned that Dean had been ill for a while and when he appeared with that familiar walk towards his host, you could see that Dean Martin was back in business. The audience gave a standing ovation in the studio and he sang 'Bumming Around' with ease. His appearance was nothing short of overwhelming; you could see the prescribed rest had done him the power of good.

This was his resurgence, and there would be a few surprises now that he was back! He felt renewed and said that he would now carry on with his work, having finally signed for *Cannonball Run II*. He was back, invigorated, and preparing himself for new roads ahead.

His former recording manager with Reprise, Jimmy Bowen, had been vice-president of Elektra/Asylum Records over in Nashville since 1978 and it was he who persuaded Dean to return to the recording studios for the first time since 1974. With this surprise move, Jimmy arranged for Dean to sign to the Warner Brothers label for just ten songs, and even talked him into travelling to Nashville for the first time ever in early 1983 to record the tracks.

But another piece of news reached me as Dean travelled to Nashville in mid-January 1983. And it was a shock.

For the first time in thirty years, Dean had decided to visit London for a series of live concerts at the Apollo Victoria - and I just could *not* believe this. I really thought his office was having me on and I'm surprised I didn't ruin my working relationship with his team by asking them to repeat what they were telling me. But they insisted it was correct, confirming that he would arrive here in June, and said they would keep me updated!

After completing 'The Nashville Sessions' between 17th and 21st January, Jimmy Bowen was pleased with the outcome of the production, saying that Dean's voice was back on excellent form (although one has to admit that it did have a slight, and understandable, weakness to it). Dean had enjoyed the sessions, with Merle Haggard and Conway Twitty joining him on a couple of tracks.

Dean was determined to get back into things, even appearing live in New York, a place he had never been too fond of, as well as various other spots during the course of this year. He was featured on *Entertainment Tonight* and made a guest appearance on a Dom de Luise special and of course, he was back in Las Vegas. He also fitted in a charity benefit for the Desert Hospital, Palm Springs with Sammy and Frank.

The Apollo management had allocated us 200 tickets for the upcoming concerts in June and we quickly sent out the good news to our DMA members, giving them the opportunity to buy them through us. Suffice to say, demand was high and we had to sell them on a first come first serve basis, suggesting that when we'd sold our allocation, our members should book with the theatre if they could.

The weeks seemed to rush by and my own excitement grew.

Dean's management called me to say he'd arrived at the Inn On The Park in London, and it seemed like he had brought the Californian sunshine with him, as it was a beautiful few days, weather-wise! I had to clear my own schedules for this period, I had been invited to some of the events where he would be appearing.

An unusual but logical decision was for Dean's new album 'The Nashville Sessions' to be released in the UK on 3rd June before the US release (15th) to tie in with his concerts. This meant sales were higher than normal (and certainly continued after his dates had ended). His first and final album on the Warner label was his very first digitally-mastered recording and, as with his previous recordings, he owned those masters outright.

His first function (one my wife and I had to dust off our respective evening dress and tuxedo for) was a 66th birthday luncheon (including a cake!) in Dean's honour on 7th June, hosted by the Princess Royal. Dean sat and listened to the many tributes given to him in the banquet hall of the Mayfair Hilton. Celebrities such as Tommy Cooper, Dickie Henderson, Ron Moody, Peter Goodwright and many others all heaped praise upon this American star who had finally made it to our shores after such a long absence. After all, he had last worked here with Jerry Lewis in 1953, when he'd vowed he would never return!

He did seem somewhat uneasy at this function, something he did not quite anticipate, and he made one slight error in Royal etiquette when he sat down before Princess Anne. Obviously Dean had not intended to break protocol, but even he himself was in awe of all of these people who were gathered there to pay him respect and adulation.

Dean had always said he was no one special, he just happened to be lucky enough to have reached the top of his chosen profession as he had hoped, and compliments made him uncomfortable. Indeed, this reminded me of Dean's embarrassment when I thanked him over the 'phone for being such a good friend and for all of the opportunities he had given to me. He curtly replied by saying that he never wanted any thanks, no matter what he would ever do for me or send to me, then softened by adding it was merely a pleasure for all that I had done for *him* for many years.

Dean gave just one press meeting at his hotel, but refused all offers for radio or television interviews, even though we and many others tried as hard as we could to change his mind.

Due to demand, his original show dates for seven nights, commencing with his Gala night on 9th June, were extended to a total of ten days, showing any doubters (were there any by now?) that he was still in demand from so many people, with an exceptional following in the United Kingdom.

I arrived nightly for all ten performances and had arranged to meet with Dean on the first Wednesday before the show. I went, as usual, through the stage door, guided by one of his staff direct to his dressing room.

I noted it was sparse, just a table and three chairs, and as I walked in, Dean stood, came towards me and embraced me, his arms as strong as they ever were. He seemed genuinely pleased to see me again.

He asked how my family were. I told them my wife Irene, daughter Carole, and son Elliot were in the audience and Elliot, then only 12 years old, knowing his live act so well, was very excited to see him performing front of him! To my surprise, he asked his staff to call them backstage and greeted them warmly, albeit only for a few minutes, before he and I returned to his dressing room.

As we sat chatting, Dean wearing just his dress shirt and trousers, no jacket nor tie, he thanked me for all my hard work over the last 23 years. He spoke of his prior illness and said that he was going to start working with Burt, Dom and Sammy again. He asked how the club was faring and I told him that we'd had such renewed interest with him being in the UK. I mentioned that many members had asked me to meet him but he shook his head.

"You do it, *you* meet them," he said. "Do it on my behalf, Bernard."

I said to him that it wouldn't quite be the same and that they'd be disappointed.

"It's impossible," he insisted. "I don't do that. I *can't* do that. Tell them how thankful I am."

Interestingly, and I wondered if this was due to his anxiety and how poorly he'd been, he was actually concerned that he wouldn't be well-received out on that stage.

"Do you really think they'll like me?" he asked me.

I assured him he didn't have a thing to worry about, pointing out that, as we talked, we could hear the audience chanting 'we want Dean' over and over. He seemed not to have noticed and his heavy-lidded eyes widened as he realised what the background noise actually was. 'Wall Street Crash', his warm-up act, had a tough crowd to please.

We continued to talk about the DMA and what he had planned in the coming months, and I asked him if he'd considered allowing the re-release of his back catalogue (being that he owned the masters). I added that EMI and Warner/Reprise had not seemed too keen on the idea (I'd approached them in 1982). He pondered and nodded as though it hadn't occurred to him (perhaps it hadn't).

"When I get back, I'll see what I can do."

The 3,000-seat theatre was packed every night and he sang his usual repertoire and told jokes on top form. He was enjoying himself and looked great up there. He told his audience he was so taken aback by the tremendous welcome he'd received. Every night, he was showered with gifts from the audience, plus those given to me to pass on to him at the hotel, which I duly did.

Naturally, the DMA had been planning a massive publicity campaign since the new year, and we sent hundreds and hundreds of letters and publicity notes to every radio and television station in the country, as well as numerous newspapers and magazines, making sure they knew all about us and Dean's acclaimed visit here. His first visit here for thirty years just could not be ignored. We visited record stores throughout the UK, asking them to present window displays to tie in with his concerts.

I knew that a concert was being recorded and filmed, so I suggested a live album plus VHS cassette to be released but this fell on deaf ears. In my opinion, these would have sold very well. The concert footage was eventually broadcast on American cable.

With astounding success at all of these appearances, Dean said he'd be back – but that remained to be seen, as this was a comment he tended to say at the end of all his appearances anywhere on stage. Although he had overcome his terrible fear of flying some time back, he still didn't like travelling so it was doubtful whether we would see him here again. He returned home amidst rumours of a visit in 1984, tying in with a European tour (possibly with Frank and Sammy), but it was all gossip and media speculation.

23

For the many years I had known and represented him through the DMA, Dean was the *gentle* gentleman. It was incredible to think that he had actually come over to London and visited us, and been a great success every single night. I must admit I was somewhat disappointed that he had not agreed with my requests that he met with some of our members whilst he was here, but it was not to be, no matter how much I pleaded with him.

Yet after thinking about it, I guess I could see his point: he was a shy person around people when he was Dino, but as Dean Martin on stage behind that mic and the apple juice, he was the total opposite. He had never been a person to meet his fans in a pre-arranged face to face situation and he would hardly change his habits at 66!

After a short break at home, he went to Nevada for his Celebrity Room appearances, to be followed by his part in *Cannonball Run II*, filmed in Tucson, Arizona. As Frank Sinatra was to appear in a cameo role, this would be the first time since 1960 that he, along with Dean, Sammy, and Shirley MacLaine, would be together in a movie.

Dean teamed up with Sammy again, their characters this time dressed as police officers (as opposed to priests in the first picture). *So this time I might get laid,* laughed Dean.

In early 1984, he recommenced his Celebrity Roasts for NBC but this time they were specials as opposed to the previous weekly shows. He also started reducing the number of cabaret appearances he would make at the MGM Grand.

He made another surprise decision by flying direct to Paris, France for just one 40-minute show at the famed Moulin Rouge on 3rd July. Here, he met with Line Renaud and they chatted about the old times (they'd recorded 'Relax-Ay-Voo' and 'Two Sleepy People' back in 1955 with Dick Stabile and his orchestra).

Back in the US, Dean and Frank had signed to appear together in a number of shows at the Golden Nugget Casino, Atlantic City, for September but it appeared that there were underhand dealings and fixed card sharking at the tables. Dean and Frank immediately cancelled the complete run, wanting no connection with (or even inferred links to) whatever was going on. Frank firmly stated that he would never appear in Atlantic City again, and never did.

Later that same month, I was invited to the Friar's Club for an honorary show on 13th September where Dean was crowned 'Man of the Year'. Hosted by Frank, tickets were available at $250 each with a meal for $1,000 if required. Asked later why he was chosen as ' Man Of The Year', Dean laughed and said he had no idea. *But I am not going to ask either, they may change their mind! I'm amused because I cannot think of anything particular I have done recently!*

Cannonball Run II had by now completed its rounds in cinemas both in the US and the UK but did not achieve impressive results at the box office, gaining returns for Warner Brothers far below the first film. In 1989, Orion Pictures made and released *Speed Zone,* also known as *Cannonball Fe*ver (or in Japan, *The Cannonball Run III: Speed Zone*). It featured an ensemble case much like the first two movies but none of the original main cast or crew, bar one: this was Jamie Farr, reprising his role in a brief cameo as Sheik Abdul ben Falafel, the only actor to link the three films together.

Once again, there were rumours of a European tour by Dean and Frank, or at least more visits to London for Dean, but nothing came of the reported concerts from either artist.

I contacted Dean to follow up on our conversation in London about re-releasing his Reprise back catalogue but his office replied saying simply that they had 'no plans at present'.

Having put his signature to paper for just the one album for Warner Brothers, it was another surprise when he recorded just the one *song* for MCA Records entitled 'L.A Is My Home'. With great production, his voice was soft and smooth, even if a little strained in places.

It was used as the end theme for a new TV series which would have Dean making a regular guest appearance in each episode. The series, *Half Nelson*, starred Joe Pesci as a private eye and bodyguard to the stars, one of his clients being Dean's character, Mr Martin. With Pesci's short stature, the promotional tag ran as 'Half Nelson - a man women can look down to! You'll Love It!' But not many people did. After the 2-hour pilot, only six more episodes were made and the 1985 series was shelved and, to date, has never been repeated or sold outside of the US.

In the UK, independent television network LWT was running a popular comedy series called *Me & My Girl*. Starring Richard O'Sullivan and Joanne Ridley, one episode had the storyline of Dean being asked to appear in cabaret at a business conference. Although he was mentioned, no footage or reference photographs were used.

This really shows the status and staying-power that Dean had and, in many ways, still has.

He is often name-checked or referenced in the most unlikely of places: in 2017, the long-awaited sequel to the 90s smash hit picture *Trainspotting* featured a sequence where one character is dancing with a full-size cardboard cut-out of Dean. The 1996 action flick *The Long Kiss Goodnight* plays 'Let It Snow! Let It Snow! Let Snow!' during a car crash sequence; the 90s comedy series *3rd Rock From the Sun* has the main cast singing a rendition of 'That's Amore'; and *Grease*, made in 1978, features *Hollywood or Bust* as a drive-in movie; Quentin Tarantino's cult success *Pulp Fiction* has a character ordering a milkshake called 'Martin & Lewis' in the fictional Jack Rabbit Slim's bar, where a photo of Dean is also seen. And it doesn't stop there: the 2008 BBC time-travel cop series *Ashes to Ashes* features a drinking establishment that shows Dean in a painted mural on a back wall; CBS/ Paramount's *Star Trek: Deep Space Nine* includes a 'holodeck' character played by James Darren that was modelled on Dean (and Frank) and Darren actually wore to the casting a pair of shoes he owned that used to be Dean's; and in 2017, *Going In Style* starring Michael Caine prominently features Dean's hit 'Memories Are Made of This.'

The places you can find Dean Martin in modern media seem endless.

As his Las Vegas shows continued (although some of his shows were again cut back on time), Dean also made further guest appearances in *Motown Revue*, *Dutch Reagan*, a Shirley MacLaine special and another Dom de Luise show. He seemed to be in reasonable health but he was most certainly taking life a little easier, although it must be noted here that he was not getting too many offers for work (a lot of which he was turning down anyway). There was an element of history repeating: as he had come out of his partnership with Jerry, he was second billing in most of his immediate films. In the mid- to late-80s, he was back in a similar position: guest starring, second or even third or fourth billing in shows and movies.

Two more of his working associates had died recently, too: the renowned and highly respected Orson Welles, who had appeared so many times on Dean's weekly shows, and Nelson Riddle, trumpeter and arranger for the Charlie Spivak orchestra back in December 1940 and who evolved his great and superb arrangement artistry for so many fine artists. It would take numerous pages to list his credits, but just listen to his album 'Hey, Let Yourself Go!' and Dean's own 'This Time I'm Swingin'!' and you will hear just a glimpse of arrangement finesse there. Once again, when Dean heard two more contemporaries had passed away, he realised that it was the era he had come from and the era he was living in.

Another landmark in Dean Martin's career came when he appeared before the one-millionth person at the MGM Grand – the lucky customer, Michelle Dolan, was taken out of the queue and presented with a special plaque by Dean on stage. She also received a free 3-night/4-day stay at the hotel complex with tickets for other shows thrown in, too. After Dean's show, Michelle and her companion even met him backstage for a brief chat.

Dean had always been the biggest success at the hotel and proved beyond doubt his international popularity. Las Vegas audiences are a cross-section of the population; they come from all over the world to visit this 'electric' town in the desert, where hundreds of entertainers have performed.

In April 1986, the Bally Manufacturing Company bought the MGM Grand, renaming it the Ballys Grand, and later, they would also buy up the Golden Nugget Casino.

As Dean got older, more ailments knocked him down. In January 1987 he was hospitalised with more stomach problems and was forced to cancel pre-booked (and confirmed) engagements in Las Vegas. Further, he acquired a small abscess in his mouth, which was dealt with quickly, after which he returned home to relax.

However, some weeks later, an event took place which was to be the most devastating in his life, affecting his future in every possible way.

His son, Dean Paul Jr, was a pilot for the National Guard and had been reported missing whilst in flight. Evidently, the weather was treacherous and when Dean was told the news, he immediately contacted Jeanne and went and stayed with her and the rest of his family. They just sat and waited for news for an agonising five days. But when the news did come, delivered personally to the family home by a USAF colonel, it was what they feared the most: what was left of his son's body had been found.

Dean Jr's jet had hit the 11,500-foot high San Gorgonio Mountains, the air-traffic controller having tried desperately to guide the experienced pilot through a massive blizzard. But heavy air traffic hampered communications and it was found after the official investigation that Dean Jr had not heard the Ontario International airport controller's instructions to change course. His last words before the F4C Phantom jet ploughed straight into the side of the mountains *was* a request for a course change and he sadly did not receive any return communication. Dean Jr was just 35 when he was killed on 21st March 1987.

Nothing whatsoever in any written word can even come close to describing how Dean felt at this time. Nothing like this had ever happened in the family. It was bad enough for him when his dear parents had died, but when he thought of how young his son was, and the tragic situation in which he had died, it all became too much for him. Dean had very small comfort in realising that perhaps his son did not have enough time to realise what was about to happen, but the loss of his son was more than he could stand. He cancelled all work and personal appearances.

With such sadness in the Martin family, once again it seemed that his own problems coincided with mine, because in April of this year my wife Irene lost her mother Connie after a massive stroke. That was a heavy loss for us, especially for Irene, who had been looking after her practically every day as part of her normal routine before Connie had to be admitted to a care home. My own mother was also experiencing bad health at that time but was not taking the medication she had been prescribed, and I was very concerned with her situation.

But Dean himself had gone into a severe and worrying state. He just could not go on: everything had completely collapsed around him and his state of mind told him he just could not work. He could not face anything, he was so shaken beyond imagination.

Jeanne and the children all encouraged him to get back to normal, at least, as normal as was possible. He had to be strong and try to overcome what had happened. He was, after all, a hugely famous and popular person, and he had to resume his career.

Dean, however, was almost ready to disappear.

24

Incredibly, after going through the trauma of his son's funeral, Dean Martin gathered himself together and listened to what his family was saying: he returned to Bally's, receiving standing ovations every night. With tears in his eyes (remember, this was a man that thus far, had showed no real emotion to the public), he made a brief reference to the family tragedy and said he would be carrying on for his son's sake, thanking everyone for their kindness and patience. He looked very strained and tired but had forced himself out of his sadness. Having completed ten nights, he returned home for a short rest, keeping in close contact with Jeanne and the rest of the family. He once again surprised everyone in the midst of all this unhappiness by announcing more concerts in London. Again, this was amazing news again for us and for all his millions of admirers.

He played at the London Palladium to packed houses between 6th and 11th July, re-tracing his steps on the same stage he had worked on with Jerry Lewis. Again, he refused all interviews and appearances on radio and television, with his official programme this time reduced from the larger-sized edition in 1983.

I met him again, but there was a marked difference.

In the four years that had gone by, he had aged tremendously and I was very concerned. Even though I said nothing to him about it, I think he knew I had noticed. His dress shirt hung around his shoulders and he was stooped, only slightly, but enough to show he was not the same man I'd known for the last 27 years. Time, emotions and life had ravaged those exceptional good looks. I gave him the deepest condolences for the loss of his son from me and my family to him and his, and he asked how *my* children were. He seemed to brighten when I told them they were now on their own two feet, with school days virtually behind them. We exchanged general pleasantries and he once again thanked me for everything I was doing.

We discussed the future of his association: the format, attitude style and distribution of our literature, plus our approach in general for the coming years. I told him the DMA needed to keep up its prestige, status and establishment of many years and move with the times, as we could never afford to be complacent. He agreed but felt I knew what I was doing and had no concerns. I didn't feel I could ask him about what he had planned or upcoming because he alluded to taking things day by day. But I did ask if he'd given any more thought to re-releasing his material. He said he had not. As he received his five minute stage call, he hugged me goodbye and wished me well for the future.

It seemed somewhat final.

He gave an outstanding performance on all nights, and mentioning his son's recent death to the audience gained sympathy and adulation at this point in his show. He filled his act with the usual jokes and his songs, but it was clear he was never to get over the tragedy, although he knew his son would have wanted him to carry on with his work and *be* Dean Martin again. In that respect, he was happy, because it did give him some motivation to pursue his career as he did before.

With Dean's tragedy combined with our own family bereavement, the London visit was somewhat tainted. A lot of gloom pervaded in our lives at the present time, as my own mother's health was deteriorating quickly. Because she was never a lady to complain about anything or tell anyone her thoughts, feelings or pain, even I myself did not realise the gravity of her situation. On the rare occasion she had said anything about herself, it was a remark that she just had backaches, her Italian stubbornness making her refuse to see her doctor. Like both Dean and me, we all have that great dislike of anything medical. She had been in poor health for most of this year and I finally insisted on medical intervention: she had been suffering quietly with lung cancer and died that August in Mayday Hospital, Croydon. Word had filtered up to Dean from the DMA to his office and I received a short handwritten note from him wishing me and my family every sympathy. Again, it was testament to his attitude: here was a man at the centre of his vast world with his own pain and suffering and problems, yet he still took a few moments to write a message of condolence.

Frank and his wife Barbara had invited Dean and Sammy to their Palm Springs home for a weekend because of the telethon she had arranged in the complex at the Eisenhower Medical Centre in September. Sammy suggested that they all do something together on stage again, but something different: they had done enough films and recordings and live acts, so a change of approach, he felt, was required.

Frank came up with an idea of something like an all-state tour, going to places via train that they had never been to before. But after research, it was found to be too impractical. Perhaps the best way to get across all states would be by air. There was a chance that this could make things easier for all three stars, particularly for getting from state to state, so thought Frank. He envisaged they could play to perhaps 20,000 at a time at indoor stadiums and the like, depending on the facilities in each venue. They would need two 'planes because of their different routines of working. Sammy and Dean liked to be in a town the night before they appeared, whereas Frank would turn up as required.

Discussing these points, Dean himself was very quiet: he had not really wanted to involve himself in another country-wide tour, particularly as he did not feel as eager and enthusiastic as he had when he was younger. He seemed uncertain anyway that all three of them could even keep up the pace --after all, Sammy was not so agile as he had been and even Frank had cut back on the amount of appearances now, so Dean did not think it would be sensible or responsible for any of them. Frank and Sammy realised too, that Dean was a broken man after his son's death. Further, Dean saw that being at a different venue each night would be very contrary to just playing in one place for several nights as he was used to and, understandably, could cope with.

Dean Martin's lifestyle could not be compared to Sammy's and Frank's: obviously, Dean was very wealthy but always dressed simply and used the minimum of clothes and properties when he was out working live. His two friends were the opposite.

But Dean was in a predicament. He agreed that it would be nice to work together like they used to, and he was never a person to let them down if they asked him for support. However, when the details were finally worked out and they all got together for press conferences at the end of 1987, he was still not really convinced and did not have his heart in it. He agreed nevertheless and 'Frank, Dean, Sammy - The Together Again Tour' was a go: a tour across *all* US states, no less, plus talk of taking the same tour to Europe. This famous trio together would be like going back 30 years. There had been nothing like them before and there certainly would be nothing like them ever, ever again.

We approached the end of 1987, 1st October to be exact, with a new-style newsletter. Now called 'Just Dino,' each edition was fully illustrated with articles and features galore. My son had begun a writing career and contributed to them, adding a new 'voice' to the association. Dean commented on the new format and looked forward to watching Elliot's career flourish! There was always so much work that could be done for Dean and we were in an exclusive position to be able to carry out this pleasurable role with such ideas and schemes that hopefully would continue to please him and our members alike.

Dean appeared in a segment for the celebration of the Las Vegas 75th Anniversary, screened in November, completing the end of a very mixed year for him. Arrangements were now fully scheduled for the 'Together Again' series of concerts (sponsored by American Express) to commence 13th March 1988. The trio's first appearances were at the Oakland Coliseum in California, with the shows planned to go on until mid-April, covering various venues, with a break mid-year scheduled to allow them to fulfil other commitment. It would be a gruelling tour, with the stamina required of men half their age.

When the tour began, Dean didn't seem right. His voice and his manner were not as they usually were and seemed as if he was elsewhere, mentally. He missed some of his cues and Sammy stepped in with a few missing lines, making a joke of it. But after just four shows, Dean couldn't cope with the punishing schedule and pulled out of the shows in Chicago after appearing there just once on 18th March.

Flying back home, he checked in at his hospital for observation, covering himself for the concert cancellations, then went home for a few days' rest. His two friends were rather frustrated at this turn of events; they understood some of his reservations, but did not quite understand why he had totally pulled out of the schedule. They felt let down.

But it seemed that Dean just did not want to carry on and there was absolutely nothing they or anyone else could do to change the mind of this stubborn man. He was replaced by Liza Minnelli.

Approaching the 1990s, Dean Martin had reached a different state of mind. He had no need to keep on going and proving himself. He had done everything he had wanted to do in his life and was happy with that. He felt within himself that he had no further need to record, make films or tour the country. He was contented to return to Vegas.

But his troubled health was rearing its ugly head again and he was certainly not at his best when appearing at Bally's. During several performances, he was seen to clutch and rub his stomach several times, as well as rubbing his forehead. He maintained his show routine and still sometimes times cut down his show lengths whenever he felt like it, often stopping mid-way through a song. His jokes were short, sometimes he slurred his speech and, on one occasion, he collapsed when he walked off stage towards his dressing room.

Once again the press had a field day; they reported in various publications that he was drunk and falling about the stage. But like Dean had showed us before, it was the drugs for his medication mixed with some alcohol, in addition to not having taken care of himself as he should have done for a person of his age and status. His medication for his ulcers, kidneys and his nerves (the latter brought on by Dean Jr's demise), when he returned home, was administered by Jeanne.

His health did improve towards the middle of the year, enough to take Jeanne and two of their children to London for five days for sight-seeing and shopping, ensuring that his hotel and staff firmly understood that he was not in residence should anyone enquire. He felt that he needed this break, and London was a nice enough place to experience a complete change of atmosphere. Even again this year, with Dean often in Jeanne's company, the media frequently informed the world that they were to re-marry. But there was no mad romance here, they were just both very happy with each other and wanted things to remain that way.

But love was certainly in the air in the form of a particular of a song that Dean had recorded way back on 13th August 1953. 'That's Amore' was re-issued as a single in May 1988, having been used as the theme for a new picture called *Moonstruck*, starring Cher. It was marvellous to hear that song again 35 years later and was Dean's very first CD single. Unfortunately and not wholly unexpectedly, it did not chart.

EMI Records, meanwhile, had created a series of albums entitled 'The Best Of The Capitol Years' and I was asked by the series producer Alan Dell (a prolific British radio DJ) to compile a selection of songs for the release featuring one of their most prominent signings. Some 45 years ago, Dean Martin had signed with them, so again it was somewhat of a task for me to choose a batch for this latest release. Once the songs had been selected and confirmed, they were to be digitally processed and the album was provisionally scheduled for the autumn release. It had to be a 'best of' compilation, of course, but I would have honestly preferred to compile something different, something of the rarer and unreleased items, but I had to more or less keep to the chart items and familiar songs that Dean had recorded.

I completed the work by September, again with my design, song choice and sleeve notes, but for reasons unexplained, EMI wouldn't be releasing it for the Christmas heavy-selling season.

All three configurations were to be issued (CD, LP and tape cassette) which gave a much bigger spread of the market. There was a gradual withdrawal of new vinyl releases, so it was pleasing that the very last new LP of Dean's ever released (albeit another compilation) was one I had been directly involved in.

Dean's health continued to improve, and he made several appearances back in Nevada, plus a special four-night season in Chicago commencing 12th November, completing another year of mixed feelings, good and bad health, but above all, this displayed a return to his public. At this present time, there was a myriad of diseases and complaints that Dean was supposedly suffering from; half of them, if he *had* had them, would have killed him years before.

To help clarify the facts and dispel the gossip and fantasy surrounding these stories, we issued a bulletin at Dean's request within our 'Just Dino' newsletter to hopefully explain to those many concerned members just how much Dean's health had improved. Meanwhile, the film magazine 'Photoplay' featured the DMA in a half-page article and we continued to progress in our 28th year of existence.

Engelbert Humperdinck was the subject of the UK version of *This Is Your Life* on 30th November and Dean gave a small tribute via satellite from his home.

'The Best of the Capitol Years' was finally released on 9th January 1989, going on to sell in considerable numbers around the world. There was a possibility of more ideas that Capitol were going to think about, which was always something to look forward to!

At this time, since Dean had no intention of recording again, all of the song masters distributed on the Reprise label were lying dormant and secure under lock and key at the Warner Brothers vaults, with a few songs appearing here and there in different parts of the world on various unusual releases (most of them on so called 'bootleg' issues). I asked them once more why there were no proper plans for these songs to be re-issued. Dean's office informed us that they would *all* be re-packaged and re-issued in the very near future. I did comment at the time that these songs could not just be left stagnating in the vaults but no one, not even Dean himself, seemed the slightest bit interested.

There were more appearances in Nevada again for Dean this year and he presented his usual act on stage for around 45 minutes, and on rare occasions he went to almost an hour, but this was the exception now. Although he was still the inimitable artist live on stage, he showed signs of strain and fatigue and was somewhat slower in his delivery and tone. In the closing moments of his show on the evening of his 72nd birthday, his former partner Jerry Lewis calmly walked on stage, pushing a trolley with a large birthday cake thereon.

Here's to 72 years of joy and happiness you have given the world, Jerry said.

Both had tears in their eyes as they looked at each other and embraced.

This was the first time that Dean and Jerry had been on the same stage since 1976 at Jerry's telethon with Frank Sinatra, yet Dean still had no interest in working with his old partner again. Director Peter Bogdanovich had attempted to get them together for *Paradise Road*, but the tentative idea for this comedy film never went further than that.

25

In the autumn of 1989, a musicians' strike caused many a problem in the US, and Dean's appearances in Las Vegas were held over when he had to cancel his engagements indefinitely. The problem arose when Bally's announced they would use taped music instead of live musicians in lavish productions, although top status performers such as Dean Martin would still be able to use full orchestras. However, pickets still caused serious problems and Dean never approached the hotel as he did not wish to cross the picket line, becoming the first headliner to cancel because of these rules.

In a strange way, this gave him a break: he was not in need of more money or work, so he had spent these last few years steadily arranging a schedule so that he was definitely around, but not overworking in any sense of the word. His health had declined and he knew he had been advised to take things easier. Sometimes he ignored this advice and sometimes he actually behaved himself and took notice! His stomach and back problems seemed to be there more or less all the time now, but he just accepted this as part of life.

When Sammy was admitted to hospital with throat cancer, Dean's depression crept slowly back. Little Sammy was very ill, under extreme and extensive chemotherapy, and Dean was devastated. He had visited Sammy, and he spoke of some of those good times they had had together, but with such extensive treatment that famous voice could not even whisper a reply.

A short while later, Dean himself was admitted to the same hospital for an abscess in his throat.

Eventually, Sammy was sent home from hospital, taking further medication and being cared for by his wife Altovise and the children.

Meanwhile, there were movements with regard to some of Dean's albums seeing the light of day again: I was delighted that 'A Winter Romance' was released in November, along with a bonus track 'The Christmas Blues'. Digitally re-mastered, we once again heard those wonderful renditions of winter and Christmas songs by Dean, sounding much richer and clearer than ever.

This same month, Dean suffered dental problems and underwent surgery, easily clearing this problem before he took part in the 60th Anniversary special tribute to Sammy. Introduced by Tony Danza, he read out a few messages to Sammy and looked very drawn and tired, joking to his old friend ...*roses are red, carnations are pink, if I had your talent, I wouldn't have to drink!* Dean had lost weight and his voice sounded weak and raspy, but he was still his old charming self.

But sadly, no matter how drawn and tired Dean looked, it was dear Sammy who brought everyone to tears. The tribute show was his last-ever appearance and, even though when you saw him on screen he was obviously in great pain, he still had that great smile for everyone and even got up on the stage for a short tap-dance sequence with Gregory Hines, with whom he had recently starred in the picture *Tap*.

But with the end of the 80s, Dean's health again was in question. He simply stayed at home, with Jeanne there quite frequently, keeping him as content as possible and trying to make sure he ate properly, because as he was now something of a recluse, he was not taking good care of himself. Living alone at his home, he would ignore family and friends on occasion, even declining the invitation to Frank's birthday party on 12th December. Occasional trips to his favourite restaurant La Famiglia or to some other eatery broke the routine, but he no longer drove anywhere himself. Dean, at 73, was deserving of better health. Perhaps he could have improved it more himself but, as I have said on numerous occasions, he was a very stubborn man and rarely took advice when it was given to him.

The following February he was admitted to hospital again with back and stomach problems, and was also suffering with muscle tightness in his hands. He had a minor operation because of an enlarged prostrate, but had delayed treatment because of his daughter Deana's wedding on 17th February. He presented the bride at the ceremony, but was in pain and very uncomfortable.

Whilst recovering in the hospital, he had visited Sammy there, who was now terminal. The fact that Sammy himself was so devastated by this appalling disease did not exactly make Dean feel any better, but he did his best to greet Sammy with words of affection and reassurance.

The DMA now entered its 30th year in 1990 and we were greatly saddened to learn from Sammy's management that the great man had died at his home on Wednesday 16th May. We issued a special tribute edition of the newsletter for May/June, featuring a whole array of photographs of Sammy with and without Dean. Sammy had been a wonderful person to know and had contacted us each and every time he had visited London, a good friend who was always very pleased to talk with me.

Meanwhile, Dean himself had surprisingly returned to Nevada for more live appearances, but he now looked very drawn and shaky on stage, slurring his words and leaning on the piano very frequently. In the midst of his act, he spoke of his son Dino Paul Jr and his friend Sammy, breaking down in tears every so often as he broke off singing. It was heart-wrenching to watch and I wondered why he had decided to return to cabaret. Almost staggering on the stage, he was met by hecklers asking him if he knew what he was doing and if he was drunk. I seethed at this disrespect: here was Dean trying to bring some normality back into life and these vile audience members saw nothing of his pain.

However, he carried on with his shows, but now took long breaks in between engagements, which made all the difference, because when he reappeared in the June, he looked much fitter and was back with his old jokes and patter with his audience.

Capitol records this year had released a Dean-related CD within their 'Collectors Series' of a selection of 25 songs, approved by Dean himself when he had taken himself down to the Capitol Tower in Hollywood to watch the digital re-mastering of this selection in their studios. An intelligent collection of some of Dean's most popular items, together with a few released in stereo for the first time, it was all in all a good compilation. Dean even included a little note on the sleeve, reminding us all that 1990 was his 50th year in show-business, as if we didn't know!

So with Dean's 50th and the DMA's 30th, we had a double celebration this year, but it seemed the media was not interested in the former (I never expected them to have any in the latter, of course): instead they were very content in telling everyone around the world that Dean Martin was drinking himself to death and falling over on stage all the time. But that was not true. He wasn't a well man, and did continue to take medication, some not always as prescribed, and sometimes mixed with alcohol, more than he had ever taken before.

Being that we had a double celebration this year, we contacted every radio and television station in the UK, every film company that Dean had worked for in the past, and many others all over the world, letting them know of his 50th anniversary. But with typical appeal and excitement, no company bothered to even write back or contact us in any way, something I must say we experienced numerous times in the past. Although Dean was always very popular here in the UK, he had never been taken very seriously, being regarded as someone who didn't take *himself* or his work seriously. It seemed that no organisation took the trouble to present anything particular and sadly, after so many years work, he was not recognised in any way. EMI Records here decided to delete 'The Classic Dino' album we had compiled in 1979, but it had been a consistent seller and had remained in their catalogue for over eleven years. I did suggest that this should be re-issued as a compact disc, together with a re-release of 'Dino – Italian Love Songs', but both of my ideas fell upon deaf ears at Capitol. The same silence came from Dean's management upon my suggestion that the Reprise issues should be re-released on CD, similar to *all* of the Frank Sinatra material, with additional and/or unreleased tracks on each disc. But jumping forward to 2009, the Reprise albums did eventually appear on CD, with two titles on one disc.

20th Century Fox released unseen footage of the ill-fated *Something's Got To Give* and Dean appeared at Las Vegas for a few more shows. Segments of him were seen on the *Crooners of the Century* special with Jerry Lewis and again in *Sinatra 75 – The Best Is Yet To Come*, screened in December.

Continuing his shows in Las Vegas however, he still managed to display the charm that was uniquely Dean, but it was painfully noticeable that he was unwell. He was attacked again by intestinal influenza in March 1991 and had to rest. He also noticed something that had been creeping up on him: he was developing stage fright. He had always suffered from anxiety, but this was now becoming something that was spilling out into his professional appearances. But with medication, he managed to control this situation and carried on with only a selected few dates in Nevada.

Meanwhile, Capitol Records had re-released on CD the complete 'Swingin' Down Yonder' plus eight extra tracks (one never before released). With the original sleeve notes and cover, this was a superb reissue and made me hope that many more were to come.

The DMA continued to promote Dean and his career and, even though he was not very much in the news now (if at all), we still had a growing band of admirers that joined us month after month.

Towards the end of this year, Dean had carried on with some occasional appearances in Las Vegas, but made a surprise move by announcing that he was to provisionally sign a two-year contract for appearances at the Desert Inn. This never came to fruition, for he did not engage any appearances there at all and completed his final shows for Las Vegas in July.

Dean Martin had finally called it a day.

26

Dean no longer wanted to appear in cabaret anywhere, bringing to an end an unprecedented career as one of Nevada's greatest ever crowd-pleasers. When Dean's name went up in lights in Las Vegas, or indeed anywhere, there was this solid gold guarantee that the crowds would come pouring in to see the man who had made a fantastic success out of everything he had attempted. The public could quite easily put someone down as easily as praise them, but Dean Martin had managed to get to the very pinnacle of success and life and had stayed there, not a small effort by any means.

When Dean worked with anyone in his career, without exception, he would play to that fellow artist and ignore the audience. Not that he didn't like the audience, he loved every one of them – but it was the art and talent within him that insisted he gave his all to the other person, in turn showing the watching audience just how good he was. Even in the most intimate surroundings, such as in cabaret or in small clubs, Dean always tended to look ahead and over the faces of those staring back up at him. This way, he got everyone there enthralled by him and so displayed no shyness whilst he was working in his own inimitable manner and unflappable style.

It was all part of his talent, and that was the way he worked, earning the respect and love of many fellow artists as well as people like Greg Garrison, Mort Viner and Mack Gray. These were the people behind this great entertainer who took away the worries of routine and complications just the way he liked it, enabling him to conquer the admirers by the multitude, making it all look so easy, but working hard at it every time!

Jimmy Bowen had begun to compile a set of songs for a double CD set of Dean's recordings to be issued on the Capitol label, a type of anthology of his songs for Capitol and Reprise, but owing to complications with Dean's ownership of Reprise sessions being married with the Capitol material, the entire project was shelved.

In 1992, John Chintala (who had been a regular DMA member) approached us regarding help with a radio documentary for Dean's 75th birthday. In 2017, John said to Elliot, "My first thought is how much [Bernard] helped with a radio (show?) Not only did he tape record answers for all the questions I wrote to him with (yes, 'wrote'...this was the pre-internet days!) but he transcribed his responses so I could have them in 'script form'. This made my job of editing his sound bites much, much easier. I did not ask him to do this; rather, he took it upon himself to go the extra mile and supply me with this information. Just one example of the generosity he showed towards me."

Dean now had all the time in the world to do nothing, a somewhat precarious situation for someone who had chronic depression. With his health not particularly good, Dean was again advised to take more exercise, so for a while he took walks in various places with an assistant. This he found quite enjoyable, although he did not carry on for more than a few weeks. He knew he should look after himself better but never getting over the loss of his loved ones and friends, he realised in his heart that he had to be strong. His dear parents and his son (as well as his living family) would not like to see him so depressed and miserable, but his state of mind made his life now so dull and routine, in total contrast to his previous experiences.

But in order to try to get to the bottom of all the stories flowing out from the media about what was wrong with Dean, we contacted the man himself via his office. One of many of Dean's short hand-written notes came back eventually in July, joking that he was living the high life! But then his management came back a couple of months later, telling me that because of increasing problems with his health, he'd been admitted to hospital on 16th September.

Certain tests were carried out but as he refused any intensive checks on himself, the hospital was unable to completely clarify his situation. Nothing was ever officially released as a bulletin from the hospital or his doctors, but we learnt that in addition to being generally debilitated, he had cancerous tumours on both lungs, which caused him terrible breathing problems. This we sadly announced in our newsletter for October 1993, which naturally caused great concern to us and our devoted members.

Contacting Dean at his home, he replied by post, remarking that he was so thankful for our concern and that it was so pleasing to have had my support for so many wonderful years. As this letter had arrived in November, it was pleasing to have actually heard from him in this way and he still thought so highly of me after all this time, even taking time out to wish me a merry Christmas.

Over the years, Dean sent me numerous small hand-written notes, expressing various remarks and comments. Occasionally we had a typewritten letter, but they were all the same: Dean always expressed how grateful he was. Many items he had also sent me and my children over the years and, as well as those letters and notes, I can only assume that many times he did this on his own. But that was Dean, a kind person in so many ways, who never truly realised just how much his public adored him and his work. Admittedly, I was always so surprised and honoured that he treated me in this way, and how he strongly expressed his feelings on paper whenever I informed him of good or tragic events within my personal life. I was so proud and sometimes even shocked with his high opinion of me.

So many of the people who have worked with Dean will all tell you the same: that he was absolutely wonderful to know and to be with, was professional, sincere and brought much needed laughter and pleasure even to the most serious situation.

During the course of 1994, very little was seen of the man.

His visits to La Famiglia (or Da Vinci's) were less frequent and sometimes he would be seen eating alone or with Jeanne. His songs were played for him and perhaps a fellow diner would acknowledge him. Dean never ignored them and occasionally even signed an autograph.

He'd ceased smoking by now but continued to mix his medication with alcohol, doing nothing for his depression or general health overall. By the middle of the year, he'd lost a lot of weight, dropping from his usual 14 stone to a worrying 10. But with the cancer in his lungs, his weight would forever be dropping. Yet, as if still defying the odds, he spent New Year's Eve at Da Vinci's restaurant with Jeanne and Ursula Andress. When asked about his well-being from those nearby, he said quite brightly ...*yes, I feel quite a lot better now, thank you.*

Meanwhile, the DMA had been asked to assist with another compilation from Capitol, with an album being titled 'Singles'. I sneaked in some of my favourites from Dean's repertoire as well as a few never before released on CD! Capitol itself was also preparing a separate collection for the American market: called 'Spotlight,' it was a random selection of material taken from various LPs, again including some songs that had never been committed to CD before. This was pleasing as it meant that Dean's work was being discovered by a whole new audience.

I'd been toying with the idea of writing Dean's life story for some time but wondered what his take on that would be. So I asked him. In March 1995, he wrote back with his blessing.

Towards the autumn of that year, Dean suffered a further decline in health, his breathing had become worse than ever, and he and shut himself away. Yet I still received a letter here and there and always responded straight away, assuring him of my and the DMA's support for him. Sometimes he replied to my letters directly, sometimes he did not, but knowing how ill he was, I knew he was with his thoughts and his family. Who was I to expect him to respond to me?

It was November that his condition became critical. He remained in hospital for a few weeks but returned home in the December.

And at 3.37am on the morning of Christmas Day 1995 in his Beverly Hills home, Dean Martin peacefully passed away from acute respiratory failure caused by lung cancer.

Without any exaggeration, I can only say I was stunned when his office called me late afternoon (UK time) that day. It seemed surreal.

For me, Dean Martin *is* Christmas…his seasonal ballads could be heard in our home throughout most of the holiday season every year. In fact, 'A Winter Romance' was playing when I got the call.

Because of the time of year, postal communication would always be sluggish but I knew I had to issue a bulletin to the loyal DMA members, who were no doubt learning the news themselves throughout the building and, I'm pleased to say, highly respectful media coverage. Our home telephone didn't stop ringing with the press asking me for my thoughts and a few quotes. I managed to get a letter out to Jeanne and the family, expressing our sincere condolences, sending them our thoughts during their terrible sadness.

With a special invitation-only funeral, it was the family wish that no flowers be sent but a contribution to charity would be welcomed. This emotional event took place on Friday 29th December, and he was laid to rest in the Crocetti family mausoleum in Westwood Park, Los Angeles.

As a magnificent and unprecedented showing of respect, all the lights on the Las Vegas strip were switched off for ten minutes that afternoon. Jerry cancelled his stage performance in Denver to attend and bid his beloved Dino farewell. Sadly, because of illness, Frank was unable to attend, his wife Barbara going on his behalf instead. Sinatra was devastated: first Sammy and now Dean. He'd lost both of his closest friends.

Dean left behind such a legacy of work and memories that he's not truly gone, not as long as we remember him.

As 1996 began, the DMA *had* to continue. For the next few years we oversaw a number of compilations with Capitol, Reprise, Charly and Joker and after much persuasion from me, EMI agreed to release two of Dean's greatest albums together, remastered, on a single CD: 'Dino – Italian Love Songs' and 'Cha de Amor'. Due to its success, it was followed up by 'Pretty Baby' coupled with 'This Time I'm Swingin''. Furthermore, EMI decided to introduce this 'two-on-one' series for many of its other artists, something which I was quietly proud of. Our working relationship with Charly saw just two titles being released, the original intention to produce with them, a whole range of compilations. The production was cut short because Dean's family gained the complete and exclusive right to all his material, and we saw over the coming years beautifully remastered editions of original studio albums. These are highly sought-after by collectors now and well worth tracking down if you can.

Following our rewarding working relationship with John Chintala, he came to us again, this time with regard to a reference book on Dean he was preparing. John said to Elliot in 2017, "Bernard took the time to answer, or at least try to answer, every question I directed toward him. In those pre-internet days, researching someone's career was much more difficult than it is today. Bernard opened up his 30+ years of files for my perusal, and even supplied his [personal contact details] so that we could correspond directly. The book would have been much less complete without his help and assistance."

As I started slowing down my work with the DMA, Elliot began to get more involved, but after much discussion and pondering, we realised that the very nature of a society such as the DMA was intrinsic to the old style of 'fan club', one that couldn't compete with the online-based appreciation groups that were springing up quickly for any number of artists, actors and movies and so on. We dabbled with an online presence but it didn't suit the DMA's approach...or perhaps it didn't suit mine?

In 2009, we started a working relationship with Mark Adams, who had approached us as he was about to embark on a tour portraying Dean Martin as part of a series of Rat Pack shows. That working relationship became a friendship and Mark's performance, along with his co-stars Daniel George Long as Sammy and Stephen Triffitt as Frank, was phenomenal and we are immensely proud and honoured to still lend our support to Mark and his incredibly talented co-stars all these years later.

In 2011, on our 51st anniversary (51 years! Surely that has to be some sort of record?), the DMA issued its last *Just Dino* newsletter and we formally ceased operations. I wondered how many words we had written about Dean since 1960? And this biography, this recollection, would likely be the very last thing I ever wrote about Dean…a coda to an incredible six decades and I called it 'Just Dino' – because, after all, everything I ever did with the DMA was *for* just Dino.

You may have gathered by now that I am one of Dean's greatest admirers and yes, you're quite right. But I am not blinkered or naïve about him to say that everything he did was perfect. Far from it. He treated people abominably sometimes, but equally, treated others with such grace and respect.

However, I have always thought myself as being very fortunate indeed regarding my association with the man, and I honestly hope that this literary effort of mine (with assistance from my son, of course) will be considered as it was intended: as a work of genuine sincerity and affection, and that my small contribution to his life and career will be perhaps something that will be remembered and referred to in the future. He was a very large part of my life and will remain so, treating my children as if he were an uncle and making such a positive difference to my own career and that of my son.

You will have your own opinions about the kind of person I am and the type of man Dean was, but the fact remains that no other performer has given me so many years of sheer pleasure with his style of entertaining.

It has been a great pleasure to work for and with him in my own way and if everything was as pleasing as his charm and talent, the way he projected such happiness and contentment to his millions of fans across the world (and still does long after his death), wouldn't it be a perfect world?

Thank you, dear Dino, for all you have done for me and this crazy world we live in.

And I'll let the man himself have the last word:

Now, I've had a special request…but I'm gonna sing anyhow.

Mutual Respect

Written by Mark Adams, 2017

When Elliot approached me in 2016 to write [what was originally] the afterword for the first edition of this exciting and unique recollection of Dean Martin, I felt honoured, delighted and a little bit apprehensive. What could I add that Bernard and Elliot hadn't already covered, each being not only huge fans and incredibly knowledgeable on the subject but also two people who have had a connection to Dean all their lives?

Then I remembered that ten years earlier I had met with Elliot in a London restaurant to ask him if he would kindly come up with something for my tour brochure of my then-forthcoming UK (and subsequent US) tour of *That's Amore- A Celebration of Dean Martin & Friends*. Elliot titled his article 'Mark of Respect' [reprinted within this work] which I guess summed up what *I* felt about Dean. So this is returning the favour, albeit ten years later, the year of Dean's centenary. I use the heading 'Mutual Respect.'

My own association with Dean Martin began in 2002. I was asked to audition for a touring show called *The Rat Pack - Live from Las Vegas*. To be perfectly honest, I was not sure I wanted to go on tour again as I had not long finished a 6-month run of another production. I had a vague idea of who the Rat Pack were, but there was to be no Peter Lawford or Joey Bishop in this show, just the triumphant trio of Frank, Dean and Sammy. In fact the full title of the show was *Frank, Dean and Sammy - The Rat Pack Live from Las Vegas* just in case anyone was in any doubt! The fact that all three artists had been dead sometime did not stop some people turning up to see who they thought were the real thing! I had also never heard of the show's producers who had made their name more through touring rock and roll shows - so I was pretty sceptical. My interest grew, however, when I googled

Dean Martin and started listening to his studio albums and live show recordings.

I then knew I had to play this man.

I was offered the role and then the real research began every book and every album I could come across and, scouring a charity shop, I struck gold. 13 LP records including 'Live at the Summit' (for £30.00 I might add, so someone in the shop knew its worth!). The voice was so good, so distinctive, it would be easy to parody. Impersonators would do that - but I wanted to nail it properly, not overdo it. I listened and listened and listened. I am *still* listening!

Finding live footage on stage was more challenging. This is well before *YouTube*! My next door neighbour at the time had a friend who was a massive Dean Martin fan. He had a VHS copy of the concert from the Keele Theatre, St Louis recorded in 1965. This was filmed live and played on closed circuit across the US. It was Frank's idea. Johnny Carson hosted in absence of Joey Bishop, and it is a cracker. I played it non-stop. Dean stole the show. The camera loved him and he it. He knew where they all were, staring down its cold lens with calculation and insouciance. This was the guy, this is who men wanted to be or at least hang out with, and who women idolised. This was the guy who could tell Frank, "No thanks pally, I'm not hanging out tonight. I shall be on the golf course at 6am!" This was the guy who made it all look so easy because he had done it thousands of times before. He could play straight or be the funny guy. Years of being with Jerry told him that.

All I had to do now is bring this into the show. It would prove difficult because the script we had was challenging. But over time I changed it: the laughs came; the interaction seemed real and not forced; the camaraderie genuine; the band got in on the jokes; I tried new things each night and if the gag landed I gave it a mark out of ten. I wrote down hundreds of one liners he used (by this time I had amassed tapes of *The Dean Martin Television Show* and the subsequent *Dean Martin Celebrity Roasts*).

To cut a long story short, the tour was a huge success and we ended up transferring to London's West end for what was supposed to be a six-week run! We ended up doing nearly three years in four different theatres! They couldn't get enough of us.

I had already been toying with the idea of a solo Dean Martin show. I'd base this more on his TV specials with different guests and of course the glamour of his backing singers, the Golddiggers. Not a tribute, much more than that. Dean Martin had Ken Lane, his brilliant pianist, I had Barry Robinson, who shared my love for Dean and was fantastic to have on stage. We toured the UK. We played the London Palladium (in Dean's very footsteps). We had a great time. And two years later we toured the US! Me, a bloke from Swindon, Wiltshire, touring the US in a show I had conceived, playing one of the biggest stars to grace the planet! Heady stuff.

Well, it is now 2018, and 101 years ago, Dino Paul Crocetti was born in Steubenville, Ohio. He became Dean Martin and he could do it all. As his partner, director/producer and friend at NBC TV, Greg Garrison, said, "Who else did it all? He played theatres, clubs, night clubs, he made million selling records, he was a super movie star, making straight appearances as well as comic, then he became perhaps the biggest star on TV the world has ever seen." No wonder after 15 years I still find things to say and do.

That's a mark of respect.

I am so excited about this new edition of the book because I know Elliot had been dreaming of it for a long time, to bring his father's lifetime's work to completion. His parents, who both sadly passed away recently, would be so proud, his dad looking over his shoulder as he types away. If you are a fan you will remember and celebrate Dean's work and life and if, like me, you enjoy reading biographies you will learn a great deal about a kind of artist, a kind of man, that we don't get too many of these days. And if you just happen to read this out of curiosity, well, you are in for a treat.

Thanks for letting me share a little bit of your dream, Elliot. Always,

MARK ADAMS

London Palladium Souvenir Brochure, 1953
(from author's personal collection)

Glasgow Empire, 1953
(from author's
personal collection)

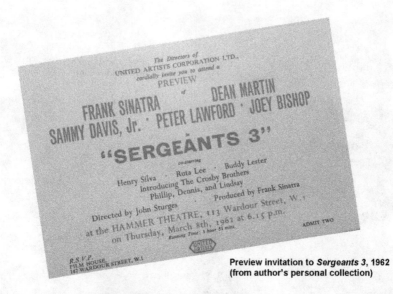

Preview invitation to *Sergeants 3*, 1962
(from author's personal collection)

Dino's Lodge, 77 Sunset Strip, Las Vegas (from author's personal collection)

with Joey Bishop, 1967 (from author's personal collection)

with Frank Sinatra, 1964 (photograph courtesy Warner-Pathe)

THIS IS YOUR FAVOURITE—DEAN MARTIN—WITH HIS
WIFE JEANNE AND THE SEVEN CHILDREN.

Photograph by kind permission of Dean Martin and Bernard Thorpe.

(from author's personal collection)

**c1970
(from author's personal collection)**

Dino

August 18, 1964

Bernard H. Thorpe, President
The International Dean Martin Club

Thornton Heath
Surrey, England

Dear Bernard:

We have just received the album, Let's Be Friendly, and the family and myself thank you. We enjoyed it and also the sleeve note comments.

We are sending you our three most recent releases. If you already have them perhaps the Club may find use for them.

Thanks again for the thoughtful congratulatory cables.

Best wishes,

DEAN MARTIN

DM:erh

4 For Texas
(photograph
courtesy
Warner-Pathe)

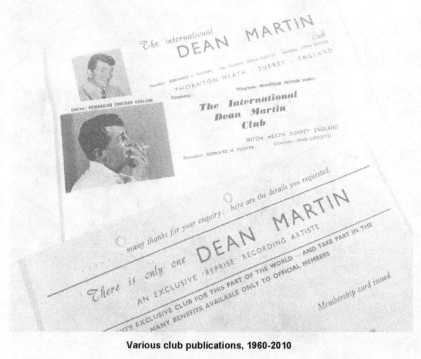

Various club publications, 1960-2010

working version of the first edition's cover from 2017, art by Steve Caldwell
(courtesy Barnaby Eaton-Jones, Chinbeard Books)

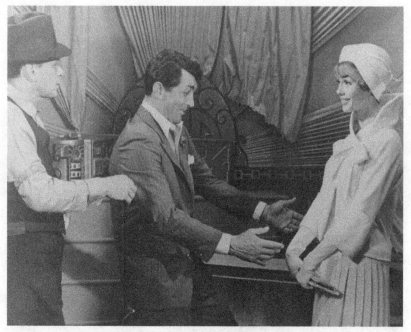

Robin and the 7 Hoods (photograph courtesy Warner-Pathe)

with Frank Sinatra, 1964
(photograph courtesy Warner-Pathe)

Bernard H Thorpe, 1983 (courtesy Croydon Advertiser)

Trade promos for 'Twenty Original Hits', October 1976

with Jimmy Stewart, c1972 (from author's personal collection)

(from author's personal collection)

On stage at the Apollo Victoria, London, June 1983
(from author's personal collection)

c1989 (from author's personal collection)

1987 (from author's personal collection)

**One of the very last
pictures of Dean taken, 1995
(from author's personal collection)**

Part Two

Compiled and edited by Elliot Thorpe

Introduction to Part Two

It is something of an understatement to say that my late father Bernard H Thorpe had always admired the talents of Dean Martin. Even through his formative years, with all the adventures and time he spent in military service and in his early working life, Bernard had thought Dino's singing voice was somewhat different to other artists of the time. Of course, in the early 1950s, the only exposure to Dino's career Bernard would have got would be via newspaper columns and the occasional magazine article and an expanding collection of available shellac 78s, radio play or cinema visits.

Young Bernard never considered himself to be a 'collector' of anything in particular, but his fascination for Dino was slowly changing that. There were any number of fan clubs in those days and he wrote to one in East London in 1953 when he was 15. With no response from them, he found that the club had in fact closed down sometime before due to 'lack of support'.

Determined to find out more about Dino, Bernard kept searching for a fan club but with nothing forthcoming, he decided that the only way would be to set one up himself!

The correct routine was to get permission from the artist concerned and so (not really knowing where to write to) Bernard sent a tentative letter to Dino care of Paramount Pictures in Hollywood. And heard nothing. And continued to hear nothing no matter what film or record company he wrote to for the next few years. His father, Henry, was convinced Bernard was being foolish because surely a man of Dean Martin's status wouldn't bother communicating with a teenager in South London!

But in 1960, Dean's office replied with full consent to create a fan club in the UK. There were two early provisos: Dean would need to approve the name of the club and the word 'fan' wouldn't be included (even though its initial moniker would be Dino's

Fan Club, until Dean soon changed it to the International Dean Martin Club. Ultimately, in 1967, he settled on the Dean Martin Association).

Bernard couldn't believe it. He shared the news with his parents. There he was, just 21 years of age, and with permission from the man himself (because, Dino said, '[he'd] been so damn insistent'). Now Bernard had to prove that he could do this, openly admitting many years later that he actually hadn't thought that far ahead, finding the initial steps to encourage membership daunting and slow. But he persevered, hoping against the odds he wouldn't let his idol down.

Little did Bernard know, of course, just how much this would affect his life going forward as amazing occurrences came and went with this huge Hollywood star.

Shortly before my father passed away in 2015, he wrote: "[Dino] took to me so much with his utter personal support and friendship...little, ordinary me! He gave me an incredible amount of backing and confidence with all the albums, gifts, opportunities and much more over the years. He was unfailing in his connections with me, all off his own back. As I try to recall what happened over the years I ran the Dean Martin Association, it does sometimes seem almost like a dream, but everything annotated here is absolutely true. Even reading it back is as if I'm reading about someone else's experiences. Dino himself had the most wonderful show business life and, with my very small part in his career, I hope did assist him. He was a genuine human being who had so much natural talent, linked with lots of luck and self-determination. I am extremely proud to have worked for Dino for so many years and did my very best to keep his name alive, even after his death in 1995, and promote his career as an important milestone in entertainment history."

My older sister, Carole, recently added this: "Having grown up listening to Dean Martin, watching his films and TV shows, it was easy to see the respect and admiration my dad had for him and continued to do so for the rest of his life. His love for Dean the performer and the man never waned and he has passed that onto myself, perhaps even from my birth when Dean sent me a doll from one of his album covers! So, thank you Dad and Dean for the love and entertainment shared by myself and millions across the world."

When I received the blessing from my father to complete the original version of this work, I began looking through the DMA Archives. The amount of time Bernard had dedicated to both Dean and the DMA was astonishing and I don't think my sister or I truly realised to what extent. I hope I have done this final version justice and that it is ultimately something both my parents (and Dean Martin himself) would have been proud of.

Here then are a small handful of selected essays and features from the DMA Archives spanning nearly seven decades, including a reproduction of the very first one-sheet publication from November 1960, as well as previously unpublished articles and new, exclusive interviews with some of the people who knew and worked with Dean.

Please don't talk about me when I'm gone, he once sang.

Sorry, Dean, but we will *always* talk about you.

✶ ✶ ✶ ✶ ✶ ✶ ✶ ✶ ✶ ✶ ✶ ✶ ✶ ✶ ✶ ✶ ✶ ✶ ✶ ✶

Letter from Dino

VOL..1.. NO....1   November 1960

Well, here we are at long last!!!

- -

After so many months organising our brand new club for you all, with
Dean giving his written permission sometime back, we can at last issue
our very first newsletter.

Obviously, to start off, we cannot advise you just how many issues we
shall be producing per year for you, but we shall DEFINITELY be issuing
our special CHRISTMAS issue for you sometime next month.

We have started advertising in the music and film   related magazines
for membership so please help us by recruiting as many people as you can
to join, after all, the more the merrier.

The membership subscription for one year is FOUR SHILLINGS for the
United Kingdom; as we hope to expand worldwide, we shall let you know the
other rates for abroad just as soon as we can.

Dean himself is very pleased we have set up his club in London and he has
told us that he will help in all ways possible to get us established for
the promotion and publicity of his career and life.

A great film that Dino made this year was of course "BELLS ARE RINGING"
with the beautiful Judy Holliday-this opened in London August 25th and
the soundtrack record SW1435 is now available of course.
It was a good UK August for Dean, because on the samedate his other great
film "OCEAN'S ELEVEN" ALSO opened in London on the same day!

His own album for Capitol "THIS TIME I'M SWINGIN'!" is released in America
for OCtober with the UK having to wait until next month for it to get
into the shops.
Backed by Nelson Riddle and his orchestra, the songs are I CAN'T BELIEVE
THAT YOU'RE IN LOVE WITH ME, YOU'RE NOBODY 'TIL SOMEBODY LOVES YOU,
TRUE LOVE, ON THE STREET WHERE YOU LIVE, IMAGINATION, UNTIL THE REAL
THING COMES ALONG, PLEASE DON'T TALK ABOUT ME WHEN I'M GONE, I'VE GROWN
ACCUSTOMED TO HER FACE, SOMEDAY, MEAN TO ME, HEAVEN CAN WAIT and his
solo version of JUST IN TIMEfrom 'Bells Are Ringing'.

But,don't forget Dean's single "AIN'T THAT A KICK IN THE HEAD" (his choice
of title) from 'Ocean's Eleven'.
Please keep your letters coming in and PLEASE recruit members for us. All
communications to our address below and, do not forget that S.A.E!!

Back next month with our very first Christmas issue of the newsletter......

Open Letter #1

Written by Dean Martin, who would occasionally send notes to the DMA for them to be reproduced in future editions of the newsletter. The one that follows was his first such correspondence, undated, but his filming references indicate he wrote it in late 1961 or early 1962 and was included in 'A Letter from Dino', Vol 2, No 8, August 1962.

Dear Friends

I am pleased to be able to write this journal letter personally to you. I'd also like to express my deep gratitude to each and every one of you for your loyalty and friendship.

Your own club president over in London and myself are really getting together to make the British club for me really great.

It's a wonderful feeling when people like you thousands of miles away take the trouble to be interested in me.

Together, the two of us hope to really got to town and do many more great things for you all.

I've just finished a role in "Sergeants 3" and enjoyed working on this film very much. I hope that you will all see it and enjoy it as much as we did filming it. Also in the cast are Frank Sinatra, Sammy Davis Jr, Peter Lawford, Joey Bishop, Henry Silva, Ruta Lee and the Crosby Brothers. Sounds like I'm a critic! But I really must say that they all are a great crowd of people to work with – really the tops.

Anyhow, it's a Western and we all think it will be enjoyable film fare for everyone.

I have another movie currently in release, which most of you have most probably seen already and know about. It's

"Ada" -- which I did for MGM. I had the good fortune of working with the very charming and lovely Susan Hayward - also a very fine actress, I might add. MGM adapted this film from the popular novel titled "Ada Dallas".

I had a bit of time off after the wind-up of "Sergeants 3" for a little rest and a little travelling.

Next, I'll be doing a film for Paramount titled "Who's Got the Action?" - and I'm looking forward to working with Lana Turner.

I have several other things lined up on the board, but nothing definite that I can mention at this time.

My wife and children are all in good health, for which I am most grateful. The children are growing more and more with each passing day.

I hope that all of you had pleasant summer vacations.

Should any of you wish to send me letters, I would be pleased if you would forward them to Bernard Thorpe in London, who will then forward them to me.*

I would like to thank you for your interest in me and I hope that all of my future efforts continue to please you.

Until next time…

All the best,

Dean Martin

*as genuine as this sentiment was, the sheer volume of correspondence quickly became too great and so the DMA, on Dino's request, retained and answered every single letter on his behalf

George Daniel Long: Well-Grounded Performer

George Daniel Long in conversation with Elliot Thorpe, April 2018

The DMA initially became involved with *The Definitive Rat Pack* after previously getting to know Mark Adams (who coolly portrays Dean Martin in their live shows). Stephen Triffitt effortlessly takes on the Frank Sinatra role and the third and vital cog is that of the multifaceted talent that is George Daniel Long who embodies Sammy Davis Jr.

I was first introduced to George by Mark some years ago now in the Matcham Room of London's Hippodrome Casino (where *The Definitive Rat Pack* has a regular slot) to talk with the three guys after being approached to write their souvenir booklet. I'd seen George perform as Sammy many times before, of course, as part of Flying Music's *Frank, Dean and Sammy: The Rat Pack Live from Las Vegas* and what struck me on meeting him was how effortless he was able to transform himself into the role. I've got to know him since over the years following that first meeting and can attest to him being a warm and generous person who always makes people smile. I asked him recently how important is it for him to be approachable.

"Oh, being approachable is *really* important for me. Of course, we all get it wrong sometimes but you have to be nice to people you meet along the way. Occasionally you can be really busy or stressed and the audience member who wants a chat with you isn't always aware of that, but a smile and a thank you goes a long way. The same goes for your work colleagues. You get more out of people if you treat them kindly."

George channels Sammy almost perfectly so I wondered if there were any preparations he went through. George laughs infectiously.

"Preparations? What's that?," he replies, tongue in cheek. "I have small routines that I go through in a certain order depending on the show, maybe the order in which I get dressed, always do my hair last, check the bowler hat is on stage and so on. I never get ready too early, which Sammy himself was known for. He would just disappear, have a nap and not warm up before a show. I tend to have a think about any new things that have cropped up, stage entrances and exits in a new venue, maybe go over song lyrics in my head if I haven't sung a particular one for a while. I find that if you overthink things then that's when they can go wrong." George can be his own critic, however, and he considers that his preparations are perhaps based on what he did or how he fared in a previous performance. "I note myself after a show. I go away and think about any mistakes I made or things I may do differently and then put them into practice the next time." Clearly, he wants to always hone his portrayal, his performance and ensure that he is the best he can possibly be when his cue to go on stage begins – but he had to have started somewhere so I was intrigued about his very first time auditioning for Sammy.

"Telling you when that was will give away my age!" laughs George with a twinkle in his eye. "It was in 2000, I believe. I had to brush up on my tap dancing with the help of Jo Kempton who was resident director on the Flying Music production and also a good friend of mine. It was being filmed for UK Living TV, something now I regret as they edited a lot of things out of context to make it better viewing which, unfortunately, didn't represent me as well as it could have. For example, I was pretending to cry on the stairs as a joke to say 'I really hope I get this,' then they used it as real footage and didn't add the bit where I was laughing immediately afterwards, so revealing it was fake! I must be the Donald Trump of show business with all this fake news!"

George, Stephen and Mark did all perform together previously for Flying Music's *Frank, Dean and Sammy: The Rat Pack Live from Las Vegas* and after hundreds of shows, they came together again to form the Definitive Rat Pack "...which is us, *our* show," says George. "We get to be in control of all creative elements, we work together developing it and we are all free to change what we want to do and experiment more. It makes everything looser and the essence of what any Rat Pack show should be is fun and camaraderie. The more natural you are, the more the audience warms to you."

Frank, Dean and Sammy all had their own individual acts and any number of Dean's over the years follows the same basic structure (you can watch one of his from the 60s, right up to his last performances in 1988 and he'd always start with the same opening song parody gag ["Drink to me only,,,that's all I aks... *ask...*"] but from then on, it varied slightly depending on the venue, the year and who was in the news. With that in mind, George says of the *Definitive Rat Pack's* interpretation: "If it's terribly scripted then it loses the main ingredient that made them so popular." And that main ingredient he is referring to is the laid-back approach, the notion that the original Frank, Dean and Sammy seemingly made it up as they went along.

George has travelled the world with *The Definitive Rat Pack* and I asked him if he had any stories he could share with me. "I'd have to kill you first!" he replies with that laugh again. "I love travelling with the show and have seen some wonderful places and met some lovely people, so it's a privilege. I can't think of many stories without saying what's not mine to say. I'm not one to gossip so you haven't heard it from me but..."

The three artists embody the spirit of the trio they portray so much that I've never perceived *The Definitive Rat Pack's* show as a 'tribute act'. It's so much more than that: Stephen, Mark and George are performers recreating a show that exists in show-business legend. Do they feel any weight of responsibility as a result? Bearing in mind their audiences (who absolutely love what they do by the standing ovations they regularly receive) would likely have never seen the real Frank, Dean and Sammy, how faithful do they need to be to the original act?

"You are incredibly responsible for the portrayal as you wouldn't want the audience going away with a slight on each of the character's legacy. People sometimes do forget that what you say is in the spirit of them and not you and perhaps can't distinguish that. Fans also have their favourites and it can be hard if you get a bad review or response as they may not have really been into the person in the first place and then you either make them like them or they don't like you either! It's all subjective, but all we can do is portray them to the best of our abilities as you can't please everyone.

"Much of the material has just morphed over time. I try to think as Sammy when in character, so before I say something I ask myself would he have said anything like it? You can't spend the whole show stuck in 1963 so we can make modern references as long as it's in character. For example, if a mobile 'phone goes off you can make a joke of it. There would have been no 'phones so rather than say something like "What is that strange contraption?" it's easier to accept that no one cares if you make out of era choices as long as it's apt. We don't do many race or Jewish gags as they aren't really necessary with what we do. I do occasionally make relevant statements but have the advantage of being in control of what is said and not have to say anything that would make anyone uncomfortable, including myself. The other problem is that if the audience don't know Sammy was Jewish and if you don't set it up, then any script relevant to that can make you look a little racist. I didn't want to spend all my time pointing out those aspects of Sammy just so the audience get the references and in-jokes. I have had a few incidents where they thought it was me saying it personally and completely missed Sammy's subtle stabs at racism. I overheard one lady call me racist and misquoted what I'd actually said on stage in character." George's respectful and protective nature of the original shows is clear and Stephen and Mark follow suit. "We used to smoke on stage, too, and now we don't. It's much easier anyway and after not being able to do it due to legislation, we actually have gotten so used to not smoking. As for the drinking...no comment!"

The camaraderie he has with Mark and Stephen on stage is clear. "Of course, with any group there will be times when you rub each other up the wrong way, you are in each others pockets a lot and you have to make decisions that suit everyone - but we never take our disagreements on stage. The good thing is once we have been on stage we have so much fun that most stuff is forgotten. I guess my role in that is being the diplomat. We have many different layers of relationships with each other so we will be different when it's all of us as opposed to when I spend time one on one with either of the other two. I'm a good go-between for the guys, too, and I am very organised, so I tend to be the person who they call to get information." And with that mischievous smile, he adds, "And at their time of life, the memory goes a bit!"

The Definitive Rat Pack has a number of CDs available and they're absolutely well worth a listen. They're not live recordings of their stage act, however, so I asked George if he enjoys studio work as much as live performances. "I prefer live as vocally I need to move around to really get into character. A live performer tends to adopt a 'studio voice' which can be softer, so I know I sound different in studio than on stage. It's a bit restrictive in the studio as you have to stay on the microphone but on stage as I can make a bigger sound when moving as well as phrase things to movement.

"I have two songs I'm not too keen on singing: 'Mr Bojangles' and 'The Candyman'. I just don't like singing 'The Candyman', and neither did Sammy apparently, because it's pop and not much you can really do with it. It's not a great song to perform as I prefer something with a bit more sentiment. 'Mr Bojangles' can be something of a struggle mainly at private events. It's a really hard song to sing as I really want to tell the story and because I get so emotionally involved, I have been known to cry by the end, I invest a lot into it. If audiences aren't really paying attention or are drunk and rowdy it makes it impossible to sing and you have to motor through it which doesn't do the song justice without pathos. Some clients request it but as it's slow, if you are doing a dinner and dance event people sometimes prefer something with more swing all evening and 'Mr Bojangles' can, as lovely as the song is, bring the mood down. Add the to the fact that it's the longest song I sing, even with the cut verses it runs at over four and a half minutes, so a long time to be up there wishing you weren't!"

George trained at the London Studio Centre but his informative years were thanks to local groups and a great music teacher at secondary school who transformed theatre there and mentored him a lot. ("Thank you, Mr David Hebden!!!") But why did he want to perform in the first place?

"I enjoyed it and some people said I should try it as they had spotted something in me. I recall I wanted to be an accountant or lawyer when I was younger and spent a lot of my teens around horses which I had to let go to progress in theatre. My first role was in *Showboat* for Oxford Operatic Society when I was 12. Over my career I've been lucky enough to be in many West End productions including *Sister Act*, *Miss Saigon*, *Porgy & Bess* and *Carmen Jones*. I was even lucky enough to be the first death in Stephen Sommers' *The Mummy Returns* in 2001. I died my socks off but didn't get a credit!"

George nods when I ask him if he would have done anything different in his performing career. "Of course, but I'm not sure all of it was within my control. I see a few places where I swerved to another path by a snap decision or courage to stick to my principles but ultimately I have had a successful and lengthy career. I'd like to think I'd be here anyway even if I had made changes, so I can't look back - it's all been a wonderful experience.

"There were roles I just missed out on due to a variety of circumstances but I never think of the as the ones that got away. I'd like to take on something again at some point, just for fun but it would have to be something I knew I could do and was comfortable with. I've never been much of a typical actor striving for roles, I would generally go up for stuff that I knew I could do and say no to being seen for something I was less confident with. I've not always had the greatest confidence with my ability and always wanted to be consistent instead of push any boundaries but I find new ways of pushing myself with Sammy. He keeps me on my toes. I don't always have time for anything else as the *Definitive Rat Pack* schedules can get quite busy, so I won't do any long West End runs again but I still go up for TV, film, commercials or other short term stuff. It also means I can work on other ventures."

As well as transforming into Sammy, George makes transformations of other well-grounded things and is about as far as one can get from the smell of the grease-paint and the roar of the crowd. Does his landscape gardening tap into a different side of his creativity?

"I love being around nature, it's not the same as performing as I can't really dance into my meetings, but I guess you still have to be a showman to sell the design or yourself as a designer. I didn't always have an interest in gardens but decided to study horticulture with the Royal Horticultural Society and see what happened. I then realised that I liked the idea of design and so took my training further. I wasn't enjoying longer contracts on shows any more, too, so wanted a quieter, more normal life. I haven't really done much 9-5 and wanted to try something that gave me flexible hours and that I could do at any age. It gives me the freedom to down the drawing board and pens and go off and join the guys on a gig."

I've talked about this with George before, but I put it to him again what he thought Sammy would make of someone taking on his persona? "I hope he would be happy about it. I don't ever pretend to be a carbon copy of him: he is Sammy, I'm George. It's more about the essence, so I'd hope he would respect me as a performer and maybe see a little of him in me. If I'd had the chance to meet Sammy himself, I don't think I'd have the words to say to him. I can get pretty tongue-tied. I think all I'd ask if he could give me some of his talent as he had enough to spare!"

For more information on **The Definitive Rat Pack,** *including international tour dates and purchasing copies of their CDs and souvenir booklets, please visit thedefinitiveratpack.com. For more information on George's exceptional landscape gardening, please visit gardens.wellgroundedgroup.com*

All the Cool Dudes

Written by Elliot Thorpe, from 'Just Dino', Vol. 42, No. 1, Issue 367, Jan-Feb 2002

On reviewing the original Rat Pack classic prior to the remake from Steven Soderbergh being released, *Ocean's 11* is actually far from being the perfect heist movie. While that criticism may be a little harsh, it in no way deflects from enjoying the movie as a fun ensemble cast piece.

Of the five main cast members, three of whom are also vocalists, it is noticeable that only Dean Martin and Sammy Davis Jr get to sing, Dean with his near-legendary 'Ain't That A Kick In the Head' (written, incidentally, specifically for Dean in reaction to this strange phrase he once uttered) and 'Eee-O-Eleven' from Sammy. Conspicuously silent is Frank Sintra, instead deciding to focus on the more dramatic side of his characterisation of Danny Ocean, the ex-commander of a parachute regiment from where he builds his eleven men.

And this is where the movie falters.

We all know how they, Sinatra, Martin, Davis, Peter Lawford and Joey Bishop had more fun off camera than they ever did on it and so, with Sinatra doing his best portrayal of a snake-like-yet-charming, wife-dropping, ex-Marine, we never quite manage to get into Ocean's head. Like the rest of the gang, the characters are superficial: literal self-painted caricatures of their real personalities.

And this is where the movie succeeds.

Dean swings his way through as Sam Harmon, fresh from Miami and having kept little in touch with Danny. He's laid back, relaxed, thinks the whole plan of Danny's is faulty but he nevertheless saunters in and out of the shots with that ease and self-assuredness we expect from Dean. And, biased or not we may be, Sam Harmon is probably the most believable of the team.

Sammy, however, has far less screen-time but his role as Josh Howard brings the comedy to the movie, playing, as he always did, on his race and size, on notable scene being as they greased up their faces, with Josh side-cracking about how he knew his colour would come in handy one day!

Peter Lawford, the British rich kid gone bad plays, ahem, a British rich kid gone bad and his character, Jimmy Foster, even falls foul of being blamed as double-crossing the gang – a chilling premonition of how Sinatra was reputedly to react some time later to Lawford's difficult position in the presidential Kennedy empire.

Oddly, with *Ocean's 11* being a vehicle solely for the Rat Pack, one wonders why Richard Conte does most of the work, has the most screen-time and has the whole plot hinged on his character's actions and reactions. If the Pack were making this film, then should not the screen-time be monopolised by *their* antics?

Nevertheless, *Ocean's 11* is the ultimate Rat Pack movie. Forget *Robin and the 7 Hoods*, don't worry about *4 For Texas* or *Sergeants 3…this* is the one, the defining movie of their heyday.

Look how it has influenced the visuals of contemporary film…

Probably the most obvious direct nod was by Quentin Tarantino in *Reservoir Dogs*, where he has his characters pacing along a sidewalk not unlike Ocean's team do at the twist ending on the 1960 classic. We can also see echoes in more than one Scorcese picture, with *Casino* being the more obvious candidate.

And surely the most gratifying tribute is for an *en vogue* director to remake it.

So, for all of us who own the original movie, pay it again (on DVD for that better quality) and get yourself caught up with the whole feel, the whole era and the whole fun.

Enjoy Frank, Dean, Sammy, Peter and Joey at their peak and recall why we admire them so – then go and see George Clooney, Brad Pitt, Andy Garcia, Matt Damon and Elliott Gould do it all over again.

And *then* decide who's best.

Open Letter #2

*Written by Bernard H Thorpe and printed in 'A Letter from Dino',
Vol 2, No 10, October 1962*

Dear Members

After so many of you writing to the club with you appreciation to us for the various services and information we supply each month, and also your letters enquiring about Dean and his career, I felt that I should first thank you, ad then attempt to explain something 'behind the scenes' about the club.

First and foremost, the reason why we have succeeded in pleasing you is because Dean himself contacts us so often and takes such an ardent interest in his club here, sending exclusive news to us as fast as he can for our use in newsletters etc.

To me, Dean is not just a showbiz personality – he is a good friend and always sends us regards from his family and, in turn, likes to hear from us on a personal level.

This is of course because of the fact that I have had the very fortunate luck to be the head of Dean's club here which now covers the world.

Plus of course I can quite proudly say that no one anywhere can be as dedicated a fan as what I am of Dean's talents!!

We have a large and growing archive already detailing the Martin story, making up a complex and concise account of the man. There are only two Dean Martin clubs in the world: while we cover nearly every country of the world, the club in California is more of a local organisation, but nevertheless we keep in constant touch and both assist each other with information.*

Dean's close friends, Frank Sinatra, Sammy Davis Jr, Peter Lawford and Joey Bishop also contact us from time to time – and they are all great fun as you can well imagine.

Dean and I have worked at making the club something worth joining for a very long time and it has taken well over two years to become established. Name changes, new ideas and all those usual events in an organisation of any size have taken their course and we can only hope that our efforts are to your liking, although really I suppose no one can ever please everyone all the time!!

Records from abroad have been the biggest headache: we continually made arrangements with distribution companies who all, in turn, let us down in the end with our orders, causing us to place the same orders to several distributors which, in turn, makes a longer wait by you.

I would like to firmly impress up on you all that Dean Martin is extremely grateful for your support, but obviously he cannot write and thank everyone individually – that is why he asks us to do that for him. He is not a 'distant figure' like some artists can be.

Finally, we'd like to thank you for your support by being a member of the International Dean Martin Club – a club which we hope will continue to grow into an organisation that you will be proud to be part of – as proud as Dino Crocetti is of it right now!!

My very best wishes to all members

Bernard H Thorpe

Dino soon wanted just one club to represent him and so ordered all others to be closed down. The DMA became the first (and was for many decades the only) fully authorised world-wide society.

Hal Espinosa: A Man of Renown

Hal Espinosa in conversation with Elliot Thorpe, April 2018

Pennsylvania-born Les Brown started his career as a band leader in 1936 with 'Les Brown and His Blue Devils', becoming 'Les Brown and His Band of Renown' from 1938. Performing with stars such as Doris Day, Tony Bennett , Ella Fitzgerald, Nat King Cole and Dean Martin, to name but a few, Les worked with his band until 2000. Les himself passed away aged 88 in 2001.

I'd been in contact with Joel Guldin, who chairs the Les Brown Big Band Festival committee (and hosts an annual event at the Williams Valley High School in Pennsylvania, where Les Brown Jr. appears) and he'd mentioned to Hal Espinosa, who was Les' lead trumpet player for many years, of my father's own association with Dean Martin.

I was very fortunate to chat with Hal about his own career, about working with Les and, of course, knowing Dean.

"Dean Martin had his own show on NBC, only one of eleven different variety shows that were being produced around that time. In those days musicians worked on multiple shows. They were staff bands and most studios had them: NBC, CBS and so on. It was the same with movie studios, too, and MGM had its own: the MGM Studio Orchestra."

Hal was in Las Vegas for six years prior to moving to LA in 1969. When he arrived in LA, Butch Stone, saxophone player for Les Brown (and who was also the musician contractor for the band), had heard about Hal from somebody and wanted to see if he'd be interested in performing with them.

"They were going out on the road for three weeks," Hal says, "and their lead trumpeter was on staff at NBC and so the studio wouldn't release him for the tour. That same musician also used to work on the Dean Martin Television Show. I accepted the offer and joined them on the tour."

Les liked the way Hal played and so, whenever cover was required, he'd sub for NBC.

At the turn of the 1970s, NBC got rid of their staff band, meaning Les was able to hire whoever he wanted. Hal continues: "Les used the majority of the members of his band for the NBC recordings and that's when I started on a regular basis for the Dean Martin Television Show. I'd previously worked on the Bob Hope Specials, going around the world entertaining the troops, but with Dean's show it was based solely in Burbank, California. Thursday evenings we rehearsed but Dean was never there. Greg Garrison [the producer] would pop his head around occasionally."

Dean would be in his dressing room, watching the show on a monitor (there'd be a stand-in for him on the soundstage). But he knew his lines, knew his cues and when he came out for the show's recording, it'd be liked he'd rehearsed properly.

"Musicians are their own worst critics," Hal laughs, "and it's got to be perfect - so anytime somebody didn't come in on cue or cracked a note then they'd ask Les to stop and start again, even though others in the band couldn't always hear it. Les would also pick up where a note was out and after a while Greg would get on the podium with Les and say, 'We're not making records here, Les – just do it one time, and that's all you need to do!' Greg was a real businessman, he was saving money!"

Hal did admit he found that way of working a little frustrating because he wanted his own performance to be perfect but when he went home and watched the show, "I couldn't hear any of the goofs so I knew it was ok." (Many years later, Hal would realise that what he thought wasn't great at the time wasn't so bad after all!)

Hal didn't see much of Dean during the recordings but remembers the entertainer as being very laid back and that he never took himself too seriously. While Hal himself never appeared on screen, he said, "The shows were a lot of fun to do and Dean was a happy guy. He was unique. There really was no one like Dean."

That relaxed approach filtered down to the crew and Hal fondly recalls one particular day: "We [the band] often used to dash over the road during a 10-minute break to a Mexican restaurant. It would take 6 minutes to get there and back so we only had 4 to down our drinks. A girlfriend I was dating back then had some sweatshirts made up one time: on the the back we'd had printed 'The Dean Martin Speed Drinking Team' (which was what a few of us called ourselves!)" On the front was a martini glass design with their respective names below it. One was made up for Dean (who of course never joined them) and Hal presented it to him.

"Dean got a kick out of it...thought it was great!" Hal laughs.

Ken Lane, Hal recalls, was a nice guy and very quiet. "One time, we all got up to start filing out for a break. We were soon questioned as to where we were all going...and much to our embarrassment and laughter we'd all misheard someone say 'Hey, Ken!' as 'Take ten'!"

Of Les Brown, Hal says; "He was good musician, easy going and, like I said, he liked the way I played. He was nice to all the guys in the band but never hung around with the us, never showed up at band parties. I think that was because Les belong to the Bel Air Country Club that attracted big stars and musicians, so he preferred to associate with them. But all the same, he was a great band leader and I've never had anything negative say about him."

I asked Hal what Les would have thought about the band still going (now with Les Jr) all these years later. With sincerity, Hal replied, "I think Les would have loved to have his son carry on the sounds of the 'Band of Renown'."

Hal is in his early 80s now and has an illustrious career behind him. Prior to his Burbank years, he worked with many East Coast bands and, after the army, joined Woody Herman's band. But Woody broke the group up after a year so Hal started with Tommy Dorsey, rejoining Woody some time later when that band reformed. At that time Bill Chase was playing lead with Woody at a good $175 per week with Hal on a little less. "But then Buddy Morrow's band offered me a higher salary. I was going to work in Basin Street East with Peggy Lee in 1963 in New York but I got a call from a friend in Las Vegas to work the Dunes Hotel on a higher pay rate - so I left for Vegas before Peggy's opening night."

Hal was a jobbing musician so there was no question he wouldn't take it. He worked in Vegas for the next 6 years then moved to LA to join Les.

"I figured I'd play 'til I was about 50 years old then get a real job because I was having too much fun as a trumpet player!" Hal's enthusiasm for his career is infectious and talking to him made me see that one can live a dream if they try hard enough.

Do You Love Me was a 20th Century Fox picture starring Maureen O'Hara. Dick Haymes played a successful singer with designs on O'Hara's music school dean. But it was Harry James as the smooth trumpet player who got the girl. On seeing the movie, Hal said to his Dad, "I want to be a trumpet player! So he bought me a $40 coronet. In High School I was once embarrassed by my music teacher...he said when I played I sounded like a billy goat! So I started practicing four or five hours every day. I remember too I would stand in front of bandstands and the trumpet section would stand and play. The power of the sound felt like my hair was blowing back!"

And so at 17 years, he knew that's what he wanted to do and when he eventually played for Harry James himself, he related his stories to him - Harry loved the anecdotes. Likewise, he had always played the Les Brown classic 'Leap Frog' at school and vowed one day he'd play it with Les Brown himself - and he did!

He stayed with the Band of Renown until 1975 and a couple of decades later Hal moved away from playing entirely: "I'd done sessions [including a few of Dean's country songs as well as tracks such as 'It's a Good Day' and 'I'm Sitting On Top of the World' and tracks for The Mamas & The Papas] and film scores [notably *WarGames* for Arthur B Rubenstein and *Forrest Gump* for Alan Silvestri]. Playing at dances were fun even though you knew that the audience wasn't really listening to the music. But the 'phone kept ringing and I kept on working. When I did stop, my friends and colleagues carried on calling me 'the trumpet player'. I still get called that to this day! I became the Musicians' Union president and even after I'd put my horn down I was still working with the guys I used to play with, but this time negotiating contracts for them." He helped many musicians over the 10 years he held the position and made sure he never took any playing offers on mainly because he didn't want to take work away from other people. Jazz, Big Band, Sinatra and so on were always his preferred tastes but he met highly-talented artists from backgrounds such as classical, hip hop and reggae. The role, however, was very intense and felt burnt out after a decade.

I asked Hal, a genuine, good-to-honest gentleman, if he felt he'd done everything he wanted to do in life. His simple and encouraging response was: "Yes."

He did wonder though who would be interested in what he'd done but I can safely say that talking with him in 2018 about his career that has spanned decades was rewarding and gave a glimpse of a work ethic that reflected determination, success, hard work, kindness and honesty - and who wouldn't want to be interested in that?

Now retired, Hal Espinosa was lead trumpet player with Les Brown and His Band of Renown. Joel Guldin is the chair of the Les Brown Big Band Festival in Pennsylvania. For more information on Les Brown and the festival, please visit lesbrownfest.org

In Studio with Dean Martin

Written by Bernard H Thorpe, from 'A Letter from Dino', Vol. 7, No. 1, Jan 1966

Dean Martin is shortly to be in studio, recording a selection of songs for future release.

The orchestra prepares the music, goes over the arrangements while a lucky few spectators (us included) are allowed in to watch the session. We wait anxiously for the man himself to show.

Bill Justis, famed US composer/arranger/conductor, discussions the upcoming session with Jimmy Bowen, both agreeing that the sound effect they've tried out will go down well on this 'Houston' ballad they're going to do tonight.

The drummer practices in one corner of the studio with the orchestra's rhythm section while everyone is patiently waiting for Dean.

Suddenly, almost unnoticed, in he walks, strictly on time and bringing with him a complete atmosphere of relaxation (he must have a large company supplyin' him with all that relaxin' talent, says one of the session guys in the orchestra!).

Dean walks up to Bill, pats him on the back and says, "We'd better start this session or else some of these folks here tonight will wonder whether they're attending a record session or a school treat!"

Tonight, he's wearing a light blue sweat shirt (with the initials 'DM' embroidered on the breast pocket), casual slacks, a pair of white woollen socks and a brilliantly shining black pair of casual shoes (best leather, or course).

The first Chesterfield is lit as he reads over the music for the first take.

"Ready when you are, fellas," he says.

Bill leads the orchestra into their first number, a great arrangement of the Boyce and Hart number 'Lovely Little One'.

Straight through in one go, this one, but Dean thinks something's gone wrong halfway in, so there's a second try.

"What d'ya think, Jimmy?" Dean asks.

"Sounds great to us here, Dean," replies the producer.

"Okay, let's get through number two," says Dean, puffing at his second – no, it's is third – Chesterfield.

Dean likes smoking. It helps him to concentrate, to relax, but Jimmy and all the boys here tonight have told him many times already that there ain't no cigarettes needed to calm this cat down. He's as relaxed as anyone can surely be.

'Everybody But Me' in the can, followed swiftly by 'Hammer and Nails'.

"Let's take a couple o' shots, Dino," requests Ed Thrasher.

"You must be mad, Ed," laughs Dean.

Ed's camera bulb pops, photo number one taken, showing Dean still laughing whilst seated on the old regulation studio stool. That's one that'll do for the album jacket, thinks Ed to himself, I'll ask Dean what he thinks later.

"Hey! You've not taken that, have ya? I didn't have a glass of Bourbon in my hand! What'll my fans think of this?!" jokes Dean.

Back to more recording.

"Yeah, this is great for you," comments Bill to Dean, after completing 'Houston'."

Jimmy makes a suggestion. "This next one, Dean, 'I Will'. Good for your next single?"

"Great! I like the up-tempo mood. Selling well," agrees Dean.

'Selling well' is an understatement.

Then we're told we need to leave, so we're ushered out.

It's been a couple of hours or so. But what a rush.

Seeing Dean Martin record and you get why his output is relaxed and charming. It oozes down the mic into the mix.

And stays with us forever.

The Boys Are Back In Town

Written by Elliot Thorpe, from 'Just Dino', Vol. 49, No. 2, Issue 408, Oct-Dec 2009

Frank, Dean and Sammy: The Rat Pack Live From Las Vegas started its 2009 run in September, at London's Adelphi Theatre. The DMA was cordially invited as guests of Rat Pack Touring Ltd, and duly went along to see for itself the latest version of the popular production.

Some background for you: it all began at the Beck Theatre, Hayes in January 2000 when *Frank, Dean and Sammy: The Rat Pack Live From Las Vegas* made its debut. It had its first London run two years later at the Peacock Theatre. Rave reviews and sell-out audiences met the show's opening night at the Theatre Royal Haymarket on 12th March 2003. Five months later, the show transferred to the Strand Theatre, where it broke box office records for the highest ever advance sales in one day. It became a world-touring production (as *The Rat Pack - Live At the Sands*), debuting in San Antonio on 3rd October 2006.

It now makes a welcome return to London's West End after playing hundreds of venues to over one million people across the UK, Ireland, Europe, Canada and the US over the last 8 years. Such is the staggering popularity of this show that we're understandably proud to be associated with it. Does that mean, though, that we can offer an objective and constructive review?

Let's try.

We're probably right to assume, perhaps a little pompously, that we, in that audience at the Adelphi on 28th September 2009, were the only ones there to have actually seen Dean Martin live on stage. Not an actor, not a performer *being* Dean Martin, but *Dean Martin himself*, the real McCoy, the definite article.

Dean Martin.

As a result, this show means more to us in the audience than anyone else. We've promoted and honoured Dino for the last 49 years, so why shouldn't it?

So there we were. London's West End. Dressed up to the nines. The theatre was packed with guests and ticket holders alike. It was hot, stuffy and bottles of water were being consumed like no one's business.

And then the band took to the stage. Compere Craige Els (Mark Adams' understudy for this show) entered stage right and told us, in a Bronx drawl, that Mr Sinatra didn't want us to take pictures. He set the scene, took us back to 1960, and, as Frank Sinatra (Louis Hoover), Sammy Davis Jr (Gils Terera) and Dean Martin (Mark Adams) ruled the stage, we forgot we were in that hot, London theatre. We were there....*really there*...at the Sands, Las Vegas.

Until someone's mobile 'phone went off and brought us back to the 21st century.

But such is the professionalism of the three performers that they weren't phased in the slightest and, in fact, made fun, completely in character, of the embarrassed audience member.

We first saw this show back in 2000 and it was then, as much as it is now, Sinatra's show. I guess that was exactly how the original, *bona fide* Rat Pack shows went as well. It was, after all, Frank's world. The rest of us just lived in it.

Because of that, Louis Hoover naturally received top billing. King of the hill. A-number one. And that wasn't a bad thing. He was Frank when we saw this show the first time around so we knew what to expect. But that said, after eight years, Hoover had honed his act, fine-tuned the nuances of Sinatra's character: from his walk to his expressions, to his mannerisms. As the show opened and Hoover stood in a single spotlight behind a gauze curtain, no hard work was required on the part of the audience to suspend their disbelief and imagine that Sinatra really was standing there.

But when he interacted with his co-stars, he got the dimension just right.

Watching the *real* Frank with the *real* Sammy and Dean, I always felt that Frank was trying very hard to fit in with Sammy and Dean's natural camaraderie. Louis tapped in to that perfectly and, while it was undeniably a show for Sinatra, he made his character almost subservient to Terera's and Adams'.

Mark Adams, as we've said before in previous editions of 'Just Dino', is a perfect Dean, so we're not going to go into any great detail here about his performance - other than to say that he does play it markedly different to that in his own show, *That's Amore - A Celebration of Dean Martin and Friends*. In *Frank, Dean and Sammy: The Rat Pack Live From Las Vegas* this Dean is the acting stage drunk, the crooning buffoon who forgets his lines, forgets his moves and plays to his audience's perceptions. And Mark captured it quite remarkably. And having seen him rehearse recently for *That's Amore...*, it's ever more apparent that Mark is a talent and then some.

But the real star of the show, of this show, was Gils Terera as Sammy Davis Jr.

When he finished his rendition of *Mr Bojangles*, I leant towards my partner sitting next to me and whispered in her ear, "He's incredible. Unbelievably so."

And that's how it was for all the time Terera was flying solo on that stage.

It could be argued that the real Sammy was the most talented out of the three. He could sing, dance and act, do uncanny impressions and be a perfect foil, a clown to two straight men. Terera's task, then, was to do all of this and do it as Sammy. He was, quite simply, outstanding. He never missed a beat, never struggled to find his mark, and showed that he was a formidable presence up there as much as Hoover and Adams.

But we mustn't forget the girls: the three Burelli sisters, played by Charlie Bull, Grace Holdstock and Lizzii Hills. While perhaps a little out of place when the three guys were on stage, they seemed much more at home when accompanying Mark Adams, and I guess that's down to the fact that we're used to seeing Dean with his Golddiggers. With only one solo number to themselves, they were, nevertheless, a welcome addition to the company.

The songs were as expected, from 'I've Got You Under My Skin', to 'What Kind of Fool Am I', to 'Everybody Loves Somebody'. The arrangements were faithful and note perfect, but after eight years one shouldn't expect otherwise.

The first act, though, with Hoover, Terera and Adams taking the stage individually, for me, didn't feel as natural as the second half (where the three rotated and interacted far more frequently). It was as if they were more comfortable after the interval, as if they had hit their stride. Now that's not to say that the first half was at fault, but you could see that it did take the three men a little while to slip back into their roles - their signature roles, even. I suppose that's to be expected on an opening night of any performance.

Above all, *Frank, Dean and Sammy: The Rat Pack Live From Las Vegas* did not disappoint. And that's the idea. It never grows dull and always entertains. If you've not had the chance to see it yet, make it your 2010 New Year's resolution.

Rich Little: The Humble Impressionist

Rich Little in conversation with Elliot Thorpe, July 2018

The Dean Martin Celebrity Roasts succeeded Dean's weekly variety shows from 1974, after initially appearing as a segment in the variety show itself.

Running until 1984, they took the form of a unique brand of American humour, in which a person being 'honoured' is subjected to jokes and insults at their expense by a group of peers and friends, usually with a genuine tribute or praise at the end of the tirade.

Growing up, my family used to gather around the TV set to watch the latest episode and, personally, I used to wait eagerly for two particular comedians to take the dais: Foster Brooks, the comedian with his 'lovable drunk' act, and Rich Little, the comedian-impressionist who effortlessly took on the personas of his peers.

Both these men brought my boyhood-self to tears of laughter and, when I watch back their performances as an adult heading towards his 50s, I'm very happy to say they still do.

So when I got the chance to speak to the great Rich Little himself, as part of the development of this book, I couldn't have been more excited.

And he was a delight to talk to.

He was born in Ottawa in 1938 and found he had a natural flair for impressions while working as an usher in his local cinema, the Elgin Movie Theatre. He moved into acting then became a DJ, incorporating his talent for mimicry into his shows. LPs followed, some satirical, but one was an interpretation of Charles Dickens' classic 'A Christmas Carol', playing all the roles himself in the guises of various Hollywood stars.

As a result of various club work and his recordings, he was asked by Mel Torme to audition for a new variety series and, successful, he debuted on American television in 1964 for CBS' *The Judy Garland Show*.

He quickly became a staple of TV, appearing on numerous entertainment and talk shows as well as taking on dramatic roles.

He is working at the Tropicana in Las Vegas when we chat, performing in a one-man retrospective show.

"I play lots of clips with some humor to go along with it. I do a whole thing on Dean."

I ask him if such a retrospective format was a conscious decision or one driven by audience desires.

"I perform for older people, those who were around when the shows were done. Young people, they don't know about Dean, or Frank Sinatra or John Wayne, unless they're interested in the past."

Certainly, the younger generation may be *aware* of the names of these classic stars, but not necessarily who they are or what they accomplished. That said, Rich points out that he's aware of teenagers who've actually seen all the *Celebrity Roasts*.

"Comics today are very crude. They use the 'f' word all the time. It's more observational now than jokes."

The *Celebrity Roasts*, while encouraging insults about the main guest star, were never crude or blue and that made the humour more palatable, more accessible and all the more funnier.

"I did 24 in all, more than anybody. There was a lot of pressure performing in front of the greatest comedians and actors of all time. Apart from the millions watching, just having [the stars] on the dais was enough to really unnerve you. To stand up in front of Lucille Ball, Orson Welles, Jack Benny, John Wayne...that was pretty terrifying in itself. You had to concentrate on what you were doing and not let [the presence of] these people bother you.

"Some people who did the *Celebrity Roasts* when they looked down the dais, they actually panicked and so there were a few who were cut to a minute or taken out of the show completely."

Rich performed in front of his idols. He grew up watching them, admiring them and impersonating them - and here he was, in Las Vegas, doing all of that *in front* of them.

I say to him that he is an idol himself now.

He replies he doesn't believe he is - and that really shows how Rich Little is genuinely and sincerely humble regarding the success he has had. He doesn't show off, he doesn't throw an ego around and his gentle manner and honesty during our conversation was clear.

Ratings for NBC's *The Dean Martin Television Show* were dropping in the early 70s, and this was one of the reasons that the format changed to become the *Celebrity Roasts*.

The other reason was, Rich says, "Dean didn't have to rehearse [for them]. That was very important to him. He didn't like to rehearse. I'd done his variety show then moved over to the *Celebrity Roasts*. He was in studio for and hour and a half or so [when he did the variety shows]. He wasn't the type to sit down and talk. He may have just put his head around the door of the Green Room and say 'How are you, pally?'

"Dean was at his best when things went wrong. He had the ability to ab lib. He wanted things to go wrong then get out of it.

"He was a man who only did what he wanted to do and he didn't care anything about Royalty or anyone with authority or presidents or anybody. He didn't want to rehearse, just wanted to get it over with. He never took anything seriously. After his son died he want totally down hill - he was just a shell, he'd gone."

Rich has also appeared in various American drama shows such as *Police Woman*, *Love American Style*, *Hawaii Five-O* (as a James Cagney-style murderer) and *The Flying Nun* (as an accident-prone priest).

"I enjoy acting. My background is theater and I always wanted to be an actor before becoming an impersonator. I love doing something dramatic." Rich adds that he would love to do more if he could.

In 2016, he released a book *Little by Little: People I've Known and Been* (from Dog Ear Publishing). It is a tremendous read and recalls many of the people he admired and worked with throughout his career and he talks about the funny things that have happened to him. I ask him if he would ever write a straight biography.

"No. My life is not that interesting," he says "I've been married 4 times, and I've got the greatest girl now, so you just gotta get lucky. I made a few people like me or laugh and forget their problems and I was able to entertain. During 1 or 2 hours on stage, people forget their problems and remember the great actors of the past.

"As Cary Grant once said, 'It's great.'"

With thanks to Rich Little and Rhea Dingess. Rich Little is a Canadian-born comedian-impersonator. For more information, please visit richlittle.com

Dean Martin: At the Riviera

Dean Martin in conversation with Jayne Kempsey, from Vol. 12, No. 3, March 1970

Dean Martin, outwardly relaxed and seemingly unconcerned about the news headlines concerning his domestic situation, received a rousing reception from a first-night audience in the hotel's Versailles Room on 27 January just gone.

The turnaway crowd accorded the easy-going comic-baritone a noisy ovation when he stepped into the spotlight and reacted enthusiastically throughout the show. Mr Martin spoofs a wide variety of subjects ranging from Frank Sinatra to Sammy Davis Jr to well-known political figures and contemporary situations.

Basically, however, the multitude came to hear him sing such songs as 'By the Time I Get To Phoenix', 'Everybody Loves Somebody' and 'Raindrops Keep Fallin' on My Head', which blends neatly with the vintage standards of another era. Surprisingly though, one of Tuesday's showstoppers was the old Eddie Cantor hit, 'If You Knew Susie'.

Mr Martin uses conductor Ken Lane, astutely bouncing numerous gags off his long-time associate who compassed the aforementioned 'Everybody Loves Somebody'.

His show, scheduled for three weeks, was a sure-fire sell out weeks before it opened. Quite often there are more than 250 people just standing outside the hotel at times whilst Dean Martin is on with just no hope of ever getting tickets for the entire engagement or of ever catching a glimpse of the man entering or leaving!

Gail Martin, his daughter, was also appearing at the same time at the hotel, in the Starlite Room and there was no prouder father than he when he slipped away in between his own shows to watch hers.

I was there 'ringside' for Dean Martin's first night performance, and nearby were Lady Bird Johnson and Gina Lollobrigida.

He graciously gave me a few moments to chat after the show and I asked him what plans he had for the future.

"Well, I don't know how much longer I can keep up at this pace," he said firmly, "but a lot of people think I'm the most relaxed guy in the world. I guess this is a nice image to project but it just isn't so. Television demands a lot of time and concentration. Movies takes months away on location and every time I play here, it takes a month of hard work. I love my home and don't like to leave it too much, but this business demands it.

"I'm not knocking it," he assured me, "and I would never want to go back to the good old days when I couldn't get arrested in this business. Now, as I have just seen Gail sing her heart out here, I know it was worth it. It damn well know it was."

I took the golden opportunity of asking Mr Martin if he was *really* thinking of leaving showbusiness (as the tabloid rumours had suggested) and also if there was any chance of a UK visit soon.

"The usual press notices state that I'm packing it all in next year while another one states I'm going on for year and years yet. You'll always get this, but I will tell you this: I can't see [my popularity] lasting much longer but I have a few commitments for a while yet, so you'll all be seeing little 'ole Dino just for a few more years yet!

"I'd love to visit England more than any other country but one thing is I'm always too busy and the other is that I hate travelling that distance. I'll have to go over one day, after all I did promise Bernard (and you can quote me here) that I would go see him in London, and I'll keep my promise even if I did make that remark in haste years ago!"

Then, Mr Martin was gone: back to another resounding stint on stage.

Mark Adams:
Mark of Respect

Mark Adams in conversation with Elliot Thorpe, featured in Vol. 49, No. 3, Issue 407, July-Sept 2009

A beautiful sunny, August lunchtime and a London restaurant not far from Broadcasting House (since 1932 the BBC's corporate headquarters and the home of BBC Radio).

The DMA meets Mark during his promotional *That's Amore: A Celebration of Dean Martin and Friends*, and Mark has been talking to national radio since 9am about the show.

Hesitantly, we ask him if he's okay to chat a bit more about Dean during what is, effectively, his lunch-break. In an easy-going manner that's almost an echo of a certain Mr Martin, Mark happily obliges, and so we settle down to some tapas (Dean would have approved - being the lover of Spanish food that he was).

To cut to the chase, *That's Amore: A Celebration of Dean Martin and Friends* is a live stage production, starring Mark (in the title role) in a live take on Dean's television shows blended in with a bit of Dean's cabaret sets. There are 'guests' (Nat King Cole, Petula Clark, Shirley Maclaine), sketches, songs and parodies - in essence, everything you'd expect the inimitable original to present to his willing audience.

It's important to mention that this show was conceived by Mark himself, borne out of his runs as Dean in *Frank, Dean and Sammy: The Rat Pack Live From Las Vegas* and *Christmas With the Rat Pack*.

What made him decide to venture out to headline as Dean, without the cosy net of the Frank/Dean/Sammy trio?

"I've become a great fan of Dino since I first started playing him (nearly 6 years ago now), and I saw the opportunity to take this character further than what I had done as part of the Rat Pack. When I first landed the role, I read books on Dino, watched his television shows, listened to his live cabaret acts and could now probably go on *Mastermind* with him as my chosen subject."

We play devil's advocate for a moment and pose the question: What makes your show different to the dozens of 'tribute' acts that are out there?

Mark looks thoughtful for a moment, seeing the angle we are coming from.

"I guess the main factor is that I interact with the audience. The audience is different every night. With tribute acts such as Abba or Elvis, they just stand up there and sing. With Dean, he can feed off the audience."

When Mark talks about Dean in the third person, it's as if he talking about a character he's playing - which he, of course, is. It takes some effort to portray someone who actually existed. There are certain nuances to achieve, a walk or a distinct mannerism. When Mark adopts his Dean persona, he becomes that man.

We were lucky enough to see Dean himself live on stage throughout his career, and we proudly state to Mark that he has captured the quintessential 'Dean-ness' in his own show.

Mark takes that, quite understandably, as a compliment. As an organisation that proudly promotes Dean and his career, we're potentially Mark's greatest critics. Mark laughs softly.

"Dean had a great sense of humour. I myself love to make people as relaxed as they can and playing Dean comes naturally to me."

Amazingly affable, Mark is very much the professional and it's lovely to see such respect he has for Dean. It would be all too easy to make a caricature out of the man, but that's not what Mark wants.

"Admittedly, some of the jokes I put into *That's Amore...* can go over peoples' heads. But that's because they're not used to seeing Dean in that context. He's primarily viewed as a singer. But Dean was an entertainer."

One of the greatest, we might add.

Does Mark feel that he has to wrestle with what the audience expects to see along with what Mark himself would like to include?

"I always look to include different songs or change the set here and there. But some of Dean's material isn't considered as popular or as well known - 'Mambo Italiano', for example, is probably more associated with Rosemary Clooney than with Dean."

That means, then, that sometimes Mark can't always include songs that he'd like. Nevertheless, Mark's clearly very proud of what he does and ensures that every performance does Dean justice. He's also careful to be as accurate as he can with regard to the era he has set his show in - primarily late 60s and early 70s - so don't expect to hear live versions of songs from 'The Nashville Sessions' album anytime soon.

In fact, the version of 'Everybody Loves Somebody' would be the one you'd expect. Mark is also keen to point out that he does the song 'straight' - as in no parodies - and is the final highlight to his show.

The accuracy even goes so far as ensuring Mark's own Golddiggers have their own melody, straight out of Dean's original TV episodes. The DMA silently wonders if Mark would ever have 'Jack Benny' guest starring with his blue-rinsed Ding-a-lings?!

Certainly no stranger to live stage performances, Mark has appeared in such diverse productions as *Nymph Errant*, *South Pacific*, *Jesus Christ Superstar*, *A Passage To India*, *Alice Through the Looking Glass* and *Tales My Lover Told Me*.

His CV is indeed packed with work, some of which features mainstream UK television such as *EastEnders*, *Holby City* and *Doctors*.

But it seems that playing Dean does indeed come natural to him, especially when he says himself that he would never have expected to still be in the same role all these years later.

From that viewpoint, then, arguably Mark is the best Dean impersonator so far. No - that's wrong and belittles Mark's undeniable talent. He's *not* impersonating Dean, no more than James Stewart impersonated Glenn Miller or Kevin Kline, Cole Porter.

What Mark does is beyond a simple impersonation. He *becomes* Dean Martin up there on that stage. Just as Dino Crocetti became Dean Martin many many times before.

But how long does Mark think he'll carry on being Dean?

"I genuinely would like to pass the baton on at some stage, and hope I inspire younger guys to want to explore the brilliance of Dean and to pick up where from where I leave off. I ain't ready to leave just yet!"

For more information on Mark Adams, please visit www. markadamsonline.com

The UK tour of That's Amore: A Celebration of Dean Martin and Friends *opened at the Bristol Hippodrome on 9th September 2009, moving to the US on 27th November, opening at the City State and Symphony Hall, Springfield MA. This article was used in the souvenir brochure for Mark's show.*

The (Oft-Told) Story of *Twenty Original Dean Martin Hits* (To Anyone Who'll Listen)

Written by Bernard H Thorpe, previously unpublished

In 1975, Dino had blocked Warner/Reprise from putting together a compilation but in 1976 he wrote to me out of the blue asking for a list of around twenty-four songs for inclusion on a forthcoming album he wanted released in the UK. He asked me if I'd also design the cover. He said he wanted my choices, my favourites of his Reprise output. I jumped at the chance and sent the list of songs with a rough idea of the cover designs to his office.

Between us, via a few lengthy 'phone calls, we shuffled the songs around and played with the designs. This was the first time I really, truly worked with Dino himself on a commercial (and major) project.

Yes, I was nervous. Of course I was. I knew that if Dino got fed up with something or it became too complex, his interest would switch off. So I ensured I drove the project and I think he welcomed that. I wasn't bowing to his position and being just a 'yes' man if he suggested something I didn't necessarily like. I stood my ground and we worked at an even pace until he let me loose with Warners in the UK!

We'd whittled the twenty-four songs down to twenty, in this order:

Side 1:   'Everybody Loves Somebody'
               'Corrine Corrina'
               'Things'
               'Houston'
               'Lay Some Happiness On Me'
               'In the Chapel In the Moonlight'
               'Little Ole Wine Drinker, Me'
               'The Birds and the Bees'
               'King of the Road'
               'Send Me the Pillow You Dream On'
Side 2:   'I'm Sittin' On Top of the World'
               'You're Nobody 'til Somebody Loves You'
               'That's When I See the Blues'
               'Tie A Yellow Ribbon'
               'The Green, Green Grass of Home'
               'The Door Is Still Open To My Heart'
               'Ramblin' Rose'
               'Amor Mio'
               'In the Misty Moonlight'
               'Detroit City'

I suggested to Dino we reproduce a small selection of previous album covers on the back of the sleeve to encourage back-catalogue sales and when he said yes, I couldn't miss the opportunity to include 'Gentle On My Mind' alongside 'Welcome To My World', 'Greatest Hits' (Volumes 1 and 2) and 'You're the Best Thing That Ever Happened To Me'.

The overall colour scheme was blue (Dino's favourite colour) and with typeface in orange and yellow, it was bright and would absolutely stand out in the record racks. After much deliberation, I named it 'Twenty Original Dean Martin Hits'.

It was then all presented to Warner Bros., who changed the song list but kept the artwork.

I disagreed.

They disagreed.

I disagreed again.

They still disagreed.

Then I used my trump card.

Dino told them what songs we'd decided and that they *would* be staying.

They agreed.

The vinyl LP, tape cassette and 8-track cartridge tape were all allocated their catalogue numbers and a synchronised release date of 20 October 1976.

We sat back and waited and, amazingly, the albums 'Gentle On My Mind' and 'Greatest Hits' (both volumes) received silver awards in the UK.

With this sudden success in mind I made a second ridiculously silly suggestion to a record company giant (if you recall elsewhere in this book I wrote about the 7" single release for 'Gentle On My Mind').

"'Twenty Original Dean Martin Hits' needs to have nationwide television advertising," I said cheerily.

They laughed.

I laughed nervously.

They laughed a bit more.

They said no.

Naturally, they thought this was insanity again from me but I kept on pushing for this because I felt that all the hard work Dino and I had put into this (and certainly Dino hadn't needed to at all), this release deserved full-blown adverts, and that meant, for me, television.

Much to my surprise, they eventually relented, saying that they would test the waters by advertising across the Tyne Tees area in the lead-up to the release date and, after just one week, album sales were in their thousands.

Warner Bros. were dumbfounded. So was I, to be honest.

They agreed national advertising and suggested I work with them further to promote the album.

I was offered an all-expenses paid nationwide campaign to speak to radio, TV and press but I turned it down, accepting instead just a visit to Manchester to chat with Piccadilly Radio.

My hesitancy in going all-guns for the promotion was nothing to do with any ego I may have had nor my initial battles with Warner Bros over this album.

You see, my dear father Henry suffered a fatal heart attack just six days after the album came out and I was devastated and unable to function let alone embark on a promotional campaign. I simply couldn't leave my mother, my wife nor my daughter and son at this awful time. My mother insisted I go as both she and my father had seen how proud I was of getting this album out there. Against what I thought was a bad decision, I relented and Warner Bros. understood and were comfortable with the revised plans. Dino was supportive in his own way, telling me that my well-being was more important than his album.

So I commenced my journey to Manchester on 26 November with thoughts of my recently buried father and my family running around my head. The train ride was a blur as a result and I remembered little of it by the time I pulled into Manchester Piccadilly to be met by Warner Bros.' representative, a charming lady called Julie. She drove me to the Piccadilly Hotel and made sure I was booked in and had everything I needed. I had the weekend to myself but was to head to Piccadilly Radio for Monday morning, so I took in the sights.

On the Sunday morning when I went to the hotel reception to hand my key in for the day, there was a familiar face who came and stood next to me. Her Swedish accent and stunning looks were impeccable. I couldn't miss this opportunity to say hello, having admired her performances alongside Hammer veteran Christopher Lee in both *The Wicker Man* and *The Man With the Golden Gun*. As Britt Ekland said hello back, Rod Stewart sidled up beside us in his slippers.

For the next ten or so minutes Mr Stewart chatted with me, interested in my connection with Dean Martin. Surprisingly, he told me that he'd always wanted to record with the Count Basie Orchestra, a revelation that never fitted his rockstar appearance! But here was a man who loved music, who was genuinely piqued by other styles of music beyond his own and was happy to chat in a hotel lobby with a chap trying to flog an American crooner's 'best of' LP! He offered me free passes to his King's Hall concert that night (his last performance there, I think) but I had to decline his kind offer as I knew I had to be up very early the next morning. I wish I'd said yes as I was and still am a great fan of his work.

Interestingly, Mr Stewart himself went on to record many years later a series of Grammy Award-winning albums of classic American big band and swing ballads.

Monday came and I was on-air on and off throughout the day talking about Dino, this new compilation and music in general. Some weeks later following this, I was offered a position as a DJ, but I turned this down as it would have meant relocating my family. Again, a regret? I wonder how life would have changed then.

With my time up, I headed back home on the Tuesday, subsequently happy with the knowledge that all my hard work had paid off.

'Twenty Original Dean Martin Hits' had gone Gold! In excess of one million copies!

Having met so many DMA members and the general public in my travels over the years, it was clear that the DMA had become larger than I had imagined. Promoting Dean Martin's career in the small way I did and continue to do has been incredibly rewarding and one letter we received was from an Elizabeth Hardy who lived in Blackpool. She wasn't a DMA member but was a huge fan of Dean Martin all the same and said that I was his greatest advocate, his greatest supporter and that if it wasn't for me, his name wouldn't be as half as well known in the UK as it was. Well, I'm not entirely convinced that is the case, but I am very proud of the work I did for him. So thank you, Ms Hardy, if you ever by chance read this, for your kind words.

Dino was overwhelmed, as we all were, with the phenomenal success of 'Twenty Original Dean Martin Hits' and told me how grateful he was that I'd put so much hard work into it, especially when my father had passed away in the midst of everything.

As we entered 1977, the album continued to still sell well and in massive quantities and our membership was growing. In fact, we were so busy I did fear that we might not have been able to cope. We were a relatively small operation, remember, even though we had 4-figure membership numbers.

My concerns during the first half of the decade of Dino's wavering popularity had not just disappeared, they'd been vaporised.

Warner Bros. suggested I be flown to Las Vegas to present Dino with the Gold Award itself during one of his live shows. He'd agreed to this but the thought of me walking onto a Vegas stage in front of thousands of people made me shudder!

His office were in the throes of setting up flights and a hotel for me when I received a call from Warner Bros. advising that the award would simply be posted to his Beverly Hills home instead, with no pomp or fanfare.

I was very disappointed and I knew it was most probably Dino himself who had decided he didn't want the fuss. But it was nice to know that he had it hung in his hallway.

Nevertheless, I do wonder where it is now.

Vincenzo Carrara: Time for the King of Cool

Vincenzo Carrara interviewed by Elliot Thorpe, July 2018

Todd & Marlon is a relatively new company, formed in 2015 in New York. Advocating luxury essentials, it produces the most amazing luxury time-pieces and in 2017, launched the *Dean Martin Exclusive Edition* watch. I spoke with company founder and owner Vincenzo Carrara while in Switzerland as to how this came about.

Vincenzo Carrara: My grandfather was an artisan jeweler and my children, Todd and Marlon, seem to have inherited the passion for the world of watches and jewelry from him. I wanted to nurture this passion, so I decided to form Todd & Marlon, a brand for them to foster and grow.

Elliot Thorpe: Your role as owner of Todd & Marlon must be both rewarding and challenging. What's your background?

VC: I believe the reward lies in the challenge. The biggest is the challenge the more satisfying is the reward, and this is the reason why I enjoy being an entrepreneur. I'm originally from Italy but spent many years abroad both in Europe and in the US. Todd & Marlon was established during my time in New York and the company is still based there despite me moving around.

ET: Your products are stunning. Where do begin when it comes to designing such intricate timepieces?

VC: We purposely wanted to create elegant watches yet not for everybody. This is one of the reasons why our first collection is made of 24-hour watches that are very particular and not used by the masses. We designed the entire watch from scratch and every element has been thought thoroughly through. For instance, the custom bracelet is made with links shaped like the shield we have in the Todd & Marlon logo. Ultimately, our effort did pay out, and soon after the introduction in 2016 we received the acclaimed A'Design Award.

ET: How did the *Dean Martin Exclusive Edition* watch come into being? Are you a fan of the man himself?

VC: I grew up watching Dean Martin movies and listening to his music. So, I had the opportunity to appreciate his unique style and elegance since my youth. Dean did create his own style and dared to be different yet elegant. In a way, this is what Todd & Marlon came to represent: daring elegance. So, when I realized that two of my passions were converging, I decided to pay homage to Dean with an exclusive watch.

ET: What was your pitch to the Dean Martin Family?

VC: Since the first talks, the Dean Martin Family and the Artist Legacy Group (ALG) team, who was managing the license, realized immediately my genuine passion for Dean Martin. We both wanted to pay homage to Dean Martin with something exclusive and this is what we did together.

ET: You describe the watch thusly: *Evoking some of Mr. Martin's style cues and passions, the treatment on the watch case is inspired by the brushed, shiny metal of a classic microphone. The strap, made of black leather, is reminiscent of the interior of his custom 1962 Ghia L6.4, and the touch of red on the hands pays homage to his signature pocket square. Finally, a transparent case back boasts a special insignia featuring Dean Martin and reveals a rotor engraved with the title that best describes him, 'KING OF COOL.'* That's a wonderful evocative tribute - so how did you settle on the design? Were there many variations until you got to the final approved version?

VC: The Dean Martin Family and I were aligned since the beginning on the design objective. I wanted to showcase Dean

Martin's passions and his unique style while maintaining the contemporary identity of Todd & Marlon. I made only few design variations that were emphasizing one passion rather than others, and we quickly and jointly agreed on the final design.

ET: The final piece, available now, is indeed a wonderful tribute to the man himself. The pride and respect which you, Vincenzo, have about your family heritage, your sons and your chosen industry, as well as the Dean Martin legacy, is clear. Thank you. It has been a genuine pleasure to talk with you.

Vincenzo Carrara is the founder and owner of Todd & Marlon. Please visit www.toddandmarlon.com

Dean Martin: Long Distance

Dean Martin interviewed by Bernard H Thorpe, from 'A Letter from Dino', Vol. 7, No. 1, July 1966

Bernard H Thorpe: One thing I've always wanted to ask you, Dean, what is your favourite song?

Dean Martin: Well, ah, let me see. I've no real favourite but 'That's Amore' I suppose I have real sentimental value for. Then there's 'Pennies From Heaven', 'Return To Me', 'Everybody Loves Somebody', 'Side by Side'…oh, I could go on and on, I guess!

BHT: And your least favourite?

DM: I work with talented guys, musicians, writers. To say I had one song I didn't like wouldn't be fair on anyone.

BHT: Which single was your biggest seller?

DM: Here, you mean?

BHT: Yes, but in overall sales anywhere but mainly in the States.

DM: In America, my most recent million-seller was 'Everybody…', but the biggest record ever was 'That's Amore', and they tell me the latest count was over four million – and that's some sellin'.

BHT: What makes you choose your songs, especially for LP?

DM: I get a whole heap of suggestions all the time from lots of people, some good, some bad, and as you know, some of the particular songs you have suggested to me yourself I've gone and cut them. But I listen to the radio a heck of a lot, especially when driving, and I think about them, then I'll get one of those tunes set on my mind and it'll be in the can at Reprise! I like those songs with that Country and Western mood, as people call it, hence the reason my recent albums have been generally of this type. I love recording, especially when I can record just exactly what I like and it becomes a real favourite for the public as well, to quote 'Everybody...' as one example, of course.

BHT: Do you ever record material for a foreign market?

DM: Not exactly. I'll make an album but on occasions I may get the chorus to sing behind me in a particular language, usually Italian. But this naturally costs my studios considerable expense for limited sales.

BHT: Italy...your home country. I notice you do not visit Italy very often.

DM: Let's face it, it's a great country, the place where my ancestry was born. But I'm Steubenville born and all my family are together in California. We are a very close family. I see my parents at least once a week, they visit Jeannie and myself very often. My home is here, my career is here. I thank God life has turned out like I wanted it to, with a great family and my children all growing up and getting married!

BHT: Club members are always asking me this question... When are you coming to England for a while?

DM: Well, I try to keep all my work near home. As I just said, I like to keep close to my family. And I can record just when I want here and I don't have much need to go anywhere abroad to film, although we are filming scenes in England and France for my new Matt Helm picture in July. But these particular scenes can be made without me so I decided not to come over for them. As regards a visit, I love London, but I honestly cannot find time for a holiday visit at the moment. Believe me, I am so much in demand here in Hollywood I haven't had a holiday for the last three and a half years, you know! But I'm far from complaining!

BHT: Turning to the subject of golf, they say you fit this in between commitments?

DM: Yeah, I find time for my favourite pastime in between work, although I like to play golf whilst I'm working on a movie. It helps me concentrate on my lines and of course improves my game.

BHT: Have you had a hole-in-one since you started playing?

DM: Wow! How I wish I had! I'm no expert!

BHT: In my notes I'd written for questions to ask you, I've put simply 'Dean's real relationship with Sinatra'. Any comments, Dean?

DM: What the hell does that mean? I guess the press have been throwing up muck again. Frank is one of the kindest persons on Earth – can't one have a close friend without all this shit thrown up all the time? Frank is my closest friend in and out of this business, he's helped me one heck of a lot and he gets on well with my family. I'm surprised you needed to ask.

BHT: But, Dean, surely you don't take any notice of the press as regards to false stories?

DM: Let's put it this way… I don't worry about what they say about me, but at the same time you have to keep your eye on them. Because some pressmen will write anything down whenever you blink! I've had some of my biggest laughs when reading a magazine with the 'startling true life and secrets of Dean Martin' heading, because although I give my consent for an article from time to time, some of the things are far-fetched to a great degree and I sometimes wonder how people think I ever do what I do in my career. I've had a great gimmick for years and a lot of people think this is true. I've always walked on stage anywhere with a glass in my hand, staggering about all over the place, looking stoned to the eye-balls. This is part of my act and I've always done this, rolling around the stage saying things like 'I don't drink anymore…but I don't drink any less, either'.

This makes my audience laugh a hell of a lot, so I've always done this.

BHT: But I know for a fact several people honestly believe you are always drunk. Surely this could injure your image as a showbusiness personality?

DM: C'mon, Bernard. You know the answer to that! All I can say is that if members of the public are so damn stupid to really believe I'm always stoned, let 'em think that way! How can I carry on my work so successfully the way I do if I really was loaded? No, they're nuts, these people who genuinely think that, although I know just what you have to put up with running my club for me, some people will believe anything they see or read. Talking of the club, how is it progressing now?

BHT: Very well, indeed. A big reason for our success, I think, indeed, I know is the fact that you keep such close contact with me all the time, a thing which must be almost unique when you're running a club for such a big star.

DM: Thank you for that remark, although if I can't keep in contact, then who can? Why shouldn't I?

BHT: You know only too well, Dean, most big people of your high calibre in showbusiness have no time whatsoever for this type of thing, but you make time and this is the great difference, for which we all thank you.

DM: But don't forget, it is only the public that have made me what I am in such a successful way. Let me please have included in this exchange here my sincere thanks to everyone in the whole world who has ever helped me, whether it be my managers right through the record-buyer. I don't say it often and I won't say it if I'm asked to. I don't want to make this sound like it's some public hymn being sung out, but I am sincerely grateful to everybody, especially to you, Bernard, who must spend a lot of time on my behalf and perhaps give up a lot of time just for me – a special thanks.

BHT: Thank you again and also thank you for spending so much time today for this interview. I could perhaps go on and on for days asking questions but perhaps they may be another time very soon.

DM: Anyhow, my club's doing well, you say, so let's hope it'll double its membership by the end of '66, huh? Give my best wishes to your wife, family and all the [club] members. Remember, anything you require, you know my number. I will help you in any way that is possible, as you already know.

Interviews anywhere with Dean outside of promotional tours were rare but Bernard was lucky enough to get him to answer a number of set questions in June 1966, transcribed above, during one of the regular telephone conversations the two men had every few weeks or so in the DMA's heyday.

Me, the Bartender and Dean Martin

Written by Mathew Todd, July 2018

In the early-mid 1990s, I was attempting to advance to the men's U.S. Open through a sectional qualifier held at Riviera Country Club in Los Angeles, CA.

During a practice round, I headed to the course's lounge to get a cup of ice water. Up, up, up the stairs I climbed until I came to a landing, found the lounge and entered through its doorway.

Inside was a simple rectangular room with leather covered tables and chairs and a large dark wooden bar in the far corner helmed by the bartender. The only other person there was a gentleman seated to my left in one of those leather chairs staring out through a course-facing east window. A tall glass on the table in front and cigarette smoke above him caught my attention as I made my way up to the bar.

I realized immediately that the man was Dean Martin.

After exchanging pleasantries with the bartender, I requested a to-go cup of ice water and thanked him as I turned to leave to get back down to the course.

I did not stop to say hello or tell Mr. Martin how much I appreciated his work.

Even in the very limited time I saw him, he looked to me like a man at peace - enveloped in the morning sun and enjoying the quiet sanctuary the lounge provided to him and I certainly was not going to interfere with that!

In the years that followed, I created (and still own) The Fundamental Golf Company and in 2017 we were contacted by Ashley Austin, CEO of Artist Legacy Group. ALG was working with Sony Entertainment to help identify and service licensing opportunities with specific artists and properties under Sony and were looking to create a line of leather golf products for Dean Martin.

At that time, my company was designing and selling replacement golf putter grips under a licensing agreement with Warner Bros. Consumer Products. The line included colorful standard and oversize putter grips designed around the DC Comics properties *Superman*, *Batman* and *Wonder Woman*. I don't know for sure, but I assume Ashley did an online search for "golf grips" and must have come across my offerings. She contacted me through email and requested to meet at the nearing Licensing Convention in Las Vegas, NV.

So, with samples of all the grips I offered at the time, I headed to Las Vegas for the scheduled meeting. During our meeting, Ashley and her husband Scott, told me about the requirements they wanted to meet based on Mr. Martin's brand. They wanted leather as the base material for any initial golf product offerings and I absolutely agreed. The other requirements were to utilize his signature and possibly incorporate his personal martini logo which featured a golf ball with a flagstick in place of an olive and toothpick. Through our discussion, we agreed that a leather putter grip would be the first product to start with. With all in agreement, we decided to move onto the next step in the process: licensing.

This step required I actually provide visuals of something that did not yet exist in order to garner a review by the Dean Martin Family Trust. Based on my 40+ years playing the game and seeing what was typically offered/accepted in the golf world, I figured it was going to be either a black leather grip with silver accents or a dark brown leather grip with gold accents. Also, the current trend in putter grip size popularity was oversize so I was able to find a traditional pistol-paddle shaped, light-weight underlisting model that would be wrapped in leather and vertically hand-stitched on the backside. From online images of the model I wanted to utilize and digital files of Mr. Martin's signature and the re-created martini glass logo, I provided the

Trust with digital images of what I wanted to create. After a few months of review and negotiations, I was granted the license to proceed!

From that point, I finalized the color (black leather with silver signature, martini logo and stitching), artwork and placement for the soon-to-be-produced oversize leather putter grips. Once the sample production grips arrived, I shared them with the Trust for their final approval and proceeded with production.

Little did I know that more than twenty five years after I'd seen him at the Riviera Country Club, I'd have the honor and opportunity to create a never-before offered line of premium leather golf grips bearing his name.

As I've stated on my website, it's my sincere hope that Mr. Martin would use these grips if alive today playing his favorite game. Based on feedback from his fan base, I believe they appreciate that I've tried to create a golf grip as classic and timeless as the man himself.

Mathew Todd is the founder and owner of The Fundamental Golf Company, specialising in exclusive golfing accessories. Please visit thefundamentalgolfcompany.com

Being Dean Martin

Written by Mark Adams, previously unpublished

It's June 2018, I am midway through a tour of Singapore, Malaysia and Dubai of a show I conceived, wrote and helped get off the ground three years ago.

The show is called *Sinatra and Friends*, born from its parent show *The Definitive Rat Pack*. Of course we have no real Sinatra, but we do have the next best thing! I'll come to that later! However first things first.

You ask me, "Is it a 'tribute show'?"

I tell you, "No, it is not!"

We *do* celebrate Sinatra and his friends, we have been doing that for over 16 years and sure we make a living out of it, but you don't get an Olivier award nomination for a tribute show. Well, not yet anyway.

For 17 years I've been a working actor with decent TV, theatre, West End and film credits to my name. A jobbing actor who can justify a modicum of success by saying I sometimes get a chance to make a choice. Look, film scripts are not blocking my letter box but I do have an agent who will often say, "You don't want to do that!"

So let's go back at bit: it's 2002 and I've have just finished a 9-month tour of a new show based on the music of Jeff Barry and Ellie Greenwich. Called *Leader of the Pack*, it was great. Katrina Leskanitch (yes, *the* Katrina of 'Katrina and the Waves') played Ellie Greenwich (Ellie Greenwich? Come on, dudes, she co-wrote 'Do Wah Diddy', 'Baby I Love You', 'River Deep Mountain High' and 'Walking In the Sand' alongside her partner and later-to-be husband Jeff Barry (who went on to write 'Sugar Sugar' for the pseudo band the Archies) Katrina was in her first stage role (and she was amazing by the way and *the* most perfect pitch singer I have ever heard - and I've heard a few).

262

I digress. So about a month later, I get offered another job. Did I want to go out on a 12-month tour of a show that had the eponymous title *Frank, Dean and Sammy: The Rat Pack Live from Las Vegas*? (I guess they left no one with any doubt as to what the show was all about!)

No, I really didn't. *But I was to play Dean Martin.*

Big deal!

Yes, a very big deal, a monster of a deal. I'd be mad, arrogant, foolish and risking career ignominy if I failed and, believe you me, there would be so many reasons why someone *could* fail.

I didn't know too much about him so let's Google him. No *YouTube* as yet but enough print, pictures and information to suggest 'this guy is good.' I buy second-hand albums in charity shops and then I have to buy a record player (who plays vinyl in 2002?). I discover a company called Guthy Renker in the US that has made DVDs of the Dean Martin Television Shows along with the Dean Martin Celebrity Roasts. I invested, heavily!

Then I get to see what all the fuss was about.

My goodness, you are so are lucky if you read this!

You don't have to spend a fortune with Guthy Renker – instead, just go to *YouTube* and I implore you do. You will see a performer like nothing else or have ever seen.

Remember this material is from the mid-sixties onwards. In the UK around that time, we were still learning the intricacies and power of the small screen. The US had it down. Yes, lots of words from the 'sponsors' but their production values were key and Dean played TV like no one before or dare I say since.

TV is relaxed, gentle, warm, honest and in your living room. TV stars drop into your lives if you let them, they'll stay a while if you like them, you'll invite them back if you trust them and you'll feel like you know them and they know you.

That was Dean Martin.

He didn't know it at the time. Of course, a movie star is set in stone, precious, precise, pertinent and outside the spectrum or mere mortals. Marlon Brando on TV variety? Clint Eastwood, not as I recall but other stars in that bracket did allow themselves to be part of Dean's world, outside of their comfort zone. Orson

Welles under a hair salon drier alongside Jimmy Stewart performing sketches? John Wayne singing 'Everybody Loves Somebody' or miming to Sinatra? So no Brando but I bet he watched the shows and thought ' That guy is the coolest guy in the planet, how does he do it?'

Well, Dean had help. In Greg Garrison, the shows' director (and later producer-director), Dean had found his perfect partner and one who wasn't going to steal his thunder but amplify it one hundred fold.

Greg Garrison totally 'got' Dean. He worked around Dean, stood in for him at rehearsals and camera rehearsals, (Dean would watch the final camera rehearsals in a monitor in his dressing room in the one day of the week he would work in the show). Garrison knew a spontaneous, dangerous Dean was what brought the best out of him. Fluffs, bloopers, ad libs were often kept in the show and, indeed often became the best parts of the show.

So I became a fan but being *just* a fan wasn't going to help me 'nail' this guy. It helped that when I started this job the guys who was to play Sinatra also started. He'd had a head-start in actual fact as he had been performing around the world as Frank for a few years (including Vegas) and had been a 'Stars In Your Eyes' finalist in the role.

His name is Stephen Triffitt (and he is here with me in the Far East).

His journey was slightly different to mine. Relatively new to show business, he was persuaded by friends to sing at a karaoke and his likeness was uncanny. Added to the fact he bears a striking resemblance to him prompts me to say he is the best.

So we entered into this together with our eyes open and aware of the responsibility we were taking on. Sinatra and Martin - these guys weren't a couple of two-bit bar-room singers - they were stars, stars that shone so bright and so loud that, along with Sammy Davis Jr, their performances became legendary and no one came after them that was even remotely like them. They were and *are* unique.

So you get what I mean when I said someone could easily fail at taking him on.

So, in the following 16 years, I honed my portrayal (I still am! There's always a nuance, an expression, a stance that I add).

When *Frank, Dean and Sammy: The Rat Pack Live from Las Vegas* ended one of its many runs (and it's being relaunched soon with a new cast), I didn't want to give up the role. So Stephen and I, along with George Daniel Long who had joined us as Sammy Davis Jr, decided we'd create our own version of the show and so *The Definitive Rat Pack* came into existence. Being the producers and directors of our own show, we have much more freedom in what songs we want to include, move around or drop, likewise with jokes and skits.

I'd also gone it alone in *That's Amore: A Celebration of Dean Martin and Friends*, which allowed me a little more scope, tapping into and drawing from Dean's variety shows (the Rat Pack shows predominantly recreating the performances that Sinatra, Martin and Davis did together, whereas 'solo', I was able to bring in different songs and 'guests' such as Shirley Maclaine and (with some artistic licence as he never actually appeared on one of Dean's shows) Nat 'King' Cole).

Back to today and the sweltering backdrop of the Far East.

It's a testament to the enduring appeal of these original artists that they find loving, appreciative audiences in any corner of the globe.

It's been decades since they died, since they left us with a legacy that spans the generations, with recordings, with movies, with TV shows.

And here I am, a jobbing actor, in a role that I adore all these years later. In fact, I've been playing Dean Martin for as long as an actor on TV would, say, encompass the role of a long-running soap character.

No, I'm not comparing the wholly incomparable Dino Paul Crocetti to a fictional character. But as Dean Martin, both he and I become something else on that stage.

And for me, it's not a tribute act: *It's an honour.*

Jimmy Bowen: Remembering Dean Martin

Jimmy Bowen interviewed by John Chintala, December 1991

Until his retirement due to health problems in 1995, Jimmy Bowen was one of the most successful record producers in music history. He began his career as a member of the Rhythm Orchids, playing bass and co-writing the Buddy Knox chart topper "Party Doll" and cutting a Top 15 pop hit of his own, "I'm Stickin' With You." In the early 1960s, Bowen headed Chancellor Records' Los Angeles office and worked with such artists as Frankie Avalon and Fabian.

In 1963, he was named A&R director for Reprise Records and scored his first hit for the label, Jack Nitzsche's classic "Lonely Surfer." But it was as the producer of Dean Martin's string of 20 Hot 100 singles between 1964-69 that put Bowen's name on the map. During that time, he also produced major hits for Dean's fellow Rat Pack pallies Frank Sinatra ("Strangers In The Night" and "That's Life") and Sammy Davis, Jr. ("I've Gotta Be Me").

In the late 1960s, Bowen formed his own record label, Amos, which issued debut albums by two future members of the Eagles: Glenn Frey (*Longbranch Pennywhistle*) and Don Henley (*Shiloh*). After working as an independent producer (which resulted in such hits as "You Gave Me A Mountain" for Frankie Laine and Bobby Vinton's "Ev'ry Day Of My Life") Bowen became president of MGM Records in 1974.

He joined MCA's Nashville division in 1977, became Vice President/General Manager of Elektra/Asylum Nashville a year later, and assumed those duties for Warner Brothers/Nashville when both labels merged in 1983. The next year, he was named president of MCA/Nashville and headed Capitol Nashville (later renamed "Liberty") from 1990 until his retirement five years later.

During the following interview (which was conducted when I was producing a radio special for Dean Martin's then-upcoming 75th birthday) Bowen recalled his two decades spent as Dean's producer, A&R man, and close friend.

John Chintala: How did you go from being a rockabilly singer, a "teen idol," to producing Dean Martin?

Jimmy Bowen: First of all, I was a teenage idol for six months (laughs); in the seventh month, I was back to square one because (Roulette Records) wanted a follow-up to "I'm Stickin' With You" and I didn't have one! So I went back and worked in radio for a year in Colorado Springs, and I hate the cold. So I escaped from there, went to California and got a job as a songwriter and song plugger at American Music in Los Angeles. Then I ran the West Coast (office) of Chancellor Records. And in late '62, a mutual friend of mine and Frank Sinatra's talked (Sinatra) into hiring me at Reprise. And when I looked over their artist roster, I said the one act I want to produce is Dean Martin. I loved him; I just loved what he did when he was with Jerry Lewis, the way he sang and the comedy and all.

He had just done a country album called *Dean "Tex" Martin*. And a few months after I met him, I produced another (album) called *Dean "Tex" Martin Rides Again*. And I told him then that this was really good and all, but we gotta cut a pop hit. So Dean said, "Well before we do that, I want to do an album called *Dream With Dean*. 'Cause in Vegas, after the show, I go out in the lounge, get up with a quartet and sing a few of these old standards and people love it." And I said, "Good, we'll do that." Well, in those days, you did 12 songs in an album; and I had 11 songs and about 30 minutes left. Dean was trying to do some song and he said, "I don't want to do this." And I came out of the booth and said, "Well, we're one short, what else do you know?" And Ken Lane, the white-haired piano player on Dean's TV show said, "How 'bout my song?" So Dean walked over to the piano and started singing (sings) 'Everybody loves somebody sometime.' I went, "Oh shit, that's the pop hit!" And Dean looked at me like I was nuts! So we did it with the four pieces as a "mood" thing, and I said, "Let's recut this, I think this is a big hit." And the manager guy said, "Oh, I don't know." And Dean said, "Hey, let the kid do what he wants." I think I was 26 at the time.

So the following week (note: it was actually a month later) I got (arranger) Ernie Freeman and Hal Blaine on drums and a big orchestra and we went in and recut "Everybody Loves Somebody." We took it over to the company and nobody cared for it. They put it out, nothing happened and they took it off the priority list. Then this one Monday in Worcester, Massachusetts and in New Orleans, two (radio) stations added it and within a week we had orders for 50,000 records, which was incredible for back then. And it was off and rockin' from then on.

JC: It hit number one in the summer of '64 at the height of Beatlemania and the British Invasion. Dean's next release, "The Door Is Still Open To My Heart," also made the Top 10. How did that one come about?

JB: Well, my best friend, a fella by the name of Don Lanier, who was the electric guitar player in our group in the '50s, and I roomed together then. I was going through this song-hunting process, 'cause the follow-up to the first big hit's the most difficult thing always. And I was saying, "Damn, I can't find a song." And he picked up a guitar and said, "Well, how 'bout this one (sings) 'And the door is still open to my heart.'" I said, "C'mon!" We got into the car and drove to 20th Century Fox where Dean was doing a picture, and when he got a break, Don played the guitar and we sang it for him and Dean said, "That's great!"

JC: Was it your idea for Dean to remake "You're Nobody 'Til Somebody Loves You" which he had already recorded for Capitol?

JB: Yeah. It had been cut a hundred times, but had never been a hit single. And I had some version that a publisher had dropped off and I put it on the turntable and said, "My God, there's one that'll fit him!"

JC: It was on the *Dean Martin Hits Again* album as was "Send Me The Pillow You Dream On."

JB: Right. That one was given to me by a guy named Dave Burgess who worked for 4 Star Music; they were primarily a country publisher. And in one of those many "song hunts," he came in with three or four songs and that was one of them. It was very obvious when a song was right for Dean, and that was one that was right!

JC: Those songs, as well as most of Dean's Reprise hits, were arranged by the late Ernie Freeman. What were his contributions to Dean's sound?

JB: Oh, Ernie was an incredible musician and a brilliant arranger. I would sing him string lines and most arrangers hate that; they want to come up with their own. But Ernie had the ego-control and the talent that if I wanted something "dumb," he wouldn't do that. He'd fix it; he wouldn't let me hang myself. He'd come up with a string line that was just brilliant, or a harmony situation between horns and voices and strings that would just be marvelous. And he had a very commercial ear where many arrangers don't have that for radio. He was one of the first people to put strings on rock and roll and rockabilly records when he did arrangements for Snuff Garrett: "Dreamin'" by Johnny Burnette and Gene McDaniels' "A Hundred Pounds Of Clay." I loved working with Ernie; he was my favorite arranger ever.

JC: Dean had two major hits in '65 that were arranged by Bill Justis. Tell me about "Houston."

JB: Lee Hazlewood came by Reprise Records around midnight. We had a little shot of Jack Daniels and he said, "Well I got a song for Dean called "Houston." I had it out by Sanford Clark on Warner Brothers." So we had to go break in the mailroom and decode the alphabetical system to find it. Got to bed about five that morning and had to get up at nine to go to Dean's house

269

and played him "Houston" and he loved it. And that gave him a big hit.

JC: How about the follow-up, "I Will," which was written by Dick Glasser?

JB: Well, I was the head of A&R for Reprise and he was head of A&R for Warner Brothers. Our offices were right next to each other, we played golf together all the time, we were friends. And one of those nights, it was about 11 and he's leaving to go home (and asked me), "What are you still doing here?" and I said, "I'm hunting songs for Dean, I gotta see him in the morning." In about 30 minutes, he came back with a demo of "I Will,". He said, "This is one of my songs; I think it would be good for Dean." And again, you put it on and you go, "Uh, oh, that's a killer thing!"

JC: Dean's final "easy listening" hit was 'Get On With Your Livin'. Was that the first time he recorded with a fuzz-tone guitar?

JB: (Laughs) Probably! We did that at a studio called TTG in Los Angeles. And it had a hum in it; some of the inputs into the control room had this distortion. And that particular guitar sound, the guitar player was messing with it on his amplifier and then I ran it through this distorted input line and it made that sound. We all thought, "Oh, this is marvelous."

JC: Dean's last LP, *The Nashville Sessions*, was the only time he recorded digitally.

JB: Yeah. Dean had been ill for a couple years and was recovering. He started feeling better and was working Vegas again. And his manager called and said, "Dean would like to come down (to Nashville) and make an album." I said, "C'mon!" We found some songs here in town and used some of the Nashville musicians and it was great fun for everybody.

JC: You mentioned Hal Blaine earlier. Who were some of the other session players that were on the Reprise hits?

JB: We had several different bass players: Chuck Berghofer and (Bill) Pitman. My favorite keyboard player for Dean was Leon

Russell. But Leon hated to play Dean's sessions 'cause I made him do all those eighth notes on the head. You know, the piano on a lot of Dean's stuff was just (sings) "da da da, da da da, da da da." And after about a minute and a half of that, a piano player's eyes start to cross! On a lot of the Dean Martin records, I had two piano players so they could alternate. One guy would play for six or eight bars, then the other guy would take over, 'cause it's a real hard thing to do. It got to where Leon wouldn't take my calls! (Laughs) So then I used different people. Don Randi could do it pretty good; he was a fine session player in L.A. On guitar: Glen Campbell played on a lot of them, also Tommy Tedesco and Al Casey. Strings were by the Sid Sharp String Section. And I used the Jack Halloran Singers, an eight-voice vocal group that did a lot of sessions in L.A.

JC: Finally, is there one particular song of Dean's that remains your favorite?

JB: "Everybody Loves Somebody." It was the highlight of everything he recorded as far as I was concerned. He had never sung with a big backbeat like that, with a big orchestra and a hip, modern rhythm section in it. He used to walk in (the studio) and in 15-20 minutes he'd have a song done. And it took me two hours to get the arrangement and the track ready. I kept walking by saying, "I'll be with you in just a minute" and he said, "That's okay." When it was all over, he said, "That's the first time I ever sang with lead drums," 'cause in that one room those drums just went everywhere. That performance he gave on "Everybody Loves Somebody" was just tremendous!

A long-time Dean Martin fan and collector, John Chintala is the author/publisher of the excellent and highly-recommended reference book Dean Martin – A Complete Guide to the 'Total Entertainer', *which was originally published in 1998 and was revised and made available as an e-book in 2012. His writings have also appeared in* Goldmine, Filmfax *and* DISCoveries *magazines and the first two Dean Martin CD box sets issued by Bear Family Records.*

Far Away Places with Dino

Written by Bernard H Thorpe, from 'Just Dino', Vol. 5, No. 1, Issue 413, Jan-Mar 2011

In the mid-90s, Charly, an independent record label, had obtained the rights under license to Dean's Reprise material and their intention was to release it all over a series of new CD-only compilations. After releasing (in January 1996) *The Best of Dean Martin 1962-1968*, they approached me to consult with them on two follow-up sets *Dean Martin Sings the All-Time Hits* (August 1996) and *Dino - The Golden Years* (December 1996). They had sold very well so there was no reason why their output wouldn't continue.

They asked me if I would like to begin preparing, long-term, for the entire catalogue to be made available going forward. I, of course, said yes! The team at Charly gave me *carte blanche* to bring all the material together in any way I felt relevant (as long as it wasn't in the format of the original Reprise albums themselves).

Far Away Places with Dino was the first and it took a good few months from concept to pre-production. A tentative release for 1997 was scheduled with a retail price of £17.99.

Then a spanner hit the works.

A £50million golden spanner!

The Dean Martin Family Trust had bought the complete and exclusive rights from EMI for the Reprise masters.

That meant that Charly was no longer in a position to release any material of Dean's and my plans were scuppered.

I wondered as time went on if the Family would do anything with the masters because there was simply no sign of any albums.

But my fears that Dean's work would never see the light of day on CD were unfounded when Collectors' Choice Music eventually began issuing fantastic two-on-one-disc complete albums in chronological order with original album artwork - licensed by the Dean Martin Family Trust ironically *back* to EMI! Our friends over at The Dean Martin Fan Center were involved and I was very happy that the releases were in safe hands and that Neil Daniels would do Dean proud.

The following, then, is an abridged version of the unpublished sleeve notes written by me that would have been included in the *Far Away Places...* set.

This double album set of 40 songs from Dean Martin is the latest in a series of releases from the great entertainer in which his recorded repertoire from 1962 has been digitally re-mastered. By the time this series is complete, there will be a comprehensive library of his work enabling all admirers to up-date their own vinyl collections on re-mastered compact discs, and for those of you who have just 'discovered' Dino, there is the golden opportunity to experience these excellent recordings, and his unique style of singing.

The title of "Far Away Places" might be otherwise misleading, for in an entertainment and a very entertaining career of over 50 years, this man was not prone to frequent travelling!

...this collection of songs recorded by Dean Martin over a ten-year period (1962-1972), takes you on an imaginary and romantic journey to places around the world. With a tongue in cheek approach to so many songs, Dean sings of romance, travel and such places as Paris, Phoenix, Houston as well as his family homeland of Italy, and taking in some other spots along the way.

Changing record labels in 1962, the French styled songs here were all recorded in one session on February 26th with that highly creative musical arranger, Neal Hefti. It was to be the birth of a new era in Dean's recordings, but his success with the new label did not come overnight as some had predicted. Commercially, he was going through a thin period, but with his 1964 hit record "Everybody Loves Somebody", Dino was back in the charts again. The disc proved so popular that he was offered his own TV show, which was [initially] called by the same name. The shows were to last for many years on TV, during which time he had the very best artists from the entertainment world as his guests.

He was kept busy in the recording studios, and in three years had cut well over a hundred song titles. The song, "South of the Border" appears twice on these CDs, but each is from a totally different session. The first version appeared on an early album, with a Latin-styled arrangement from Don Costa, where Dean ends up 'soused at the Border. A completely different recording appears on Disc Two, which came from the first of four Matt Helm stories that he made for Columbia Pictures, entitled "The Silencers". The combined orchestras of Gene Page and Ernie Freeman made this version more powerful musically in its presentation. His regular recording dates continued and in 5 years had issued no less than 16 solo albums. He began to slow down this rate during the 1970's, but a new Dean Martin album was always welcome.

After a protracted and painful illness, Dean Martin died on Christmas Day 1995, and we had lost a great personality, unique in his field who seemed to epitomise something we would all like to do, and that was not to take life too seriously. This happy and carefree nature was reflected in all his work, especially his music. The Dean Martin Association will continue with the legacy of his work, and I hope that this song collection will give you much lasting pleasure. There are many more compact discs of his still to be issued on Charly, and they will be a fine tribute to a much missed entertainer.

See the Discography section of this book for the full track details of this intriguing, unreleased collection.

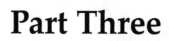

Part Three

Discography

Any omissions or errors in the data hereunder are accidental.

Singles *(all vinyl except where indicated)*

DIAMOND

[78rpm]

September 1946	All of Me / Which Way Did My Heart Go?
October 1946	I Got the Sun in the Mornin' / Sweetheart of Sigma Chi

NATIONAL MASK & PUPPET CORPORATION

[78rpm]

May 1947	The Puppet Show [promotion only; lost recording]

EMBASSY

[78rpm]

July 1947	One Foot in Heaven / The Night Is Young (and You're So Beautiful)

APOLLO

[78rpm]

August 1947	Oh Marie / Walkin' My Baby Back Home
November 1947	Memory Lane / Louise
March 1948	Santa Lucia / Hold Me

CAPITOL

[78rpm]

November 1948	The Money Song (w. Jerry Lewis) / That Certain Party (w. Jerry Lewis)
December 1948	Tarra Ta-Lara Ta-Lar / Once in Love With Amy
January 1949	You Was (w. Peggy Lee) / b-side Peggy Lee solo
January 1949	Powder Your Face with Sunshine / Absence Makes the Heart Grow Fonder
March 1949	Powder Your Face with Sunshine / You Was (w. Peggy Lee)
March 1949	Johnny Get Your Girl / Have A Little Sympathy
April 1949	Johnny Get Your Girl / Tarra Ta-Lara Ta-Lar
April 1949	Dreamy Old New England Moon (w. The Martingales) / Three Wishes (w. The Martingales)

[78/45rpm]

May 1949	Just For Fun / My Own, My Only, My All
	(from *My Friend Irma*)
August 1949	Vieni Su / That Lucky Old Sun
August 1949	Vieni Su [promotion only] / b-side Red Ingle solo (78rpm only)
December 1949	That Lucky Old Sun / Three Wishes (w. The Martingales)
	(78rpm only)
February 1950	Rain / Zing-A-Zing-A-Zoom
February 1950	Choo'n Gum / Zing-A-Zing-A-Zoom

April 1950	I'm Gonna Paper All My Walls With Your Love Letters / Muskrat Ramble
April 1950	Muskrat Ramble / Choo'n Gum (78rpm only)
May 1950	I Don't Care If the Sun Don't Shine / Choo'n Gum
May 1950	Be Honest With Me / I Still Get A Thrill (Thinking Of You)
May 1950	Baby, Obey Me! / I'll Always Love You (from *My Friend Irma Goes West*)
June 1950	Bye Blackbird / Happy Feet
July 1950	I Don't Care If The Sun Don't Shine / Have A Little Sympathy (78rpm only)
August 1950	The Peddler's Serenade (w. The Starlighters) / Wham! Bam! Thank You Mam! (w. The Starlighters)
September 1950	Don't Rock the Boat, Dear (w. Margaret Whiting) / I'm In Love With You (w. Margaret Whiting)
September 1950	Don't Rock the Boat, Dear (w. Margaret Whiting) / Happy Feet (78rpm only)
November 1950	Johnny Get Your Girl / Have A Little Sympathy
January 1951	I'll Always Love You (My Friend Irma Goes West) / I'm Gonna Paper All My Walls With Your Love Letters (78rpm only)
January 1951	If / I Love the Way You Say Goodnight
February 1951	If / Baby, Obey Me! (from *My Friend Irma Goes West*) (78rpm only)
February 1951	Three Wishes (w. The Martingales) / Dreamy Old New England Moon (w. The Martingales)

March 1951	You and Your Beautiful Eyes / Tonda Wonda Hoy (from *At War With The Army*) (UK 78rpm only)
April 1951	Who's Sorry Now? / Beside You
May 1951	Bye Blackbird / The Money Song (w. Jerry Lewis) (78rpm only)
May 1951	How D'Ya Like Your Eggs In the Mornin'? (w. Helen O'Connell) / We Never Talk Much (w. Helen O'Connell) (UK 78rpm only)
December 1951	Meanderin' / I'm In Love With You (w. Margaret Whiting) (78rpm only)
December 1951	Solitaire / I Ran All The Way Home (UK 78rpm only)
February 1952	Blue Smoke / Night Train To Memphis
February 1952	Sailor's Polka / Never Before (from *Sailor Beware*) (UK 78rpm only)
March 1952	As You Are / Oh Boy! Oh Boy! Oh Boy!
June 1952	You Belong To Me / Hominy Grits (UK 78rpm only)
July 1952	I Know A Dream When I See One (from *Jumping Jacks*) / Second Chance (w. The Encores) (UK 78rpm only)
July 1952	What Could Be More Beautiful / Kiss
July 1952	There's My Lover / Little Did We Know
August 1952	Until You Love Someone / My Heart Has Found A Home Now

VOGUE

[78rpm]

December 1952	Santa Lucia (w. Jerry Jerome and his All-Stars) / Hold Me (w. Jerry Jerome and his All-Stars)

CAPITOL

[78/45rpm]

February 1953	I Don't Care If the Sun Don't Shine / Choo'n Gum
March 1953	Won't You Surrender / Pretty As A Picture
May 1953	I Passed Your House Tonight / Bet-I-Cha
June 1953	Oh Marie / Come Back To Sorrento
August 1953	Oh Marie / I'll Always Love You (from *My Friend Irma Goes West*)
August 1953	Love Me, Love Me (w. The Herman McCoy Singers) / 'Til I Find You (UK 78rpm only)
August 1953	Kiss / There's My Lover (78rpm only)
August 1953	When You're Smiling / Who's Your Little Who-Zis? (from *The Stooge*) (78rpm only)
August 1953	Don't You Remember? / If I Could Sing Like Bing (w. The Herman McCoy Singers)
September 1953	In the Cool, Cool, Cool of the Evening / Bonne Nuit
	(UK 78rpm only)
September 1953	That's Amore (from *The Caddy*) / You're The Right One (from *The Caddy*) (UK 78rpm only)
October 1953	I Love the Way You Say Goodnight / Hanging Around With You (78rpm only)

October 1953	Go / Luna Mezzo Mare
October 1953	Hanging Around With You / Aw C'Mon
November 1953	Aw C'Mon / Go Go Go Go (78rpm only)
November 1953	Meanderin' / (Ma Come Bali) Bella Bimba
November 1953	The Christmas Blues / If I Should Love Again (UK 78rpm only)
January 1954	When You're Smiling / All I Have To Give You
April 1954	Hey Brother Pour the Wine / I'd Cry Like A Baby
May 1954	Sway / Money Burns A Hole In My Pocket (from *Living It Up*)
July 1954	Sway / Pretty As A Picture
July 1954	The Peddlerman (Ten I Loved) / That's What I Like (from *Living It Up*)
September 1954	Money Burns A Hole In My Pocket / That's What I Like (from *Living It Up*)
September 1954	How Do You Speak To An Angel? / Ev'ry Street's A Boulevard (In Old New York) (w. Jerry Lewis) (from *Living It Up*)
October 1954	The Peddlerman (Ten I Loved) / Try Again
November 1954	One More Time / If I Could Sing Like Bing (w. The Herman McCoy Singers)
November 1954	Try Again / One More Time
January 1955	Open Up the Doghouse (w. Nat 'King' Cole) / Long, Long Ago (w. Nat 'King' Cole)
January 1955	The Naughty Lady of Shady Lane / Let Me Go, Lover
January 1955	Mambo Italiano / That's All I Want From You

February 1955	Belle From Barcelona / Confused
March 1955	Young and Foolish / Under the Bridges Of Paris
April 1955	Under the Bridges Of Paris / What Could Be More Beautiful
June 1955	Chee Chee-oo-Chee / Ridin' Into Love
July 1955	Simpatico / Love Is All That Matters (from *You're Never Too Young*)
November 1955	Relax-Ay-Voo (w. Line Renaud) (from *You're Never Too Young*) / Two Sleepy People (w. Line Renaud)
November 1955	In Napoli / I Like Them All
December 1955	Memories Are Made Of This (w. The Easyriders) / Change Of Heart
January 1956	When You Pretend / The Lucky Song (from *Artists and Models*)
February 1956	Innamorata / You Look So Familiar (from *Artists and Models*)
February 1956	Young and Foolish / Just One More Chance (from *The Stooge*)
February 1956	Innamorata (from *Artists and Models*) / The Lady With the Big Umbrella
April 1956	Standing On the Corner / Watching the World Go By
July 1956	Watching the World Go By / The Lady With the Big Umbrella
July 1956	I'm Gonna Steal You Away (w. The Nuggetts) / Rue De Mon Amour
August 1956	I'm Gonna Steal You Away (w. The Nuggetts) / The Test of Time

September 1956	Me 'n' You 'n' the Moon / The Wind, The Wind (from *Pardners*)
November 1956	Pardners (w. Jerry Lewis) (from *Pardners*) / b-side Jerry Lewis Solo
November 1956	Mississippi Dreamboat / The Test of Time
December 1956	Give Me A Sign / Mississippi Dreamboat
December 1956	Give Me A Sign / The Look
February 1957	Just Kiss Me / I Know I Can't Forget
March 1957	The Man Who Plays the Mandolino (*from Ten Thousand Bedrooms*) / I Know I Can't Forget
March 1957	The Man Who Plays the Mandolino (from *Ten Thousand Bedrooms*) / Captured
April 1957	Bamboozled / Only Trust Your Heart (from *Ten Thousand Bedrooms*)
June 1957	I Can't Give You Anything But Love / I Never Had A Chance
July 1957	Beau James / Write To Me From Naples
September 1957	The Triche Trache / Promise Her Anything
December 1957	Just Kiss Me / The Look
December 1957	Good Mornin' Life / Makin' Love Ukulele Style
February 1958	Return To Me / Forgetting You (US 45rpm only)
April 1958	It's 1200 Miles From Palm Springs To Texas [Promotional Single Only] (45rpm only)
June 1958	Angel Baby / I'll Gladly Make the Same Mistake Again
	(US 45rpm only)

July 1958	Once Upon A Time / The Magician (45rpm only)
August 1958 [45rpm]	Volare / Outta My Mind (US 45rpm only)
November 1958	Sleep Warm / All I Do Is Dream of You [Promotion Release Only]
December 1958	It Takes So Long / You Were Made For Love
January 1959	My Rifle, My Pony and Me (w. Ricky Nelson and Introduction by John Wayne) [Promotion Release Only] (from *Rio Bravo*)
February 1959	Rio Bravo / My Rifle, My Pony and Me (from *Rio Bravo*)
August 1959	On An Evening In Roma / You Can't Love 'Em All
September 1959	Ain't Gonna Lead This Life / Maybe
October 1959	(Love Is A) Career (from *Career*) / For You
November 1959	(Love Is A) Career (from *Career*) / Ain't Gonna Lead This Life
January 1960	Who Was That Lady? (from *Who Was That Lady?*) / Love Me, My Love
February 1960	Who Was That Lady? (from *Who Was That Lady?*) / (Love Is A) Career (from *Career*)
April 1960	Napoli / Professor Professor
May 1960	Buttercup A Golden Hair / Napoli
July 1960	Buttercup A Golden Hair / Just In Time (from *Bells Are Ringing*)
August 1960	Just In Time (from *Bells Are Ringing*) / Humdinger
August 1960	Ain't That A Kick In the Head (from *Ocean's 11*) / Humdinger

October 1960	Sogni D'oro / How Sweet It Is
January 1961	Sparkelin' Eyes / Tu Sei Bella, Signorina
May 1961	That's Amore (from *The Caddy*) / Memories Are Made Of This
May 1961	All In A Night's Work (from *All In A Nights Work*) / Bella Bella Bambina
May 1961	Giuggiola / The Story of Life
February 1962	Return To Me / Volare

REPRISE

[45rpm]

February 1962	Tik-A-Tee, Tik-A-Tay / Just Close Your Eyes
April 1962	C'est Si Bon / The Poor People of Paris
April 1962	C'est Si Bon / April In Paris (33rpm only)
April 1962	The Poor People Of Paris / Mimi (33rpm only)
April 1962	The River Seine / The Last Time I Saw Paris (33rpm only)
April 1962	C'est Magnifique / Mam'selle (33rpm only)
April 1962	Gigi / I Love Paris (33rpm only)
May 1962	Dame Su Amor / Baby O
October 1962	In A Little Spanish Town / From the Bottom of My Heart
November 1962	Sam's Song (w. Sammy Davis Jr) / b-side Frank Sinatra and Sammy Davis Jr duet
November 1962	Senza Fine / Who's Got The Action? (from *Who's Got The Action?*)
February 1963	Who's Got The Action? (from *Who's Got The Action?*) / From the Bottom of My Heart
February 1963	Face In A Crowd / Ain't Gonna Try Anymore

| March 1963 | Who's Got The Action? (from *Who's Got The Action?*) / In A Little Spanish Town |

CAPITOL

[45rpm]

| March 1963 | Cha Cha Cha d'Amour / I Wish You Love |

REPRISE

[45rpm]

| July 1963 | My Sugar's Gone / Corrine, Corrina |

| August 1963 | The Middle of the Night (Is My Crying Time) / My Sugar's Gone |

| October 1963 | The Oldest Established (Permanent Floating Crap Game In New York) (w. Bing Crosby and Frank Sinatra) / b-side Frank Sinatra and Bing Crosby duet |

| November 1963 | Via Veneto / Mama Roma |

| November 1963 | Via Veneto / La Giostra [Promotion Only] |

| January 1964 | La Giostra / Grazie, Prego, Scusie |

| May 1964 | Everybody Loves Somebody / Your Other Love (33rpm only) |

| May 1964 | Everybody Loves Somebody / A Little Voice (w. Keely Smith) |

| May 1964 | Shutters and Boards / Baby O (33rpm only) |

| June 1964 | My Heart Cries For You / A Little Voice [Promotion Only] (33rpm only) |

| July 1964 | Siesta Fiesta / Corrine, Corrina [Promotion Only] (33rpm only) |

| September 1964 | The Door Is Still Open To My Heart / Every Minute, Every Hour |

CAPITOL

[45rpm]

October 1964	Somebody Loves You / A Hundred Years From Today

REPRISE

[45rpm]

December 1964	Face In A Crowd / Siesta Fiesta [Promotion Only] (33rpm only)
December 1964	You're Nobody 'til Somebody Loves You / You'll Always Be the One I Love
February 1965	Send Me the Pillow You Dream On / I'll Be Seeing You
February 1965	Things / Face In A Crowd [Promotion Only] (33rpm only)
May 1965	(Remember Me) I'm the One Who Loves You / Born To Lose
May 1965	Sophia (from *Kiss Me, Stupid*) / same b-side [Promotion Only]
July 1965	Houston (w. The Jack Halloran Singers) / Bumming Around
October 1965	I Will (w. The Jack Halloran Singers) / You're The Reason I'm In Love (w. The Jack Halloran Singers)
February 1966	Somewhere There's A Someone / That Old Clock On the Wall
March 1966	Come Running Back / Bouquet of Roses
March 1966	The Silencers (score - no vocal) (from *The Silencers*) / Hammer and Nails (w. The Jack Halloran Singers) (33rpm only)
July 1966	A Million and One / Shades
September 1966	Nobody's Baby Again / It Just Happened That Way

November 1966	(Open Up The Door) Let the Good Times In / I'm Not the Marrying Kind (from *Murderer's Row*)
December 1966	Marshmallow World / Blue Christmas
December 1966	Silver Bells / Same b-side [Promotion Only]
January 1967	I'm Not the Marrying Kind (from *Murderer's Row*) / no b-side
April 1967	Lay Some Happiness On Me / Think About Me
June 1967	In the Chapel In the Moonlight / Welcome To My World
August 1967	Little Ole Wine Drinker, Me / I Can't Help Remembering You
November 1967	In the Misty Moonlight / Wallpaper Roses
January 1968	The Glory of Love / Wallpaper Roses
March 1968	You've Still Got A Place In My Heart / Old Yellow Line (w. The Jack Halloran Singers)
May 1968	Bumming Around / Home (w. Don Lanier)
July 1968	April Again / That Old Time Feelin'
August 1968	Five Card Stud (from *Five Card Stud*) / same b-side [Promotion Only]
August 1968	Five Card Stud (from *Five Card Stud*) / One Lonely Boy
October 1968	(Open Up the Door) Let the Good Times In / Lay Some Happiness On Me
October 1968	Everybody Loves Somebody / A Million and One
October 1968	Come Running Back / Somewhere There's A Someone

October 1968	Houston (w. The Jack Halloran Singers) / I Will (w. The Jack Halloran Singers)
October 1968	(Remember Me) I'm the One Who Loves You / You're Nobody 'til Somebody Loves You
October 1968	Send Me the Pillow You Dream On / The Door Is Still Open To My Heart
October 1968	Little Ole Wine Drinker, Me / In the Chapel In the Moonlight
October 1968	Not Enough Indians / In the Misty Moonlight
October 1968	Not Enough Indians / Rainbows Are Back In Style
January 1969	Gentle On My Mind *[release suggested by Bernard H. Thorpe]* / That Old Time Feelin'
February 1969	Gentle On My Mind *[release suggested by Bernard H. Thorpe]* / That's When I See the Blues
May 1969	By the Time I Get To Phoenix / Things
July 1969	I Take A Lot of Pride In What I Am / Drowning In My Tears
October 1969	One Cup of Happiness (and One Peace of Mind) / Cryin' Time
April 1970	Come On Down / Down Home
May 1970	For the Love of A Woman / The Tracks of My Tears
July 1970	My Woman, My Woman, My Wife / Here We Go Again
September 1970	Detroit City / Turn the World Around
December 1970	Jingle Bells / White Christmas *[release suggested by Bernard H. Thorpe]*
January 1971	Georgia Sunshine / For Once In My Life

January 1971	Georgia Sunshine / For the Good Times
April 1971	Raining In My Heart / She's A Little Bit Country
January 1972	What's Yesterday / The Right Kind of Woman
January 1972	The Right Kind of Woman *[alternative arrangement]* / What's Yesterday
April 1972	Guess Who / I Can Give You What You Want Now
March 1973	Amor Mio / You Made Me Love You
October 1973	Get On With Your Livin' / Smile
November 1973	You're The Best Thing That Ever Happened To Me / Free To Carry On

CAPITOL

[45rpm]

| May 1975 | Memories Are Made Of This (w. The Easyriders) / That's Amore (from *The Caddy*) |

REPRISE

[45rpm]

| July 1981 | Gentle On My Mind / King of The Road |

WARNER

[45rpm]

June 1983	Drinking Champagne / Don't Give Up On Me
June 1983	Drinking Champagne / Since I Met You Baby
July 1983	Hangin' Around / My First Country Song (w. Conway Twitty)

MCA

[45rpm]

August 1985   L.A Is My Home (from *Half Nelson*) / Drinking Champagne

OLDGOLD

[45rpm]

March 1988   Memories Are Made Of This (w. The Easyriders) [released in conjunction with the Peugeot 306 radio & TV advertising campaign] / Return To Me

CAPITOL

[45rpm]

May 1988   That's Amore (from *The Caddy*) [released as part of the *Moonstruck* motion picture soundtrack] / b-side Vikki Carr solo

June 1996   That's Amore (from *The Caddy*) [featured as the main theme to the 'Loyal Supporters' TV & cinema campaign for the 1996 European Football Championship] / On An Evening In Roma [Promotion Only]

[5" Compact Disc]

June 1996   That's Amore (from *The Caddy*) / On An Evening In Roma / Standing On the Corner [released to coincide with the 'Loyal Supporters' TV & cinema campaign for the 1996 European Football Championship]

June 1996   That's Amore (from *The Caddy*) [Promotion Only - to coincide with the 'Loyal Supporters' TV & cinema campaign for the 1996 European Football Championship]

[Tape Cassette]

June 1996   That's Amore (from *The Caddy*) / On An Evening In Roma [released to coincide with the 'Loyal Supporters' TV & cinema campaign for the 1996 European Football Championship]

[5″ Compact Disc]

August 1999   Sway / That's Amore (from *The Caddy*) / Sway - The Rip-Off Artist Mix (w. Julie London) [remix used by the BBC as part of the 'BBC1 is the One' campaign]

EPs *(all vinyl)*

APOLLO
[45rpm]

August 1951   **EIGHTEEN TOP HITS!** (Various Artists)

Walkin' My Baby Back Home / Hold Me /
Louise / Santa Lucia

LLOYDS
[45rpm]

August 1951   **DEAN MARTIN**

Oh Marie / Walking My Baby Back Home /
Santa Lucia / Hold Me

(original Apollo recordings)

CAPITOL
[45rpm]

July 1954   **SUNNY ITALY**

That's Amore / Luna Mezzo / Oh Marie /
Come Back to Sorrento

July 1954   ***LIVING IT UP***

How Do You Speak To An Angel? / Money
Burns A Hole In My Pocket / *Jerry Lewis solo* /
That's What I Like / Ev'ry Street's A
Boulevard (In Old New York)

June 1955   **DEAN MARTIN**

Mambo Italiano / Let Me Go, Lover / That's
All I Want From You / Naughty Lady of
Shady Lane

May 1956   **DEAN MARTIN SINGS (Volume 1)**

I Feel Like A Feather In the Breeze / A Girl
Named Mary and A Boy Named Bill / Who's
Your Little Who-zis? / I'm Yours

May 1956	**DEAN MARTIN SINGS (Volume 2)**
	I Feel A Song Comin' On / With My Eyes Wide Open I'm Dreaming / Just One More Chance / When You're Smiling
July 1956	*PARDNERS*
	Pardners / Me 'n' You 'n'the Moon / The Wind, the Wind / *Jerry Lewis solo*
November 1956	**SWINGIN' DOWN YONDER (Part 1)**
	Is It True What They Say About Dixie? / Carolina Moon / Basin Street Blues / Waiting for the Robert E Lee
December 1956	**SWINGIN' DOWN YONDER (Part 2)**
	Mississippi Mud / When It's Sleepy Time Down South / Georgia On My Mind / Just A Little Bit South of North Carolina
December 1956	*ARTISTS AND MODELS*
	Innamorata / You Look So Familiar / The Lucky Song / When You Pretend
September 1956	**SWINGIN' DOWN YONDER (Part 3)**
	Way Down Yonder In New Orleans / Alabamy Bound / Dinah / Carolina In the Morning
October 1956	**MEMORIES ARE MADE OF THIS**
	Memories Are Made of This / Ridin' Into Love / Change of Heart / I Like Them All
December 1956	*HOLLYWOOD OR BUST*
	Hollywood Or Bust / It Looks Like Love / Let's Be Friendly / A Day In the Country
April 1957	*TEN THOUSAND BEDROOMS*
	Ten Thousand Bedrooms / You I Love / Only Trust Your Heart / Money Is A Problem

September 1957   **PRETTY BABY (Part 1)**

Pretty Baby / Only Forever / Maybe / I Can't Give You Anything But Love

September 1957   **PRETTY BABY (Part 2)**

Sleepy Time Gal / Once In A While / I Don't Know Why (I Love You Like I Do) / You've Got Me Crying Again

September 1957   **PRETTY BABY (Part 3)**

The Object of My Affection / Nevertheless (I'm In Love With You) / For You / It's Easy To Remember

May 1958   **RETURN TO ME**

Return to Me / Buona Sera / Forgetting You / Don't You Remember?

September 1958   **VOLARE**

Angel Baby / Outta My Mind / I'll Gladly Make the Same Mistake Again / Volare

January 1959   **SLEEP WARM**

Sleep Warm / Hit the Road to Dreamland / Sleepy Time Gal / Goodnight Sweetheart

February 1959   **BRAVO!! IT'S BIG!! IT'S *RIO BRAVO*!!** [Promotion only]

Rio Bravo / My Rifle, My Pony and Me / *Nelson Riddle instrumentals*

February 1959   ***RIO BRAVO***

Rio Bravo / My Rifle, My Pony and Me / *Nelson Riddle instrumentals*

September 1959   **A WINTER ROMANCE (Part 1)**

A Winter Romance / Let It Snow! Let It Snow! Let It Snow! / I've Got My Love To Keep Me Warm / Winter Wonderland

September 1959   **A WINTER ROMANCE (Part 2)**

Baby, It's Cold Outside / June In January / Canadian Sunset / Out In the Cold Again

September 1959   **A WINTER ROMANCE (Part 3)**

White Christmas / Rudolph the Red-Nosed Reindeer / The Things We Did Last Summer / It Won't Cool Off

May 1960   **MERRY CHRISTMAS TO YOU** *(Various Artists)*

The Christmas Blues

February 1961   *WHO WAS THAT LADY?*

Who Was That Lady? / Professor Professor / Napoli / Love Me, My Love

June 1961   **LINE AND DINO**

Relax-Ay-Voo (w. Line Renaud) / Two Sleep People (w. Line Renaud) / *Line Renaud solos*

August 1961   **RELAXIN' WITH DEAN MARTIN**

Just One More Chance / You Belong to Me / When You're Smiling / Under the Bridges of Paris

December 1961   **AIN'T THAT A KICK IN THE HEAD**

Ain't That A Kick In the Head / Buttercup A Golden Hair / Humdinger / Just In Time

1962   **DINO**

Just Say I Love Her / Arrivederci, Roma / Vieni Su / Non Dimenticar / Take Me In Your Arms / I Have But One Heart

July 1962   **SOGNI D'ORO**

Sogni d'Oro / How Sweet It Is / Tu Sei Bella, Signorina / Sparkelin' Eyes

August 1962	**I'M YOURS**
	Money Burns A Hole In My Pocket / Kiss / How Do You Speak To An Angel? / I'm Yours
August 1962	**SOGNI D'ORO WITH DEAN MARTIN**
	Innamorata / Return To Me / True Love / Sogni d'Oro
September 1962	**DEAN MARTIN IN MOVIELAND**
	Who Was That Lady? / Ain't That A Kick In the Head / (Love Is A) Career / Just In Time
September 1962	**DEAN MARTIN**
	That's Amore / Memories Are Made of This / Return To Me / Volare
November 1962	**GIUGGIOLA**
	Guiggiola / All In A Night's Work / Bella Bella Bambina / The Story of Life
December 1965	**SOMEBODY LOVES YOU**
	Somebody Loves You / If Love Is Good To Me / A Hundred Years From Today / Two Loves Have I
1966	**THE BEST OF DEAN MARTIN (Volume 1)**
	Memories Are Made of This / Just In Time / That's Amore / Come Back to Sorrento / Return To Me / Volare
January 1966	**CHA CHA CHA D'AMOUR**
	Cha Cha Cha d'Amour / My One and Only Love / I Wish You Love / I Love You Too Much
1967	**DINO - ITALIAN LOVE SONGS**
	On An Evening In Roma / My Heart Reminds Me / Just Say I Love Her / Vieni Su

REPRISE

[45rpm]

May 1963   **FRENCH STYLE**

C'est Magnifique / The River Seine / La Vie En Rose / Mimi

July 1964   **COUNTRY STYLE** [33rpm only]

Any Time / Room Full of Roses / I Walk the Line / Hey Good Lookin' / Singing the Blues / Face In A Crowd / Shutters and Boards

August 1964   **DINO LATINO** [33rpm only]

Tangerine / South of the Border / What A Diff'rence A Day Made / In A Little Spanish Town / Magic Is the Moonlight / Besame Mucho

August 1964   **DREAM WITH DEAN** [33rpm only]

I Don't Know Why (I Just Do) / Baby, Won't You Please Come Home / I'm Confessin' / Gimme A Little Kiss, Will Ya, Huh! / I'll Buy That Dream / Smile

August 1964   **DEAN 'TEX' MARTIN RIDES AGAIN** [33rpm only]

I Can't Help It (If I'm Still In Love With You) / Bouquet of Roses / Second Hand Rose / Just A Little Lovin'

September 1964   *KISS ME KATE* (Various Artists [Reprise Repertory Theatre])

We Open In Venice (w. Frank Sinatra & Sammy Davis Jr)

September 1964   *FINIAN'S RAINBOW* (Various Artists [Reprise Repertory Theatre])

If This Isn't Love

October 1964	**EVERYBODY LOVES SOMEBODY** [33rpm only]

Everybody Loves Somebody / Corrine Corrina / Face In A Crowd / Just Close Your Eyes / Things / My Heart Cries For You

October 1964 **DINO LATINO**

South of the Border / La Paloma / Besame Mucho / In A Little Spanish Town

October 1964 **HAVE YOURSELF A MERRY LITTLE CHRISTMAS**

(Various Artists)

Peace On Earth / Silent Night

October 1964 *GUYS AND DOLLS* (Various Artists [Reprise Repertory Theatre])

Guys and Dolls (w. Frank Sinatra)

December 1964 **EVERYBODY LOVES SOMEBODY**

Everybody Loves Somebody / A Little Voice / Every Minute, Every Hour / The Door Is Still Open To My Heart

March 1965 **WE'LL SING IN THE SUNSHINE**

We'll Sing In the Sunshine / Things / My Heart Cries For You / I'm Gonna Change Everything

March 1965 *ROBIN AND THE 7 HOODS* (Various Artists)

Mister Booze (w. Bing Crosby, Frank Sinatra and Sammy Davis Jr) / Any Man Who Loves His Mother

August 1965 **I'LL BE SEEING YOU**

In the Chapel In the Moonlight / I'll Be Seeing You / You're Nobody 'til Somebody Loves You / Wedding Bells

September 1965 **I'M THE ONE WHO LOVES YOU** [33rpm only]

Walk On By / King of the Road / (Remember Me) I'm the One Who Loves You / Here Comes My Baby / My Shoes Keep Walking Back To You / The Birds and the Bees

November 1965 **HOUSTON** [33rpm only]

Snap Your Fingers / Houston / Little Lovely One / The First Thing (Every Morning) / I Will / Down Home

October 1965 **SEND ME SOME LOVIN'**

Send Me Some Lovin' / My Heart Is An Open Book / You'll Always Be the One I Love / Send Me the Pillow You Dream On

February 1966 **THE BIRDS AND THE BEES**

Welcome To My World / King of the Road / The Birds and the Bees / Take These Chains From My Heart

March 1966 **DEAN MARTIN SINGS SONGS FROM *THE SILENCERS*** [33rpm only]

The Glory of Love / Empty Saddles In the Old Corral / Side by Side / On the Sunny Side of the Street / The Last Round-Up / Red Sails In the Sunset

March 1966 **RED ROSES FOR A BLUE LADY**

Red Rose For A Blue Lady / Walk On By / Bumming Around / My Shoes Keep Walking Back To You

June 1966 **THE HIT SOUND OF DEAN MARTIN** [33rpm only]

Don't Let the Blues Make You Bad / A Million and One / I'm Living In Two Worlds

/ Shades / Today Is Not the Day / Ain't Gonna Try Anymore

November 1966   **LOVE LOVE LOVE**

Everybody But Me / Love Love Love / Down Home / You're the Reason I'm In Love

March 1966   **SOMEWHERE THERE'S A SOMEONE** [33rpm only]

Second Hand Rose / Bouquet of Roses / Just A Little Lovin' / Somewhere There's A Someone / I Can't Help It (If I'm Still In Love With You)

February 1967   **THE GLORY OF LOVE**

The Glory of Love / On the Sunny Side of the Street / If You Knew Susie / Side by Side

August 1967   **WELCOME TO MY WORLD** [33rpm only]

Little Ole Wine Drinker, Me / The Green, Green Grass of Home / Wallpaper Roses / In the Chapel In the Moonlight / Welcome To My World / Release Me

October 1967   **MISTER HAPPINESS**

Lay Some Happiness On Me / I'm Not the Marrying Kind / Corrine Corrina / Things

November 1968   **WINTER WONDERLAND**

White Christmas / Winter Wonderland / Clinging Vine / In the Misty Moonlight

May 1968   **DEAN MARTIN'S GREATEST HITS (Volume 1)** [33rpm only]

Everybody Loves Somebody / You're Nobody 'til Somebody Loves You / In the Chapel In the Moonlight / Every Minute, Every Hour / Bumming Around / You'll Always Be the One I Love

| August 1968 | **DEAN MARTIN'S GREATEST HITS (Volume 2)** [33rpm only] |

In the Misty Moonlight / Send Me the Pillow You Dream On / Little Ole Wine Drinker, Me / Lay Some Happiness On Me / You've Still Got A Place In My Heart / King of the Road

| December 1968 | **GENTLE ON MY MIND** [33rpm only] |

By the Time I Get To Phoenix / April Again / Honey / That Old Time Feelin' / Rainbows Are Back In Style / Not Enough Indians

| August 1970 | **MY WOMAN, MY WOMAN, MY WIFE** [33rpm only] |

Here We Go Again / Make the World Go Away / It Keeps Right On A-Hurtin' / My Woman, My Woman, My Wife / Together Again / Turn the World Around

| January 1972 | **DINO** [33rpm only] |

Guess Who / Just the Other Side of Nowhere / Blue Memories / What's Yesterday / I Can Give You What You Want Now / Party Dolls and Wine

| May 1973 | **SITTIN' ON TOP OF THE WORLD** [33rpm only] |

I Wonder Who's Kissing Her Now / At Sundown / Almost Like Being In Love / It's A Good Day / Ramblin' Rose / I'm Sitting On Top of the World

| December 1973 | **YOU'RE THE BEST THING THAT EVER HAPPENED TO** ME [33rpm only] |

I Don't Know Why (I Love You Like I Do) / You're the Best Thing That Ever Happened To Me / I'm Confessin' / Free To Carry On / Tie A Yellow Ribbon

June 1974	**LITTLE OLE WINE DRINKER, ME**

Little Ole Wine Drinker, Me / Bumming Around / Not Enough Indians / By the Time I Get To Phoenix

June 1974	**GENTLE ON MY MIND**

Gentle On My Mind / King of the Road / Georgia Sunshine / You're Nobody 'til Somebody Loves You

Albums *(all vinyl except where indicated)*

WALDORF

1949   **DEAN MARTIN SINGS**

Walkin' My Baby Back Home / Hold Me / Santa Lucia / Louise / Memory Lane / Oh Marie

(reissued 1954, UK June 1959)

CAPITOL

April 1953   **DEAN MARTIN SINGS**

Who's Your Little Who-zis? / I'm Yours / I Feel A Song Comin' On / With My Eyes Wide Open I'm Dreaming / Just Once More Chance / Louise / I Feel Like A Feather In the Breeze / A Girl Named Mary and A Boy Named Bill

May 1953   **CAPITOL PRESENTS DEAN MARTIN**

When You're Smiling / With My Eyes Wide Open I'm Dreaming / I Feel Like A Feather In the Breeze / I Feel A Song Comin' On / Who's Your Little Who-zis? / Muskrat Ramble / Be Honest With Me / Rain

September 1953   **DEAN MARTIN SINGS**

Who's Your Little Who-zis? / I'm Yours / I Feel A Song Comin' On / With My Eyes Wide Open I'm Dreaming / Just Once More Chance / Louise / I Feel Like A Feather In the Breeze / A Girl Named Mary and A Boy Named Bill / Come Back To Sorrento / Oh Marie / That's Amore / When You're Smiling

August 1955   **SWINGIN' DOWN YONDER**

Carolina Moon / Waiting For the Robert E Lee / When It's Sleepy Time Down South /

Mississippi Mud / Alabamy Bound / Dinah / Carolina In the Morning / Way Down Yonder In New Orleans / Georgia On My Mind / Just A Little Bit South of North Carolina / Basin Street Blues / Is It True What They Say About Dixie?

(also on TC; re-issue UK March 1974)

February 1957   **PRETTY BABY**

I Can't Give You Anything But Love / Only Forever / Sleepy Time Gal / Maybe / I Don't Know Why (I Just Do) / Pretty Baby / You've Got Me Crying Again / Once In A While / The Object of My Affection / For You / It's Easy To Remember / Nevertheless (I'm In Love With You)

(straight reissue via World Record Club, August 1965; Music For Pleasure, April 1969; Capitol, November 1996 [coupled with THIS TIME I'M SWINGIN', CD only])

REGAL

June 1957   **DEAN MARTIN**

In the Cool, Cool, Cool of the Evening / Baby, Obey Me / I Love the Way You Say Goodnight / If I Should Love Again / Belle from Barcelona / Muskrat Ramble / Go Go Go Go / Just For Fun / I Don't Care If the Sun Don't Shine / My Own, My Only, My Ally / I'm Gonna Paper My Walls With Your Love Letters / That Lucky Old Sun

CAPITOL

October 1958   **THIS IS DEAN MARTIN!**

Volare / Write To Me From Naples / The Test of Time / Don't You Remember? / The Look /

Return To Me / Buona Sera / I Know I Can't Forget / Angel Baby / When You're Smiling / Makin' Love Ukulele Style / Promise Her Anything

(also Tapereel & TC; reissued World Record Club, July 1971)

April 1959 **SLEEP WARM**

Sleep Warm / Hit the Road to Dreamland / Dream / Cuddle Up A Little Closer / Sleepy Time Gal / Goodnight Sweetheart / All I Do Is Dream of You / Let's Put Out the Lights (and Go to Sleep) / Dream A Little Dream of Me / Wrap Your Troubles in Dreams / Goodnight, My Love / Brahms' Lullaby

(also Tapereel & TC; reissued UK, July 1985 [LP/TC]; reissued UK, April 1996 [CD]; reissued April 1965 [TC, coupled with THIS TIME I'M SWINGIN'])

REGAL

September 1959 **THAT'S AMORE**

I've Got My Love To Keep Me Warm / Just One More Chance / Under the Bridges of Paris / Baby, It's Cold Outside / Canadian Sunset / Who's Your Little Who-zis? / That's Amore / June In January / The Things We Did Last Summer / The Man Who Plays the Mandolino / Out In the Cold Again / When You're Smiling

CAPITOL

November 1959 **A WINTER ROMANCE**

A Winter Romance / Let it Snow! Let it Snow! Let it Snow! / The Things We Did Last Summer / I've Got My Love To Keep Me

Warm / June In January / Canadian Sunset / Winter Wonderland / Out In the Cold Again / Baby, It's Cold Outside / Rudolph the Red-Nosed Reindeer / White Christmas / It Won't Cool Off

July 1960   **BELLS ARE RINGING** (Various Artists)

Do It Yourself / Better Than A Dream (w. Judy Holliday) / I Met A Girl / Just In Time (w. Judy Holliday)

(also Tapereel; reissued World Record Club, June 1969 [LP, Tapereel, TC]; reissued Stet, 1982; reissued January 1992 [CD])

October 1960   **THIS TIME I'M SWINGIN'**

I Can't Believe You're In Love With Me / True Love / You're Nobody 'til Somebody Loves You / On the Street Where You Live / Imagination / Until the Real Thing Comes Along / Please Don't Talk About Me When I'm Gone / I've Grown Accustomed To Her Face / Someday / Mean To Me / Heaven Can Wait / Just In Time

(also Tapereel; reissued April 1965 [TC, coupled with SLEEP WARM]; reissued Starline, October 1973 [LP, TC, cartridge]; reissued November 1996 [CD, coupled with PRETTY BABY])

WORLD RECORD CLUB

February 1961   **THE DEAN SINGS**

I Ran All the Way Home / Love me, Love Me / I Know A Dream When I See One / Hanging Around With You / Never Before / Aw C'mon / Try Again / 'Til I Find You / Solitaire / You Belong To Me / Second Chance / If I Could Sing Like Bing

(reissued Music For Pleasure, November 1965)

November 1961   **THE DEAN SINGS AGAIN**

In the Cool Cool, Cool of the Evening / Baby, Obey Me! / I Love the Way You Say Goodnight / If I Should Love Again / Belle From Barcelona / Muskrat Ramble / Go Go Go Go / Just For Fun / I Don't Care If the Sun Don't Shine / My Own, My Only, My All / I'm Going To Paper All My Walls With Your Love Letters / That Lucky Old Sun

CAPITOL

Unreleased   **LOVERS IN ROME**

Just Say I Love Her / Arrivederci, Roma / My Heart Reminds Me / You're Breaking My Heart . Non Dimenticar / Return To Me / Vieni Su / On An Evening In Roma / Pardon / Take Me In Your Arms / I Have But One Heart / There's No Tomorrow

February 1962   **DINO - ITALIAN LOVE SONGS**

Just Say I Love Her / Arrivederci, Roma / My Heart Reminds Me / You're Breaking My Heart . Non Dimenticar / Return To Me / Vieni Su / On An Evening In Roma / Pardon / Take Me In Your Arms / I Have But One Heart / There's No Tomorrow

(also Tapereel, TC & cartridge; reissued UK, September 1962; reissued May 1965 [TC, coupled with CHA CHA DE AMOR]; reissued, USA January 1973; reissued January 1997 [CD, coupled with CHA CHA DE AMOR])

REPRISE

April 1962   **FRENCH STYLE**

C'est Si Bon / April In Paris / Mimi / Darling, Je Vous Aime Beaucoup / La Vie En Rose /

The Poor People of Paris / The River Seine / The Last Time I Saw Paris / Mam'selle / C'est Magnifique / Gigi / I Love Paris

(also TC & cartridge; reissued UK, May 1962; reissued 2001 [CD, coupled with DEAN LATINO])

CAPITOL

November 1962 **CHA CHA DE AMOR**

Somebody Loves You / My One and Only Love / Love (Your Magic Spell Is Everywhere) / I Wish You Love / Cha Cha Cha d'Amour / A Hundred Years From Today / I Love You Too Much / (I Love You) For Sentimental Reasons / Let Me Love You Tonight / Amor / Two Loves Have I / If Love Is Good To Me

(also Tapereel; reissued Starline, November 1971 [LP, TC, cartridge]; reissued January 1997 [CD, coupled with DEAN - ITALIAN LOVE SONGS[)

July 1962 **DEAN GOES DIXIE**

Carolina Moon / Waiting For the Robert E Lee / When It's Sleepy Time Down South / Mississipi Mud / Alabamy Bound / Dinah / Carolina In the Morning / Way Down Yonder In New Orleans / Georgia On My Mind / Just A Little Bit South of North Carolina / Basin Street Blues / Is It True What They Say About Dixie?

REPRISE

November 1962 **DINO LATINO**

Alla en le Rancho Grande / Manana / Tangerine / South of the Border / In A Little Spanish Town / What A Diff'rence A Day

310

Made / Magic Is the Moonlight / Always In My Heart / Besame Mucho / La Paloma

(also TC & cartridge; reissued UK, January 1963; reissued 2001 [CD, coupled with FRENCH STYLE])

January 1963   **DEAN 'TEX' MARTIN - COUNTRY STYLE**

I'm So Lonesome I Could Cry / Face In A Crowd / Things / Room Full of Roses / I Walk the Line / My Heart Cries For You / Anytime / Shutters and Boards / Blue, Blue Day / Singin' the Blues / Hey, Good Lookin' / Ain't Gonna Try Anymore

(also TC & cartridge; reissued UK, July 1963; reissued 2001 [CD, coupled with DEAN 'TEX' MARTIN RIDES AGAIN])

June 1963   **DEAN 'TEX' MARTIN RIDES AGAIN**

I'm Gonna Change Everything / Candy Kisses / Rockin' Alone (In An Old Rocking Chair) / Just A Little Lovin' / I Can't Help It (If I'm Still In Love With You) / My Sugar's Gone / Corrine, Corrina / Take Good Care of Her / The Middle of the Night (Is My Crying Time) / From Lover To Loser / Bouquet of Roses / Second Hand Rose

(also TC & cartridge; reissued UK, July 1973 [TC & cartridge]; reissued 2001 [CD, coupled with DEAN 'TEX' MARTIN - COUNTRY STYLE])

WORLD RECORD CLUB

June 1964   **LET'S BE FRIENDLY**

Let's Be Friendly / With My Eyes Wide Open I'm Dreaming / Rain / I Feel Like A Feather In the Breeze / Who's Your Little Who-zis? /

Let Me Go, Lover / I Feel A Song Comin' On / Be Honest With Me / Mambo Italiano / That's All I Want From You / It Looks Like Love / A Day In the Country

(compilation, design and sleeve notes by Bernard H Thorpe)

REPRISE

August 1964 | **DREAM WITH DEAN**

I'm Confessin' / Fools Rush In / I'll Buy That Dream / If You Were the Only Girl In the World / Blue Moon / Everybody Loves Somebody / I Don't Know Why (I Just Do) / Gimme A Little Kiss, Will Ya Huh? / Hands Across the Table / Smile / My Melancholy Baby / Baby, Won't You Please Come Home

(also TC & cartridge; reissued 2001 [CD, coupled with EVERYBODY LOVES SOMEBODY - THE HIT VERSION!]; reissued Sony, 2015 [CD, boxed with EVERYBODY BODY LOVES SOMEBODY / THE DOOR IS STILL OPEN TO MY HEART / HOUSTON / THE DEAN MARTIN TELEVISION SHOW])

August 1964 | **EVERYBODY LOVES SOMEBODY - THE HIT VERSION!**

Everybody Loves Somebody / Your Other Love / Shutters and Boards / Baby-O / A Little Voice / Things / My Heart Cries For You / Siesta Fiesta / From Lover To Loser / Just Close Your Eyes / Corrine Corrina / Face In A Crowd

(also TC & cartridge; reissued 2001 [CD, coupled with DREAM WITH DEAN]; reissued Sony, 2015 [CD, boxed with DREAM WITH DEAN / THE DOOR IS STILL OPEN TO MY HEART

/ HOUSTON / THE DEAN MARTIN TELEVISION SHOW*])*

October 1964 **THE DOOR IS STILL OPEN TO MY HEART**

The Door Is Still Open To My Heart / We'll Sing In the Sunshine / I'm Gonna Change Everything / The Middle of the Night (Is My Crying Time) / Every Minute, Every Hour / Clinging Vine / In the Misty Moonlight / Always Together / My Sugar's Gone / You're Nobody 'til Somebody Loves You / Take Me / So Long Baby

(also TC; reissued 2001 [CD, coupled with (REMEMBER ME) I'M THE ONE WHO LOVES YOU]; reissued Sony, 2015 [CD, boxed with DREAM WITH DEAN / EVERYBODY BODY LOVES SOMEBODY / HOUSTON / THE DEAN MARTIN TELEVISION SHOW])

CAPITOL

December 1964 **HEY BROTHER POUR THE WINE**

Hey Brother Pour the Wine / Sway / Try Again / The Man Who Plays the Mandolino / Memories Are Made of This / The Peddlerman (Ten I Loved) / Standing On the Corner / Love me, Love Me / That's What I Like / Solitaire / Just In Time

(also TC & cartridge)

REPRISE

February 1965 **DEAN MARTIN HITS AGAIN**

You're Nobody 'til Somebody Loves You / I'll Hold You In My Heart / Have A Heart / My Heart Is An Open Book / You'll Always Be the One I Love / Send Me the Pillow You

Dream On / In the Chapel In the Moonlight / Send Me Some Lovin' / Wedding Bells / I'll Be Seeing You

(also TC; reissued 2001 [CD, coupled with HOUSTON])

April 1965   **DEAN MARTIN SINGS, FRANK SINATRA CONDUCTS**

Sleep Warm / Hit the Road to Dreamland / Cuddle Up A Little Closer / Sleepy Time Gal / Goodnight Sweetheart / All I Do Is Dream of You / Let's Put Out the Lights (and Go to Sleep) / Dream A Little Dream of Me / Wrap Your Troubles in Dreams / Goodnight, My Love / Brahms' Lullaby

(reissued 1974)

CAPITOL

June 1965   **SOUTHERN STYLE**

Carolina Moon / Waiting For the Robert E Lee / When It's Sleepy Time Down South / Mississippi Mud / Alabamy Bound / Carolina In the Morning / Way Down Yonder In New Orleans / Georgia On My Mind / Just A Little Bit South of North Carolina / Basin Street Blues / Is It True What They Say About Dixie?

REPRISE

August 1965   **(REMEMBER ME) I'M THE ONE WHO LOVES YOU**

(Remember Me) I'm the One Who Loves You / King of the Road / Welcome To My World / My Shoes Keep Walking Back To You / Born To Lose / The Birds and the Bees / Walk On By / Red Roses For A Blue Lady / Take These

Chains From My Heart / Here Comes My Baby / I Don't Think You Love Me Anymore / Bumming Around

(also TC & cartridge; reissued 2001 [CD, coupled with THE DOOR IS STILL OPEN TO MY HEART])

CAPITOL

November 1965   **HOLIDAY CHEER**

Let it Snow! Let it Snow! Let it Snow! / The Things We Did Last Summer / I've Got My Love To Keep Me Warm / June In January / Canadian Sunset / Winter Wonderland / Out In the Cold Again / Baby, It's Cold Outside / Rudolph the Red-Nosed Reindeer / White Christmas / It Won't Cool Off

TOWER

November 1965   **THE LUSH YEARS**

Love Me My Love / Be An Angel / Off Again, On Again / Where Can I Go Without You? / Hear My Heart / I Never Had A Chance / Rio Bravo / (Love Is A) Career / The Story of Life / It Takes So Long

REPRISE

November 1965   **HOUSTON**

Houston / The First Thing Ev'ry Mornin' / Hammer and Nails / Little Lovely One / Love, Love, Love / Down Home / I Will / Snap Your Fingers / Everybody But Me / Old Yellow Line / Detour / You're the Reason I'm In Love

(also TC; reissued US, 2001 [CD, coupled with DEAN MARTIN HITS AGAIN]; reissued

Sony, 2015 [CD, boxed with DREAM WITH DEAN / EVERYBODY BODY LOVES SOMEBODY / THE DOOR IS STILL OPEN TO MY HEART / THE DEAN MARTIN TELEVISION SHOW])

TOWER

March 1966 **RELAXIN'**

Little Did We Know / Pennies From Heaven / In Napoli / Chee-Chee-Oo-Chee / I Want You / Sparkelin' Eyes / Cheatin' On Me / Let Me Know / How Sweet It Is / Who Was That Lady?

REPRISE

March 1966 **SOMEWHERE THERE'S A SOMEONE**

Somewhere There's A Someone / Anytime / Blue, Blue Day / I'm So Lonesome (I Could Cry) / Candy Kisses / I Can't Help It (If I'm In Still In Love With You) / That Old Clock On the Wall / Bouquet of Roses / I Walk the Line / Just A Little Lovin' / Room Full of Roses / Second Hand Rose

(also TC; reissued US, 2001 [CD, coupled with THE HIT SOUND OF DEAN MARTIN])

April 1966 **DEAN MARTIN SING SONGS FROM *THE SILENCERS***

The Glory of Love / Empty Saddles / Lovey Kravezit / The Last Round-Up / Anniversary Song / Side by Side / South of the Border / Red Sails In the Sunset / Lord, You Made the Night Too Long / If You Knew Susie / On the Sunny Side of the Street / The Silencers (instrumental)

(also TC; reissued US, 2001 [CD, coupled with THE DEAN MARTIN TELEVISION SHOW])

July 1966 **THE HIT SOUND OF DEAN MARTIN**

A Million and One / Don't Let the Blues Make You Bad / Any Time / One Lonely Boy / I'm Living In Two Worlds / Come Running Back / Shades / Today Is Not the Day / Terrible, Tangled Web / Nobody But A Fool / Ain't Gonna Try Anymore

(also TC; reissued US, 2001 [CD, coupled with SOMEWHERE THERE'S A SOMEONE])

September 1966 **DEAN MARTIN SPECIAL**

Everybody Loves Somebody / The Door Is Still Open To My Heart / You're Nobody 'til Somebody Loves You / You'll Always Be the One I Love / Send Me the Pillow You Dream On / (Remember Me) I'm the One Who Loves You / Houston / I Will / Somewhere There's A Someone / Come Running Back / It Just Happened That Way / Nobody's Baby Again

TOWER

August 1966 **HAPPY IN LOVE**

Love Is All That Matters / I Love the Way You Say Goodnight / I'll Always Love You / You I Love / All I Have To Give You / Until You Love Someone / If I Should Love Again / Rue de Mon Amour / You Were Made For Love / I'm Gonna Paper All My Walls With Your Love Letters

CAPITOL

October 1966 **THE BEST OF DEAN MARTIN**

That's Amore / You're Nobody 'til Somebody Loves You / Volare / Sway / Return To Me / Memories Are Made of This / Come Back to

Sorrento / Just In Time / I'm Yours / Hey Brother Pour the Wine / It's Easy To Remember

(also TC & cartridge; reissued US, May 1988 [CD])

REPRISE

October 1966   **THE DEAN MARTIN CHRISTMAS ALBUM**

White Christmas / Jingle Bells / I'll Be Home For Christmas / Blue Christmas / Let It Snow! Let It Snow! Let It Snow! / Marshmallow World / Silver Bells / Winter Wonderland / The Things We Did Last Summer / Silent Night

(also TC)

November 1966   *THE DEAN MARTIN TELEVISION SHOW*

If I Had You / What Can I Say After I'm Sorry / The One I Love (Belongs To Somebody Else) / S'posin' / It's the Talk of the Town / Baby, Won't You Please Come Home / I've Grown Accustomed To Her Face / Just Friends / The Things We Did Last Summer / Home

(also TC; reissued US, 2001 [CD, coupled with DEAN MARTIN SINGS SONGS FROM THE SILENCERS]; reissued Sony, 2015 [CD, boxed with DREAM WITH DEAN / EVERYBODY BODY LOVES SOMEBODY / THE DOOR IS STILL OPEN TO MY HEART / HOUSTON])

February 1967   **AT EASE WITH DEAN**

If I Had You / What Can I Say After I'm Sorry / The One I Love (Belongs To Somebody Else) / S'posin' / It's the Talk of the Town / Baby, Won't You Please Come

318

Home / I've Grown Accustomed To Her Face / Just Friends / The Things We Did Last Summer / Home

PICKWICK

January 1967 **YOU CAN'T LOVE 'EM ALL**

You Can't Love 'Em All / I'm Yours / That Lucky Old Sun / Be Honest With Me / I Still Get A Thrill Thinking of You / Who's Sorry Now? / Ain't Gonna Lead This Life / Once In Love With Amy / If / Ain't That A Kick In the Head

(also TC & cartridge)

REPRISE

November 1967 **ON THE SUNNY SIDE**

Side By Side / I Walk the Line / In the Misty Moonlight / Lay Some Happiness On Me / Release Me / In the Chapel In the Moonlight / Just A Little Lovin' / Bumming Around / Red Sails In the Sunset / You're the Reason I'm In Love / The Glory of Love / Anytime / Send Me the Pillow You Dream On / On the Sunny Side of the Street / That Old Clock On the Wall / Detour / Candy Kisses / Wallpaper Roses / South of the Border / Bouquet of Roses

STATESIDE

May 1967 **LOVE IS A CAREER**

(Love Is A) Career / If I Should Love Again / You Were Made For Love / Pennies From Heaven / Where Can I Go Without You? / How Sweet It Is / Rue de Mon Amour / Off Again, On Again / The Story of Life / It Takes So Long / Sparkelin' Eyes / Hear My Heart / Cheatin' On Me / Rio Bravo

REPRISE

May 1967 **HAPPINESS IS DEAN MARTIN**

Lay Some Happiness On Me / Think About Me / I'm Not the Marrying Kind / If I Ever Get Back to Georgia / It Just Happened That Way / (Open Up the Door) Let the Good Times In / You've Still Got A Place In My Heart / Sweet, Sweet Lovable You / He's Got You / Thirty More Miles To San Diego / Nobody's Baby Again

(also TC; reissued US, 2001 [CD, couple with WELCOME TO MY WORLD]; reissued US, 2009 [CD])

August 1967 **WELCOME TO MY WORLD**

In the Chapel In the Moonlight / Release Me / I Can't Help Remembering You / Turn To Me / Wallpaper Roses / Little Ole Wine Drinker, Me / The Green, Green Grass of Home / A Place In the Shade / Pride / Welcome To My World

(also TC; reissued US, 2001 [CD, coupled with HAPPINESS IS DEAN MARTIN])

TOWER

August 1967 **DINO - LIKE NEVER BEFORE**

I Ran All the Way Home / What Could Be More Beautiful? / Second Chance / There's My Lover / 'Til I Find You / Never Before / Try Again / Beside You / That's What I Like

CAPITOL

October 1967 **THE DEAN MARTIN DELUXE SET**

Just Say I Love Her / Arrivederci, Roma / My Heart Reminds Me / You're Breaking My

Heart . Non Dimenticar / Return To Me /
Vieni Su / On An Evening In Roma / Pardon /
Take Me In Your Arms / I Have But One
Heart / There's No Tomorrow / Hey Brother
Pour the Wine / Sway / Try Again / The Man
Who Plays the Mandolino / Memories Are
Made of This / The Peddlerman (Ten I
Loved) / Standing On the Corner / Love me,
Love Me / That's What I Like / Solitaire / Just
In Time / That's Amore / You're Nobody 'til
Somebody Loves You / Volare / It's Easy To
Remember / June In January / Come Back To
Sorrento / I'm Yours / Write To Me From
Naples / Don't You Remember? / The Look /
Buona Sera

REPRISE

May 1968

DEAN MARTIN'S GREATEST HITS VOLUME ONE

Everybody Loves Somebody / You're
Nobody 'til Somebody Loves You / In the
Chapel In the Moonlight / Houston /
(Remember Me) I'm the One Who Loves You
/ I Can't Help Remembering You / Nobody's
Baby Again / Every Minute, Every Hour /
Bumming Around / You'll Always Be the
One I Love / Come Running Back / The Birds
and the Bees

(also TC & cartridge)

August 1968

DEAN MARTIN'S GREATEST HITS VOLUME TWO

The Door Is Still Open To My Heart / I Will /
Send Me the Pillow You Dream On / Little
Ole Wine Drinker, Me / You've Still Got A
Place In My Heart / In the Misty Moonlight /
Lay Some Happiness On Me / (Open Up the

Door) Let the Good Times In / Somewhere There's A Someone / The Glory of Love / Old Yellow Line / King of the Road

(also TC & cartridge)

December 1968   **GENTLE ON MY MIND**

Not Enough Indians / That Old Time Feelin' / That's When I See the Blues / Welcome To My Heart / Drowning In My Tears / Honey / By the Time I Get To Phoenix / Gentle On My Mind / Rainbows Are Back In Style / April Again

(also TC & cartridge; reissued US, 2001 [CD, coupled with I TAKE A LOT OF PRIDE IN WHAT I AM])

PICKWICK

January 1969   **I CAN'T GIVE YOU ANYTHING BUT LOVE**

I Can't Give You Anything But Love / Innamorata / All In A Night's Work / You Look So Familiar / It Looks Like Love / Just One More Chance / When You're Smiling / When You Pretend / The Test of Time / A Day In the Country

(also TC & cartridge)

January 1969   **YOUNG AND FOOLISH**

Young and Foolish / Oh Marie / Little Did We Know / Pennies From Heaven / Let Me Go, Lover / That's All I Want From You / In the Cool, Cool, Cool of the Evening / Rain / Absence Makes the Heart Grow Fonder

(also TC & cartridge)

January 1969   **DEAN MARTIN SWINGIN'!**

You Can't Love 'Em All / I'm Yours / That Lucky Old Sun / Be Honest With Me / I Still Get A Thrill Thinking of You / Who's Sorry Now? / Ain't Gonna Lead This Life / Once In Love With Amy / If / Ain't That A Kick In the Head / I Can't Give You Anything But Love / Innamorata / All In A Night's Work / You Look So Familiar / It Looks Like Love / Just One More Chance / When You're Smiling / When You Pretend / The Test of Time / A Day In the Country

CAPITOL

January 1969   **THE BEST OF DEAN MARTIN VOLUME TWO**

Just Say I Love Her / If Love Is Good To Me / Standing On the Corner / Vieni Su / Cha Cha Cha d'Amour / Arrivederci, Roma / I've Grown Accustomed To Her Face / Canadian Sunset / Pretty Baby / My One and Only Love

(also TC & cartridge)

January 1969   **DEAN MARTIN FAVOURITES**

Who's Your Little Who-zis? / I'm Yours / I Feel A Song Comin' On / With My Eyes Wide Open I'm Dreaming / Just Once More Chance / Louise / I Feel Like A Feather In the Breeze / Come Back To Sorrento / Oh Marie / That's Amore / When You're Smiling

February 1969   **THE BEST OF DEAN MARTIN**

Volare / Sway / Memories Are Made of This / Please Don't Talk About Me When I'm Gone / I'm Yours / Pretty Baby / That's Amore / Come Back To Sorrento / Just In Time /

Dream A Little Dream of Me / Sleepy Time
Gal / Arrivederci, Roma / Non Dimenticar /
You're Nobody 'til Somebody Loves You /
My One and Only Love / Return To Me

(also TC & cartridge)

MUSIC FOR PLEASURE

March 1969   **DEAN OF MUSIC**

I've Got My Love To Keep Me Warm / Just
One More Chance / Under the Bridges of
Paris / Baby, It's Cold Outside / Canadian
Sunset / Who's Your Little Who-zis? / That's
Amore / June In January / The Things We
Did Last Summer / The Man Who Plays the
Mandolino / Out In the Cold Again / When
You're Smiling

REPRISE

August 1969   **I TAKE A LOT OF PRIDE IN WHAT I AM**

I Take A Lot of Pride In What I Am / Make It
Rain / Where the Blue and Lonely Go / If You
Ever Get Around To Loving Me / Do You
Believe This Town / One Cup of Happiness
(and One Piece of Mind) / The Sun Is Shinin'
(On Everybody But Me) / The Sneaky Little
Side of Me / Crying Time / Little Green
Apples

*(also TC; reissued US, 2001 [CD, coupled with
GENTLE ON MY MIND])*

October 1969   **THE DEAN MARTIN SONGBOOK
(VOLUMES 1 & 2)**

Honey / Nobody But A Fool / Corrine
Corrina / Wedding Bells / Here Comes My
Baby / I'm Gonna Change Everything / What
Can I Say After I Say I'm Sorry? / Everybody

But Me / Pride / Little Green Apples / Red
Roses For A Blue Lady / I'm So Lonesome I
Could Cry / If I Had You / Crying Time / I'll
Be Seeing You / Release Me / We'll Sing In
the Sunshine / Room Full of Roses / My
Heart Cries For You / Anytime

CAPITOL

October 1969 **DEAN MARTIN'S GREATEST!**

That's Amore / You're Nobody 'til Somebody
Loves You / Volare / Sway / Return To Me /
Memories Are Made of This / Come Back to
Sorrento / Just In Time / Hey Brother Pour
the Wine

October 1969 **THE BEST OF DEAN MARTIN VOLUME
TWO**

Cha Cha Cha d'Amour / Buona Sera / You're
Breaking My Heart / Standing On the Corner
/ Mean To Me / Vieni Su / Cuddle Up A Little
Closer / Is It True What They Say About
Dixie? / I've Got My Love To Keep Me Warm
/ The Things We Did Last Summer / I Can't
Believe That You're In Love With Me /
Somebody Loves You / On An Evening In
Roma / I Feel A Song Comin' On / Hey
Brother Pour the Wine / Wrap Your Troubles
In Dreams

(also TC & cartridge)

WORLD RECORD CLUB

January 1970 **THE DEAN MARTIN 6 LP COLLECTION**

You're Nobody 'til Somebody Loves You / I
Can't Believe That You're In Love With Me /
Canadian Sunset / In the Cool, Cool, Cool of
the Evening / Memories Are Made of This /

Return To Me / On the Street Where You Live / You Can't Love 'Em All / Volare / Alabamy Bound / Just In Time / It Takes So Long / Imagination / Mississippi Mud / Basin Street Blues / True Love / Sleepy Time Gal / Louise / If / When You're Smiling / Cuddle Up A Little Closer / Let Me Love You Tonight / Who's Sorry Now? / Innamorata / Way Down Yonder In New Orleans / Hit the Road to Dreamland / Two Loves Have I / The Object of My Affection / It's Easy To Remember / That's All I Want From You / All I Do I Dream of You / Take Me In Your Arms / All In A Night's Work / I Don't Know Why (I Just Do) / Money Burns A Hole In My Pocket / Good Night Sweetheart / (Love) Your Magic Spell Is Everywhere / I Feel A Song Comin' On / How Do You Speak To An Angel? / I Feel Like A Feather In the Breeze / A Hundred Years From Today / Goodnight, My Love / That's Amore / Rain / Watching the World Go By / Wrap Your Troubles In Dreams / I've Grown Accustomed To Her Face / Hear My Heart / With My Eyes Wide Open I'm Dreaming / Captured / Nevertheless (I'm In Love With You) / I Can't Give You Anything But Love / Young and Foolish / June In January / Brahms' Lullaby / Once In A While / When It's Sleepy Time Down South / That Lucky Old Sun

(compilation by Bernard H Thorpe)

(also TC; reissued September 1981 [4xLP])

PICKWICK

March 1970

YOU WERE MADE FOR LOVE

The Object of My Affection / You Were Made For Love / Come Back To Sorrento / Cheatin'

On Me / Until You Love Someone / I Love the Way You Say Goodnight / Let Me Know / I'll Always Love You / You I Love

(also TC & cartridge)

CAPITOL

March 1970

RETURN TO ME /

YOU'RE NOBODY 'TIL SOMEBODY LOVES YOU

Just Say I Love Her / Arrivederci, Roma / You're Breaking My Heart / Non Dimenticar / Return To Me / Vieni Su / On An Evening In Roma / Take Me In Your Arms / I Have But One Heart / There's No Tomorrow / I Can't Believe You're In Love With Me / True Love / You're Nobody 'til Somebody Loves You / On the Street Where You Live / Imagination / Please Don't Talk About Me When I'm Gone / I've Grown Accustomed To Her Face / Someday / Mean To Me / Just In Time

(also TC & cartridge)

July 1970

YOU'RE NOBODY 'TIL SOMEBODY LOVES YOU

I Can't Believe You're In Love With Me / True Love / You're Nobody 'til Somebody Loves You / On the Street Where You Live / Imagination / Please Don't Talk About Me When I'm Gone / I've Grown Accustomed To Her Face / Someday / Mean To Me / Just In Time

July 1970

RETURN TO ME

Just Say I Love Her / Arrivederci, Roma / You're Breaking My Heart . Non Dimenticar

/ Return To Me / Vieni Su / On An Evening In Roma / Take Me In Your Arms / I Have But One Heart / There's No Tomorrow

MUSIC FOR PLEASURE

July 1970   **HEY BROTHER POUR THE WINE**

I Feel A Song Comin' On / Mississippi Dreamboat / Let Me Go, Lover / Louise / Let's Be Friendly / Forgetting You / Hey Brother Pour the Wine / Be Honest With Me / Young and Foolish / On An Evening In Roma / I Can't Give You Anything But Love / Watching the World Go By

REPRISE

August 1970   **MY WOMAN, MY WOMAN, MY WIFE**

My Woman, My Woman, My Wife / Once A Day / Here We Go Again / Make the World Go Away / The Tips of My Fingers / Detroit City / Together Again / Heart Over Mind / Turn the World Around / It Keeps Right On A-Hurtin'

(also TC & cartridge; reissued US, 2001 [CD, coupled with FOR THE GOOD TIMES])

WORLD RECORD CLUB

October 1970   **ONE MORE TIME**

One More Time / If / Winter Wonderland / Let It Snow! Let It Snow! Let It Snow! / I'll Always Love You / Happy Feet / Bye Bye Blackbird / Come Back To Sorrento / Oh Marie / A Winter Romance / I'm Yours / Luna Mezzo Mare

VALIANT

Unreleased

(UNTITLED)

C'est Si Bon / April In Paris / Mimi / Darling, Je Vouse Aime Beaucoup / La Vie En Rose / The Poor People of Paris / South of the Border / Red Sails In the Sunset / The Glory of Love / If You Knew Susie / Side By Side / On the Sunny Side of the Street

LONGINES

December 1970

MEMORIES ARE MADE OF THIS

Memories Are Made of This / I Feel A Song Comin' On / It's Easy To Remember / All I Do Is Dream of You / On the Street Where You Live / A Hundred Years From Today / Take Me In Your Arms / Let's Put Out the Lights / When You're Smiling / Cuddle Up A Little Closer / Please Don't Talk About Me When I'm Gone / That's All I Want From You / Volare / Innamorata / Once In A While / Mississippi Mud / True Love / Only Forever / Louise / Pretty Baby / Hear My Heart / If / June In January / Alabamy Bound / Imagination / You're Nobody 'til Somebody Loves You / In the Cool, Cool, Cool of the Evening / I Can't Give You Anything But Love / Way Down Yonder In New Orleans / Hit the Road to Dreamland / Love (Your Magic Spell Is Everywhere) / I Can't Believe That You're In Love With Me) / The Object of My Affection / Wrap Your Troubles In Dreams / I've Grown Accustomed To Her Face / I Feel Like A Feather In the Breeze / With My Eyes Wide Open I'm Dreaming / Until the Real Thing Comes Along / Return

To Me / Arrivederci, Roma / Young and Foolish / Good Night Sweetheart / Two Loves Have I / Canadian Sunset / Brahms' Lullaby / Basin Street Blues / Sleep Time Gal / Goodnight, My Love / Heaven Can Wait / That Lucky Old Sun / That's Amore / Somebody Loves You / Who's Sorry Now? / Rain / Pennies From Heaven / Just In Time / Carolina In the Morning / Nevertheless (I'm In Love With You) / When It's Sleepy Time Down South / Watching the World Go By

REPRISE

February 1971 **FOR THE GOOD TIMES**

For the Good Times / Marry Me / Georgia Sunshine / Invisible Tears / Raindrops Keep Fallin' On My Head / A Perfect Mountain / Raining In My Heart / She's A Little Bit Country / For Once In My Life / Sweetheart

(also TC & cartridge; reissued US, 2001 [CD, coupled with MY WOMAN, MY WOMAN, MY WIFE)

MUSIC FOR PLEASURE

March 1971 **NAT, DEAN AND FRIENDS**

Open Up the Doghouse (w. Nat 'King' Cole) / Relax-Ay-Voo (w. Line Renaud) / Ev'ry Street's A Boulevard (In Old New York) (w. Jerry Lewis) / You Was (w. Peggy Lee) / Long, Long Ago (w. Nat 'King' Cole) / Don't Rock the Boat (w. Margaret Whiting) / We Never Talk Much (w. Helen O'Connell) / Two Sleepy People (w. Line Renaud)

REPRISE

October 1971 **DEAN MARTIN COUNTRY!**

Welcome To My World / Heart Over Mind / She's A Little Bit Country / Take These

Chains From My Heart / Candy Kisses / I Walk the Line / I'll Hold You In My Heart / My Shoes Keep Walkin' Back To You / I'm Living In Two Worlds / King of the Road / Bouquet of Roses / Send Me the Pillow You Dream On / I Take A Lot of Pride In What I Am / The Tips of My Fingers / The Green, Green Grass of Home / Gentle On My Mind / The First Thing (Ev'ry Mornin') / Make the World Go Away / Blue, Blue Day / Walk On By

MUSIC FOR PLEASURE

October 1971 **WHITE CHRISTMAS**

WITH NAT 'KING' COLE AND DEAN MARTIN

Winter Wonderland / White Christmas / Brahms' Lullaby / Rudolph the Red-Nosed Reindeer / The Christmas Blues / Let It Snow! Let It Snow! Let It Snow!

(reissued 1979; reissued 1990 [CD & TC]; reissued 1995 [CD])

REPRISE

January 1972 **DINO**

What's Yesterday? / The Small Exception of Me / Just the Other Side of Nowhere / Blue Memories / Guess Who / Party Dolls and Wine / I Don't Know What I'm Doing / I Can Give You What You Want Now / The Right Kind of Woman / Kiss the World Goodbye

(also TC & cartridge; reissued US, 2001 [CD, coupled with YOU'RE THE BEST THING THAT EVER HAPPENED TO ME])

PICKWICK

February 1972   **I HAVE BUT ONE HEART**

I Have But One Heart / Don't You Remember? / Return To Me / My One and Only Love / A Hundred Years From today / Standing On the Corner / Imagination / Non Dimenticar / If Love Is Good To Me

(reissued 1973 [2xLP gatefold, with DEAN MARTIN! DELUXE!])

February 1972   **DEAN MARTIN! DELUXE!**

I Can't Believe You're In Love With Me / True Love / On the Street Where You Live / Imagination / Until the Real Thing Comes Along / Please Don't Talk About Me When I'm Gone / I've Grown Accustomed To Her Face / Someday / Heaven Can Wait / Just In Time

(reissued 1973 [2xLP gatefold, with I HAVE BUT ONE HEART])

REPRISE

December 1972   **THE MOST BEAUTIFUL SONGS OF DEAN MARTIN**

Houston / My Heart Is An Open Book / Shades / Release Me / Gentle On My Mind / The Green, Green Grass of Home / Red Roses For A Blue Lady / Blue Moon / Gigi / April in Paris / By the Time I Get To Phoenix / Fools Rush In / C'est Si Bon / Baby, Won't You Please Come Home? / Things / (Open Up the Door) Let the Good Times In / Everybody Loves Somebody / King of the Road / My Woman, My Woman, My Wife / Welcome To My World / Rainbows Are Back

In Style / Lay Some Happiness On Me / Send
Me the Pillow You Dream On

(also TC & cartridge)

May 1973

SITTIN' ON TOP OF THE WORLD

I'm Sittin' On Top of the World / I Wonder
Who's Kissing Her Now / Smile / Ramblin'
Rose / Almost Like Being In Love / It's A
Good Day / At Sundown / When the Red,
Red Robin Comes Bob, Bob, Bobbin' Along /
You Made Me Love You (I Didn't Want To
Do It) / I'm Forever Blowing Bubbles

*(also TC & cartridge; reissued US, 2001 [CD,
coupled with ONCE IN A WHILE])*

December 1973

**YOU'RE THE BEST THING THAT EVER
HAPPENED TO ME**

Free To Carry On / You're the Best Thing
That Ever Happened To Me / I'm Confessin'
/ Amor Mio / You Better Move On / Tie A
Yellow Ribbon / Baby, Won't You Please
Come Home / I Don't Know Why (I Love
You Like I Do) / Gimme A Little Kiss, Will Ya
Huh! / Get On With Your Livin'

*(also TC & cartridge; reissued US, 2001 [CD,
coupled with DINO])*

CAPITOL

December 1973

THE VERY BEST OF DEAN MARTIN

Return To Me / Angel Baby / Volare / Rio
Bravo / Hey Brother Pour the Wine / I've Got
My Love To Keep Me Warm / That's Amore /
Memories Are Made of This / Baby, It's Cold
Outside / Buona Sera / Good Night
Sweetheart / Come Back To Sorrento / Write
Me From Naples / June In January / Cha Cha
Cha d'Amour / I Have But One Heart

(also TC & cartridge; reissued 1983; reissued 1985 [LP & CD]; reissued January 1998 [CD])

July 1975 **MEMORIES ARE MADE OF THIS**

Memories Are Made of This / That's Amore / Volare / Makin' Love Ukulele Style / Let Me Go, Lover / Two Sleepy People / Arrivederci, Roma / I Love the Way You Say Goodnight / Just One More Chance / Solitaire / I've Got My Love To Keep Me Warm / Wrap Your Troubles In Dreams / Nevertheless / Just In Time / Dream A Little Dream of Me / Don't You Remember? / A Hundred Years From Today / There's No Tomorrow / That Lucky Old Sun / Innamorata

(released as part of the UK's Kodak national photographic competition for 1975; compilation by Bernard H Thorpe)

(also TC & cartridge; reissued Music For Pleasure, October 1981)

MUSIC FOR PLEASURE

September 1975 **WHEN YOU'RE SMILING**

When You're Smiling / Just Say I Love Her / You're Breaking My Heart / My Heart Reminds Me / There's No Tomorrow / That's Amore / You're Nobody 'til Somebody Loves You / Buona Sera / Take Me In Your Arms / I Have But One Heart / Return To Me / Arrivederci, Roma

(also TC)

REPRISE

October 1976 **TWENTY ORIGINAL DEAN MARTIN HITS**

Everybody Loves Somebody / Corrine Corrina / Things / Houston / Lay Some

Happiness On Me / In the Chapel In the Moonlight / Little Ole Wine Drinker, Me / The Birds and the Bees / King of the Road / Send Me the Pillow You Dream On / I'm Sittin' On Top of the World / You're Nobody 'til Somebody Loves You / That's When I See the Blues / Tie A Yellow Ribbon / The Green, Green Grass of Home / The Door Is Still Open To My Heart / Ramblin' Rose / Amor Mio / In the Misty Moonlight / Detroit City

(compilation by Dean Martin & Bernard H Thorpe, design by Bernard H Thorpe)

(also TC)

August 1978 **ONCE IN A WHILE**

Twilight On the Trail / Love Thy Neighbour / Without A Word of Warning / That Old Gang of Mine / The Day You Came Along / It's Magic / If I Had You / Only Forever / I Cried For You / Once In A While

(also TC & cartridge; reissued US, 2001 [CD, coupled with SITTIN' ON TOP OF THE WORLD])

TEEVEE

September 1978 **TWENTY GREAT HITS**

Memories Are Made of This / That's Amore / I've Grown Accustomed To Her Face / Just Say I Love Her / All I Do Is Dream of You / Volare / Standing On the Corner / Just In Time / You Belong To Me / Angel Baby / You're Nobody 'til Somebody Loves You / Cha Cha Cha d'Amour / Dream A Little Dream of Me / I'll Always Love You / It's Easy To Remember / When You're Smiling / Return To Me / Sway / Someday / Dream

(reissued Goodmusic, 2001 [CD only])

CAPITOL

June 1979

THE CLASSIC DINO

Watching the World Go By / The Lucky Song / Simpatico / In Napoli / I'm Gonna Steal You Away / Giuggiola / How Do You Speak To An Angel? / What Could Be More Beautiful? / Me'n'You'n'the Moon / If / Where Can I Go Without You? / Be An Angel / Money Burn A Hole In My Pocket / Only Trust Your Heart / You Belong To Me / Good Mornin' Life

(compilation by Bernard H Thorpe)

(also TC)

HEARTLAND

1980

GOLDEN MEMORIES

I Don't Know Why / Someday / When You're Smiling / I've Grown Accustomed To Her Face / True Love / That's Amore / Once In A While / Innamorata / Non Dimenticar / Volare / You Belong To Me / Just Say I Love Her / Dream A Little Dream of Me / Just In Time / Return To Me / Come Back To Sorrento / You're Nobody 'til Somebody Loves You / Dream / Standing On the Corner / You're Breaking My Heart / Memories Are Made of This / I'll Always Love You

SEARS

1980

I'M YOURS

You Can't Love 'Em All / I'm Yours / That Lucky Old Sun / Be Honest With Me / I Still Get A Thrill Thinking of You / Who's Sorry Now? / Ain't Gonna Lead This Life / Once In Love With Amy / If / Ain't That A Kick In the Head

1980	**JUST ONE MORE CHANCE**

I Can't Give You Anything But Love / Innamorata / All In A Night's Work / You Look So Familiar / It Looks Like Love / Just One More Chance / When You're Smiling / When You Pretend / The Test of Time / A Day In the Country

1980	**I'LL ALWAYS LOVE YOU**

The Object of My Affection / You Were Made For Love / Come Back To Sorrento / Cheatin' On Me / Until You Love Someone / I Love the Way You Say Goodnight / Let Me Know / I'll Always Love You / You I Love

CAPITOL

1982	**ALL I DO IS DREAM OF YOU**

I've Grown Accustomed To Her Face / Just In Time / Imagination / Nevertheless / You're Nobody 'til Somebody Loves You / All I Do Is Dream of You / You Belong To Me / Once In A While

WARNER BROS.

June 1983	**THE NASHVILLE SESSIONS**

Old Bones / Everybody's Had the Blues / Don't Give Up On Me / In Love Up To My Heart / Shoulder To Shoulder / Since I Met You Baby / My First Country Song / Drinking Champagne / Hangin' Around / Love Put A Song in My Heart

(also TC)

Due to the sheer number of compilations that appeared from 1983, a selection are included hereafter by title only, or detailed if a major or unusual release.

PAIR

September 1983 **DREAMS AND MEMORIES**

SUFFOLK

1984 **HEART TOUCHING TREASURY**

1984 **FAMOUS LOVE SONGS**

CAPITOL

1984 **DEAN MARTIN SINGS ITALIAN FAVOURITES**

1986 **GREATEST HITS!**

(TC only)

PAIR

1986 **HAPPY HOUR WITH DEAN MARTIN**

(CD only)

CAPITOL

May 1998 **YOU'RE NOBODY 'TIL SOMEBODY LOVES YOU**

(TC only)

SILVER EAGLE

1988 **GREATEST HITS**

(CD only; also issued 1988 [LP only, coupled with FAVOURITE SONGS])

1988 **FAVOURITE SONGS**

(CD only; also issued 1988 [LP only, coupled with GREATEST HITS])

CAPITOL

January 1989 **CAPITOL COLLECTOR'S SERIES**

(CD only)

January 1989   **THE BEST OF THE CAPITOL YEARS**

That's Amore / Kiss / Memories Are Made of This / Sway / Money Burns A Hole In My Pocket/ Hey Brother Pour the Wine / The Naughty Lady of Shady Lane / The Man Who Plays the Mandolino / Mambo Italiano / Innamorata / Volare / Relax-Ay-Voo (w. Line Renaud) / All In A Night's Work / Return To Me / Cha Cha Cha d'Amour / Just In Time

(compilation by Alan Dell & Bernard H Thorpe; sleeve notes by Bernard H Thorpe)

(also CD & TC; reissued March 2003 [CD only, as THE ESSENTIAL DEAN MARTIN])

November 1989   **A WINTER ROMANCE**

A Winter Romance / Let it Snow! Let it Snow! Let it Snow! / The Things We Did Last Summer / I've Got My Love To Keep Me Warm / June In January / Canadian Sunset / Winter Wonderland / Out In the Cold Again / Baby, It's Cold Outside / Rudolph the Red-Nosed Reindeer / White Christmas / It Won't Cool Off / The Christmas Blues

(CD only)

July 1990   **THE GREATEST HITS OF DEAN MARTIN**

(CD only)

1991   **SWINGIN' DOWN YONDER**

Carolina Moon / Waiting For the Robert E Lee / When It's Sleepy Time Down South / Mississipi Mud / Alabamy Bound / Dinah / Carolina In the Morning / Way Down Yonder In New Orleans / Georgia On My Mind / Just A Little Bit South of North Carolina / Basin

Street Blues / Is It True What They Say About Dixie? / Hominy Grits / I'm Gonna Paper All My Walls With Your Love Letters / Muskrat Ramble / Be Honest With Me / I Don't Care If the Sun Don't Shine / Bye Bye Blackbird / Happy Feet / Darktown Strutters Ball

(CD & TC only)

MUSIC FOR PLEASURE

August 1994   **THE SINGLES**

(conception and compilation by Gerald Mahlowe with Bernard H Thorpe)

(CD & TC only; reissued July 2001)

CAPITOL

July 1995   **GREAT GENTLEMEN OF SONG:**
SPOTLIGHT ON DEAN MARTIN

(CD only)

RADIO SPIRITS

October 1995   *THE MARTIN AND LEWIS SHOW*

18 original shows from 1949, with guests: Lucille Ball, William Bendix, Peter Lorre, Madeleine Carroll, Burl Ives, Arthur Treacher, John Garfield, Henry Fonda, Marilyn Maxwell, Tony Martin, John Carradine, Ralph Bellamy, Frances Longford, William Boyd, Burt Lancaster, Victor Moore, Billie Burke and Jane Russell

(released with permission from Jerry Lewis)

(CD & TC only)

CHARLY

January 1996   **THE BEST OF DEAN MARTIN 1962-1968**

(CD only)

CAPITOL

August 1996   **THE CAPITOL YEARS**

(CD only)

April 1996   **THE BEST OF DEAN MARTIN – THAT'S AMORE**

(CD only)

CHARLY

August 1996   **DEAN MARTIN SINGS THE ALL-TIME HITS**

(compilation by Bernard H Thorpe)

(CD only)

December 1996   **DINO – THE GOLDEN YEARS**

(songs selected in consultation with Bernard H Thorpe)

(CD only)

RETRO

1997   **THE GOLD COLLECTION - 40 CLASSIC PERFORMANCES**

(CD only)

CHARLY

1997 (unreleased)   **FAR AWAY PLACES WITH DINO**

From Georgia To Rome – The Long Route: Georgia Sunshine / South of the Border / Darling, Je Vous Aime Beaucoup / (Alla En) Rancho Grande / The Poor People of Paris /

Detroit City / Magic Is the Moonlight / Amor Mio / C'est Magnifique / La Paloma / From the Bottom of My Heart / Siesta Fiesta / Besame Mucho / The River Seine / Manana / Houston / Mimi / Senza Fine / Tangerine / Mama Roma. **Here, There – But Not Everywhere:** In A Little Spanish Town / La Vie En Rose / Grazie, Prego, Scusie / What A Diff'rence A Day Made / April In Paris / By the Time I Get To Phoenix / Gigi / Via Veneto / C'est Si Bon / South of the Border (from *The Silencers*) / I Love Paris / Thirty More Miles To San Diego . La Giostra / If I Ever Get Back To Georgia / Dame Su Amor / The Last Time I Saw Paris / Just Close Your Eyes / Mam'selle / Tik-A-Tee, Tik-A-Tay / Always In My Heart

(compilation by Bernard H Thorpe)

(CD only)

RANWOOD

May 1997   **LOVE SONGS BY DEAN MARTIN**

(CD only)

READER'S DIGEST

June 1997   **THE CAPITOL YEARS**

(CD only)

CAPITOL

October 1997   **THE BEST OF DEAN MARTIN**

(CD only)

November 1998   **A WINTER ROMANCE**

([not the studio album] CD & TC; reissued September 2003 [CD only]; reissued 2003 [CD only, couple with SINGLES])

CASTLE

August 1998   **THE DEAN MARTIN COLLECTION**

(also CD & TC)

CAPITOL

November 1998   **MAKING SPIRITS BRIGHT!**

(CD only; reissued 2002 [CD only, boxed with HURTIN' COUNTRY SONGS])

October 1998   **THE VERY BEST OF DEAN MARTIN:**

THE CAPITOL AND REPRISE YEARS

(songs selected in consultation with Bernard H Thorpe)

(CD & TC; reissued 2003 [CD only, coupled with THE VERY BEST OF DEAN MARTIN: THE CAPITOL AND REPRISE YEARS – VOLUME TWO])

JOKER

August 1999   **AGAIN**

(compilation by Bernard H Thorpe)

(CD only)

CAPITOL

October 1999   **LATE AT NIGHT WITH DEAN MARTIN**

(CD only)

October 1999   **HURTIN' COUNTRY SONGS**

(CD only; reissued 2002 [CD only, boxed with MAKING SPIRITS BRIGHT])

August 2000   **THE VERY BEST OF DEAN MARTIN:**

THE CAPITOL AND REPRISE YEARS – VOLUME TWO

(songs selected in consultation with Bernard H Thorpe)

(CD & TC; reissued 2003 [CD only, coupled with THE VERY BEST OF DEAN MARTIN: THE CAPITOL AND REPRISE YEARS])

JOKER

September 2000   **SOMEONE LIKE YOU**

(compilation by Bernard H Thorpe)

(CD only)

CAPITOL

2001   **EEE-0 ELEVEN – THE BEST OF THE RAT PACK**

Ain't That A Kick In the Head / Volare / Sam's Song (w. Sammy Davis Jr) / When You're Smiling / You're Nobody 'til Somebody Loves You / Sittin' On Top of the World

(CD only)

2001   **THE RAT PACK LIVE AT THE SANDS**

Medley: Drink To Me Only-I Don't Care If the Sun Don't Shine-I Love Vegas / monologue / June In January / monologue / Via Veneto / Medley: Volare-On An Evening In Roma / Dialogue (w. Frank Sinatra) / Medley (w. Frank Sinatra): Marianne-Dance With A Dolly-You Are Too Beautiful-You Made Me Love You-Carolina In the Morning-Beautiful Dreamer-Dancing With Tears In My Eyes-Maria-Try A Little Tenderness-What Is This Thing Called Love / Dialogue (w. Frank Sinatra and Sammy Davis Jr) / Guys and Dolls (w. Frank Sinatra) / The Oldest Established (Permanent Floating Crap Game In New York) (w. Frank Sinatra) / Introductions (w. Frank Sinatra and Sammy Davis Jr) / The Oldest Established

(Permanent Floating Crap Game In New York) (w. Frank Sinatra and Sammy Davis Jr)

(CD only)

February 2002 **LOVE SONGS**

(CD only)

DEMON MUSIC

2003 **A NIGHT ON THE TOWN WITH THE RAT PACK**

(CD only)

EMI

July 2003 **DEAN MARTIN AND JERRY LEWIS**

(CD only)

CAPITOL

September 2003 **CHRISTMAS TOGETHER:**

NAT 'KING' COLE AND DEAN MARTIN

(CD only)

November 2003 **THE DEAN MARTIN COLLECTION**

Kiss / That's Amore / You Belong To Me / Who's Sorry Now? / Powder Your Face With Sunshine / Just For Fun / In the Cool, Cool, Cool of the Evening / That Lucky Old Sun / Rain / When You're Smiling / I'm Gonna Paper All My Walls With Your Love Letters / Bye Bye Blackbird / Wham! Bam! Thank You Mam! / If / Oh Marie / Luna Mezzo Mare / Solitaire / Blue Smoke / I Know A Dream When I See One / 'Til I Find You / Come Back To Sorrento / Hey Brother Pour the Wine

(compilation by Bernard H Thorpe)

(CD only, exclusive to HMV stores)

EMPORIO

2004 **THE ESSENTIAL DEAN MARTIN**

(CD only)

CAPITOL

September 2004 **DINO – THE ESSENTIAL DEAN MARTIN**

Ain't That A Kick In the Head / That's Amore / Memories Are Made of This / Just In Time / Sway / I'd Cry Like A Baby / Volare / Under the Bridges of Paris / Love Me, Love Me / If / Mambo Italiano / Let Me Go, Lover / Standing On the Corner / You Belong To Me / Powder Your Face With Sunshine / Innamorata / I'll Always Love You / Kiss / You're Nobody 'til Somebody Loves You / Return To Me / The Door Is Still Open To My Heart / Houston / Send Me the Pillow You Dream On / Everybody Loves Somebody / In the Chapel In the Moonlight / I Will / Little Ole Wine Drinker, Me / Somewhere There's A Someone / In the Misty Moonlight / Gentle On My Mind

(CD only; reissued May 2005 with bonus DVD 'That's Amore')

November 2004 **CHRISTMAS WITH DINO**

Let It Snow! Let It Snow! Let It Snow! / White Christmas / Silver Bells / I've Got My Love To Keep Me Warm / Winter Wonderland / Baby, It's Cold Outside / Blue Christmas / Jingle Bells / A Winter Romance / Marshmallow World / The Christmas Blues / Rudolph the Red-Nosed Reindeer / Silent Night / I'll Be Home For Christmas / Let It Snow! Let It Snow! Let It Snow! / Winter Wonderland / White Christmas

(CD only)

May 2005

LIVE FROM LAS VEGAS

Introduction / Everybody Loves Somebody / Drink To Me Only / Pennies From Heaven / Hello Dolly / monologue / June In January / Everybody Loves Somebody / Baby Face / That's Amore / monologue / Try A Little Tenderness / Love Walked In / Cecilia / Me and My Gal / Swing Low, Sweet Chariot / My Heart Sings / There's No Tomorrow / It Was A Very Good Year / You Made Me Love You / It Had To Be You / Nevertheless (I'm In Love With You) / Welcome To My World / If You Knew Susie / Volare / On An Evening In Roma / monologue / theme / closing theme

(CD only)

May 2005

DINO – THE ESSENTIAL DEAN MARTIN
[SPECIAL PLATINUM EDITION]

Ain't That A Kick In the Head / That's Amore / Memories Are Made of This / Just In Time / Sway / I'd Cry Like A Baby / Volare / Under the Bridges of Paris / Love Me, Love Me / If / Mambo Italiano / Let Me Go, Lover / Standing On the Corner / You Belong To Me / Powder Your Face With Sunshine / Innamorata / I'll Always Love You / Kiss / You're Nobody 'til Somebody Loves You / Return To Me / The Door Is Still Open To My Heart / Houston / Send Me the Pillow You Dream On / Everybody Loves Somebody / In the Chapel In the Moonlight / I Will / Little Ole Wine Drinker, Me / Somewhere There's A Someone / In the Misty Moonlight / Gentle On My Mind / Drink To Me Only / Almost Like Being In Love / I Love Paris / My Kind of Girl / monologue / June In January / I'm

Gonna Sit Right Down (and Write Myself A Letter) / Volare / On An Evening In Roma / Rock-A-Bye Your Baby / Break It To Me

(CD only; reissued October 2005 with bonus DVD 'That's Amore')

July 2006	**THAT'S AMORE (20 SONGS OF ROMANCE)**

(CD only)

August 2007	**FOREVER COOL**

Who's Got the Action? (w. Big Bad Voodoo Daddy) / Ain't That A Kick In the Head (w. Kevin Spacey) / I've Grown Accustomed To Her Face (w. Chris Botti) / Baby-O (w. Paris Bennett) / Who Was That Lady? / Please Don't Talk About Me When I'm Gone (w. Robbie Williams) / I Can't Believe That You're In Love With me (w. Joss Stone) / Just In Time (w. Dave Koz) / Baby, It's Cold Outside (w. Martina McBride) / King of the Road (w. Kevin Spacey) / You're Nobody 'til Somebody Loves You (w. Shelby Lynne & Big Bad Voodoo Daddy) / Arrivederci, Roma (w. Tiziano Ferro) / Everybody Loves Somebody (w. Charles Aznavour) / Brahms' Lullaby [acapella version]

(CD only [contains bonus 'behind the scenes' DVD])

SONY MUSIC

2014	**THE REAL... DEAN MARTIN**

(CD only)

CRIMSON

2015   **LET IT SNOW! LET IT SNOW! LET IT SNOW!**

(A RAT PACK CHRISTMAS)

(CD only)

BBC WORLDWIDE

2015   **VOLARE - THE COLLECTION**

(CD only)

Filmography

Any omissions or errors in the data hereunder are accidental.

MY FRIEND IRMA

John Lund (Al); Diana Lynn (Jane Stacey); Irma (Marie Wilson); Steve Laird (Dean Martin); Seymour (Jerry Lewis)

Director - George Marshall; Screenwriters - Cy Howard & Parke Levy.

Based on the CBS radio series *My Friend Irma*

A Paramount Release. A Hal Wallis Production

Wrapped 14 July 1949. Duration 86mins

Released September 1949 (USA), 14 August 1950 (UK)

MY FRIEND IRMA GOES WEST

Al (John Lund); Jane Stacey (Diana Lynn); Irma (Marie Wilson); Steve Laird (Dean Martin); Seymour (Jerry Lewis)

Director – Hal Walker; Screenwriters – Cy Howard & Parke Levy

Based on the CBS radio series *My Friend Irma*

A Paramount Release. A Hal Wallis Production

Wrapped 18 May 1950. Duration 85mins

Released August 1950 (USA), 1 January 1951 (UK)

AT WAR WITH THE ARMY

Sergeant Puccinelli (Dean Martin); Private Korwin (Jerry Lewis); Sergeant McVey (Mike Kellin); Pokey (Dick Stabile); Helen (Polly Bergen)

Director – Hal Walker; Producer/Screenwriter – Fred F Finkelhoffe

A Paramount Release. A York Picture Corporation Production

Wrapped 23 January 1951. Duration 92mins

Released January 1951 (USA), August 1951 (UK)

HOLLYWOOD AT PLAY

Featurette cameo [with Jerry Lewis]

Columbia Pictures 1951

THAT'S MY BOY

Bill Baker (Dean Martin); 'Junior' Jackson (Jerry Lewis); Ann Jackson (Ruth Hussey); 'Jarring Jack' Jackson (Eddie Mayehoff); Betty Hunter (Polly Bergen)

Director - Hal Walker; Screenwriter/Associate Producer – Cy Howard

A Paramount Release. A Hal Wallis Production

Wrapped 1 August 1951. Duration 89mins

Released August 1951 (USA), 2 June 1952 (UK)

SAILOR BEWARE

Al Crowthers (Dean Martin); Melvin Jones (Jerry Lewis): Herself (Corrine Calvet); Hilda Jones (Marion Marshall); Themselves (The Mayo Brothers)

Director – Hal Walker; Screenwriters – James Allardice & Martin Rackin

A Paramount Release. A Hal Wallis Production

Wrapped 4 December 1951. Duration 104mins

Released February 1952 (USA), 10 March 1952 (UK)

ROAD TO BALI

Cameo [with Jerry Lewis]

Paramount Pictures, 1952

JUMPING JACKS

Chick Allen (Dean Martin); Hap Smith (Jerry Lewis); Betty Carver (Mona Freeman); Sergeant McClusky (Robert Strauss)

Director – Norman Taurog; Screenwriters – Herbert Baker, Robert Lees & Fred Rinaldo

A Paramount Release. A Hal Wallis Production

Wrapped 9 July 1952. Duration 96mins

Released July 1952 (USA), 3 November 1952 (UK)

THE STOOGE

Bill (Dean Martin); Ted (Jerry Lewis); Mary (Polly Bergen); Leo Lyman (Eddie Mayehoff); Frecklehead (Marion Marshall); Frank Darling (Freeman Lusk)

Director – Norman Taurog; Screenwriters – Fred F Finklehoffe & Martin Rackin

A Paramount Release. A Hal Wallis Production

Wrapped March 1951. Duration 100mins

Released February 1953 (USA), 10 December 1953 (UK)

SCARED STIFF

Larry Todd (Dean Martin); Myron Mertz (Jerry Lewis); Mary Caroll (Lizabeth Scott); Carmelita Castina (Carmen Miranda); Mr. Ortega (George Dolenz); Rosie (Dorothy Malone)

Director – George Marshall; Screenwriters – Herbert Baker & Walter DeLeon

A Paramount Release. A Hal Wallis Production

Wrapped June 1953. Duration 107mins

Released July 1953 (USA), 17 August 1953 (UK)

THE CADDY

Joe Anthony (Dean Martin); Harvey Miller (Jerry Lewis); Kathy Taylor (Donna Reed); Lisa Anthony (Barbara Bates); Papa Anthony (Joseph Galleia); Mama Anthony (Argentina Brunetti)

Director – Norman Taurog; Screenwriters – Edmund Hartmannn & Danny Arnold

A Paramount Release. A Hal Wallis Production

Wrapped 4 September 1953. Duration 94mins

Released September 1953 (USA), 9 November 1953 (UK)

MONEY FROM HOME

Honeytalk Nelson (Dean Martin); Virgil Yokum (Jerry Lewis); Phyllis Leigh (Marjie Miller); Autumn Claypool (Pat Crowley); Bertie Searles (Richard Haydn); Seldom Seen Kid (Robert Strauss); Jumbo (Sheldon Leonard)

Director – George Marshall; Screenwriter – Hal Kanter

From a story by Damon Runyon, adapted by James Allardice & Hal Kanter

A Paramount Release. A Hal Wallis Production

Wrapped May 1953. Duration 100mins

Released February 1954 (USA), 8 February 1954 (UK)

LIVING IT UP

Dr. Steve Harris (Dean Martin); Homer Flagg (Jerry Lewis); Wally Cook (Janet Leigh); Oliver Stone (Fred Clark)

Director – Norman Taurog; Producer – Paul Jones; Screenwriters – Jack Rose & Melville Nelson

Based on the story by James Street from the musical comedy 'Hazel Flagg'

A Paramount Release. A York Pictures Corporation Production

Wrapped July 1953. Duration 95mins

Released 1 August 1954 (USA), 13 September 1954 (UK)

THREE RING CIRCUS

Pete Nelson (Dean Martin); Jerry Hotchkiss (Jerry Lewis); Jill Brent (Joanne Dru); Saadia (Zsa Gabor); Sam Morley (Wallace Ford); Bearded Lady (Elsa Lanchester)

Director – Joseph Peveney; Screenwriter – Don McGuire

A Paramount Release. A Hal Wallis Production

Wrapped December 1954. Duration 108mins

Released 22 December 1954 (USA), 24 January 1956 (UK)

YOU'RE NEVER TOO YOUNG

Bob Miles (Dean Martin); Wilbur Hoolick (Jerry Lewis); Nancy Collins (Diana Lyn); Noonan (Raymond Burr)

Director – Norman Taurog; Producer – Paul Jones; Screenwriter – Sidney Sheldon

From the play by Edward Childs Carpenter and based on the book by Fannie Kilbourne

A Paramount Release. A York Pictures Corporation Production

Wrapped August 1955. Duration 102mins

Released 2 August 1955 (USA), 14 November 1955 (UK)

ARTISTS AND MODELS

Rick (Dean Martin); Eugene (Jerry Lewis); Bessie (Shirley MacLaine); Abigail (Dorothy Malone); Mr. Murdock (Eddie Mayehoff); Anita (Anita Ekberg); Ivan (Jack Elam)

Director – Frank Tashlin; Screenwriters – Hal Kantner, Herbert Baker & Frank Tashlin

A Paramount Release. A Hal Wallis Production

In VistaVision & Technicolor

Wrapped December 1951. Duration 109mins

Released December 1955 (USA), 23 January 1956 (UK)

PARDNERS

Slim Moseley Jr (Dean Martin); Wade Kingsley Jr (Jerry Lewis); Carol Kinglsey (Lori Nelson); Dolly Riley (Jackie Loughrey); Rio (Jeff Morrow); Mrs. Kingsley (Agnes Moorhead); Whitey (Lon Chaney Jr)

Director – Norman Taurog; Producer – Paul Jones; Screenwriter – Sidney Sheldon

Screenstory by Jerry Davis from the original story by Mervin J Houser

A Paramount Release. A York Pictures Corporation Production

In VistaVision & Technicolor

Wrapped July 1956. Duration 87mins

Released 25 July 1956 (USA), 10 September 1956 (UK)

HOLLYWOOD OR BUST

Steve Wiley (Dean Martin); Malcolm Smith (Jerry Lewis); Terry Roberts (Pat Crowley); 'Bookie' (Maxie Rosebloom); Herself (Anita Ekberg); Himself (Mr Bascom)

Director – Frank Tashlin; Screenwriter – Erna Lazarus

A Paramount Release. A Hal Wallis Production

In VistaVision & Technicolor

Wrapped December 1956. Duration 95mins

Released December 1956 (USA), 4 December 1956 (UK)

TEN THOUSAND BEDROOMS

Ray Hunter (Dean Martin); Maria Martelli (Eva Bartok); Nina Martelli (Anna Maria Alberghetti); Mike Clark (Dewey Martin); Vittorio Martelli (Walter Slezak)

Director – Richard Thorpe; Producer – Joseph Pasternak; Screenwriters – Lalso Vadnay, William Ludwig, Art Cohn & Leonard Spigelglass

A Metro-Goldwyn-Mayer Release

Wrapped April 1956. Duration 114mins

Released 12 February 1957 (USA), 28 March 1957 (UK)

THE YOUNG LIONS

Christian Diestl (Marlon Brando); Noah Ackerman (Montgomery Clift); Michael Whiteacre (Dean Martin); Hope Plowman (Hope Lange); Margaret Freemantle (Barbara Rush); Gretchen Hardenberg (May Britt); Hardenberg (Maximilian Schell); Simone (Dora Doll); Rickett (Lee Van Cleef)

Director – Edward Dmytryk; Producer – Al Lichtman; Screenwriter – Edward Anhalt

Based on the novel by Irwin Shaw

A Twentieth Century Fox Film Corporation Release.

In CinemaScope

Wrapped March 1958. Duration 167mins

Released April 1958 (USA), 22 May 1958 (UK)

SOME CAME RUNNING

Dave Hirsh (Frank Sinatra); Alabama Dillert (Dean Martin); Ginny Moorhead (Shirley MacLaine); Gwen French (Martha Hyer)

Director – Vincente Minelli; Screenwriters – John Patrick & Arthur Skeekman

Based on the novel by James Jones

A Metro-Goldwyn-Mayer Release. A Sol C Siegel Production

In CinemaScope & Metrocolor

Wrapped December 1958. Duration 140mins

Released January 1959 (USA), 22 April 1959 (UK)

RIO BRAVO

Sheriff Chance (John Wayne); Dude (Dean Martin); Colorado (Ricky Nelson); Feathers (Angie Dickinson); Joe Burdette (Claude Akins)

Director – Howard Hawks; Screenwriter – Leigh Brackett & Jules Fordham

From a story by B H McCampbell

A Warner Brothers Release. A Howard Hawks Production

In Technicolor

Wrapped May 1958. Duration 140mins

Released April 1959 (USA), 23 July 1959 (UK)

CAREER

Maury Novak (Dean Martin); Sam Lawson (Anthony Franciosa); Sharon Kensington (Shirley MacLaine); Shirley Drake (Joan Blackman)

Director – Joseph Anthony; Screenwriter – James Lee

A Paramount Release. A Hal Wallis Production

Wrapped October 1959. Duration 105mins

Released October 1959 (USA), 17 December 1959 (UK)

WHO WAS THAT LADY?

David Wilson (Tony Curtis); Michael Haney (Dean Martin); Ann Wilson (Janet Leigh); Harry Powell (James Whitmore); Bob Doyle (John McIntire); Gloria Coogle (Barbara Nichols)

Director – George Sidney; Screenwriter – Norman Krasna (based upon his play)

A Columbia Pictures Corporation Release. An Ansark/George Sidney Production

Wrapped July 1958. Duration 114mins

Released April 1960 (USA), 14 May 1960 (UK)

BELLS ARE RINGING

Ella Peterson (Judy Holliday); Jeffery Moss (Dean Martin); Larry Hastings (Fred Clark); J Otto Prantz (Eddie Foy Jr); Blake Barton (Frank Gorshin)

Director – Vincente Minelli; Screenwriters – Betty Comden & Adolph Green

Based on the musical play

A Metro-Goldwyn-Mayer Release. An Arthur Freed Producton

In CinemaScope & Metrocolor

Wrapped May 1960. Duration 126mins

Released June 1960 (USA), 25 August 1960 (UK)

OCEAN'S 11

Danny Ocean (Frank Sinatra); Sam Harmon (Dean Martin); Josh Howard (Sammy Davis Jr); Jimmy Foster (Peter Lawford); Beatrice Ocean (Angie Dickinson); Anthony Bergdorf (Richard Conte); Duke Santos (Cesar Romero); Adele Ekstrom (Patrice Wymore); 'Mushy' O'Connors (Joey Bishop); Spyros Acebos (Akim Tamiroff)

Director – Lewis Milestone; Screenwriters – Harry Brown & Charles Lederer

A Warner Brothers Release. A Dorchester Production

In Panavision & Technicolor

Wrapped August 1960. Duration 127mins

Released 4 August 1960 (USA), 25 August 1960 (UK)

ALL IN A NIGHT'S WORK

Tony Ryder (Dean Martin); Katie Robbins (Shirley MacLaine); Warren Kingsley Jr (Cliff Robertson); Oliver Dunning (Gale Gordon)

Director – Joseph Anthony; Screenwriters – Maurice Richlin & Sidney Sheldon

Based on a story by Margit Veszi and the play by Owen Elford

A Paramount Release. A Hal Wallis Production

In Technicolor

Wrapped December 1960. Duration 94mins

Released March 1961 (USA), 11 May 1961 (UK)

PEPE

Cameo

Columbia Pictures, 1961

ADA

Ada Dallas (Susan Hayward); Bo Gillis (Dean Martin); Sylvester Marin (Wilfrid Hyde White); Colonel Yancy (Ralph Meeker); Steve Jackson (Martin Balsam); Ronnie Hallerton (Frank Maxwell)

Director – Daniel Mann; Producer – Lawrence Weingarten; Screenwriters – Arthur Sheekman & William Driskill

Based on the novel *Ada Dallas* by Wirt Williams

A Metro-Goldwyn-Mayer Release.

In CinemaScope & Metrocolor

Wrapped June 1961. Duration 108mins

Released August 1961 (USA), 18 January 1962 (UK)

SERGEANTS 3

Mike Merry (Frank Sinatra); Chip Deal (Dean Martin); Jonah Williams (Sammy Davis Jr); Larry Barrett (Peter Lawford); Roger

Boswell (Joey Bishop); Mountain Hawk (Henry Silva); Amelia Parent (Ruta Lee); Willie Sharpknife (Buddy Lester) with Philip, Lindsay and Dennis Crosby

Director – John Sturges; Producer – Frank Sinatra; Screenwriter – WR Burnett

A United Artists Release. In Panavision & Technicolor

Wrapped July 1961. Duration 112mins

Released 9 February 1962 (USA), 5 April 1962 (UK)

ROAD TO HONG KONG

Cameo [with Frank Sinatra]

United Artists, 1962

SOMETHING'S GOT TO GIVE

Ellen Wagstaff Arden (Marilyn Monroe); Nicholas Arden (Dean Martin); Bianca Russell Arden (Cyd Charisse); Stephen Burkett (Tom Tryon); Shoe Salesman (Wally Cox); Insurance Salesman (Phil Silvers); Psychiatrist (Steve Allen); Tommy Arden (Robert Christopher Morley); Lia Arden (Alexandria Heilweil)

Director – Frank Tashlin (replaced by George Cukor); Producers – David Brown (replaced by Harry Weinstein); Screenwriters – Arnold Schulman, Nunally Johnson & Walter Bernstein

Based on the film *My Favorite Wife* by Leo McCarey & Samuel and Bella Spewack, in turn, based on the poem *Enoch Arden* by Alfred, Lord Tennyson

Twentieth Century Fox/Claude Productions

Production cancelled 11 June 1962

Footage released 1990/2001

WHO'S GOT THE ACTION?

Steve Flood (Dean Martin); Melanie Flood (Lana Turner); Clint Morgan (Eddie Albert); Saturday Knight (Nita Talbot); Tony Gagoots (Walter Matthau); Roza (Margo)

Director – Daniel Mann; Producer – Jack Rose; Screenwriter – Jack Rose

Based on the novel *Four Horse-players Are Missing* by Alexander Rose

A Paramount Release. An Amro/Claude/Mea/Paramount Production

Wrapped December 1962. Duration 95mins

Released 21 December 1962 (USA), 21 February 1963 (UK)

COME BLOW YOUR HORN

Cameo

Paramount Pictures, 1963

TOYS IN THE ATTIC

Carrie Berniers (Geraldine Page); Anna Berniers (Wendy Hiller); Julian Berniers (Dean Martin); Lilly Prine Berniers (Yvette Mimieux); Albertine Prine (Gene Tierney); Henry (Frank Silvera); Charlotte Warkins (Nan Martin); Cyrus Warkins (Larry Gates)

Director – George Roy Hill; Producer – Walter Mirisch; Screenwriter – James Poe

Based on the play by Lillian Hellman

A United Artists Release. A Mirisch-Claude Production

Wrapped June 1963. Duration 90mins

Released August 1963 (USA), 24 November 1963 (UK)

WHO'S BEEN SLEEPING IN MY BED?

Jason Steel (Dean Martin); Melissa Morris (Elizabeth Montgomery); Sanford Kaufman (Martin Balsam); Tony Tobler (Jill St. John); Leonard Ashley (Richard Conte); Stella (Carol Burnett)

Director – Daniel Mann; Producer/Screenwriter – Jack Rose

A Paramount Release. An Amro/Claude/Mea/Paramount Production

In Panavision & Technicolor

Wrapped October 1963. Duration 102mins

Released December 1963 (USA), 9 January 1964 (UK)

4 FOR TEXAS

Zack Thomas (Frank Sinatra); Joe Jarrett (Dean Martin); Elya Carlson (Anita Ekberg); Maxine Richter (Ursula Andress); Matson (Charles Bronson); Harvey Burden (Victor Buono)

Director/Producer – Robert Aldrich; Screenwriters – Teddi Sherman & Robert Aldrich

A Warner Brothers Release. A SAM Company Production

In Technicolor

Wrapped December 1963. Duration 115mins

Released 25 December 1963 (UK), 4 January 1964 (USA)

WORLD BY NIGHT (38-24-36)

Cameo

Warner Brothers, 1964

WHAT A WAY TO GO!

Louisa (Shirley MacLaine); Larry Flint (Paul Newman); Rod Anderson (Robert Mitchum); Leonard Crawley (Dean Martin); Jerry Benson (Gene Kelly); Dr Steffanson (Bob Cummings); Edgar Hopper (Dick Van Dyke)

Director – AJ Lee Thompson; Producer – Arthur P Jacobs; Screenwriters – Betty Comden & Adolph Green

Based on the story by Gwen Davis

A Twentieth Century Fox Film Corporation Release. An A J Lee Thompson Production

In CinemaScope. Color by Deluxe

Wrapped May 1964. Duration 111mins

Released May 1964 (USA); 2 July 1964 (UK)

ROBIN AND THE 7 HOODS

Robbo (Frank Sinatra); John (Dean Martin); Will (Sammy Davis Jr); Allen A Dale (Bing Crosby); Guy Gisborne (Peter Falk); Marian (Barbara Rush); Big Jim (Edward G Robinson); Sheriff Potts (Victor Buono)

Director – Gordon Douglas; Producer – Frank Sinatra; Screenwriter – David R Schwartz

A Warner Brothers Release. A Panama/Claude Production

In Panavision & Technicolor

Wrapped June 1964. Duration 123mins

Released August 1964 (USA), 2 August 1964 (UK)

KISS ME, STUPID

Dino (Dean Martin); Polly the Pistol (Kim Novak); Orville J Spooner (Ray Walston); Zelda Spooner (Felicia Farr); Barney Millsap (Cliff Osmond); Big Bertha (Barbara Pepper); Doctor Sheldrake (Mel Blanc)

Director/Producer – Billy Wilder; Screenwriters – Billy Wilder & I A L Diamond

From the stage comedy *The Dazzling Hour* by Anna Bonacci

A United Artists Release. A Claude/Mirisch/Phalanx Production

In Panavision

Wrapped December 1964. Duration 126mins

Released December 1964 (USA), 25 February 1965 (UK)

THE SONS OF KATIE ELDER

John Elder (John Wayne); Tom Elder (Dean Martin); Mary Gordon (Martha Hyer); Bud Elder (Michael Anderson Jr); Matt

Elder (Earl Holliman); Morgan Hastings (James Gregory); Curley (George Kennedy); Sheriff Wilson (Paul Fix); David Hastings (Dennis Hopper)

Director – Henry Hathaway; Screenwriters – Harry Essex, Allan Weiss & William H Wright

Based on the story by Talbot Jennings

A Paramount Release. A Hal Wallis Production

In Panavision & Technicolor

Wrapped June 1965. Duration 122mins

Released August 1965 (USA); 28 October 1965 (UK)

MARRIAGE ON THE ROCKS

Dan Edwards (Frank Sinatra); Valerie Edwards (Deborah Kerr); Ernie Brewer (Dean Martin); Miguel Santos (Cesar Romero); Jeannie MacPherson (Hermione Baddeley); Jim Blake (Tony Bill); Tracy Edwards (Nancy Sinatra); Himself (Trini Lopez); Shad Nathan (John McGiver)

Director - Jack Donohue; Producer - William H Daniels; Screenwriter - Cy Howard

A Warner Brothers Release. An Artanis/Claude Production

In Panavision & Technicolor

Wrapped September 1965. Duration 101mins

Released October 1965 (USA); 16 September 1965 (UK)

THE SILENCERS

Matt Helm (Dean Martin); Gail Hendricks (Stella Stevens); Tina Batori (Daliah Lavi); Tung-Tze (Victor Buono); Wigman (Arthur O'Connell); Sam Gunther (Robert Webber); MacDonald (James Gregory); Barbara (Nancy Kovak); Sarita (Cyd Charisse); Lovey Kravezit (Beverly Adams)

Director - Phil Karlson; Producer - Irving Allen; Screenwriter - Oscar Saul

Based on the novels *The Silencers* & *Death of A Citizen* by Donald Hamilton

A Columbia Pictures Corporation Release. A Meadway/Claude Production

In Technicolor & Columbiacolor

Wrapped March 1966. Duration 105mins

Released March 1966 (USA); 7 April 1966 (UK)

TEXAS ACROSS THE RIVER

Sam Hollis (Dean Martin); Don Andrea (Alain Delon); Phoebe Naylor (Rosemary Forsyth); Kronk (Joey Bishop); Lonetta (Tina Marquand); Captain Stimpson (Peter Graves); Iron Jacket (Michael Ansara); Yellow Knife (Linden Chiles)

Director - Michael Gordon; Producer - Harry Keller; Screenwriters - Harold Green, Wells Root, Ben Starr

A Universal Pictures Release

In Technicolor

Wrapped October 1966. Duration 101mins

Released November 1966 (USA); 9 June 1967 (UK)

MURDERERS' ROW

Matt Helm (Dean Martin); Suzie Solaris (Ann-Margret); Julian Wall (Karl Malden); Coco Duquette (Camilla Sparv); MacDonald (James Gregory); Lovey Kravezit (Beverly Adams); Dr. Norman Solaris (Richard Eastham); Ironhead (Tom Reese); featuring Dino, Desi & Billy

Director - Henry Levin; Producer - Irving Allen; Screenwriter - Herbert Baker

Based on the novel by Donald Hamilton

A Columbia Pictures Corporation Release. A Meadway/Claude Production

In Technicolor & Columbiacolor

Wrapped December 1966. Duration 108mins

Released December 1966 (USA); 19 February 1967 (UK)

ROUGH NIGHT IN JERICHO

Alex Flood (Dean Martin); Dolan (George Peppard); Mollie (Jean Simmons); Ben (John McIntire); Yarborough (Slim Pickens); Jace (Don Galloway)

Director - Arnold Laven; Producer - Martin Rackin; Screenwriters - Sydney Boehm & Marvin H Albert

Based on the novel *The Man In Black* by Marvin H Albert

A Universal Pictures Release

In Technicolor

Wrapped October 1967. Duration 102mins

Released October 1967 (USA); 27 October 1967 (UK)

THE AMBUSHERS

Matt Helm (Dean Martin); Francesca Madeiros (Senta Berger); Sheila Sommers (Janice Rule); MacDonald (James Gregory); Jose Ortega (Albert Salmi); Quintana (Kurt Kasznar); Lovey Kravezit (Beverly Adams)

Director - Henry Levin; Producer - Irving Allen; Screenwriter - Herbert Baker

Based on the novel by Donald Hamilton

A Columbia Pictures Corporation Release. A Meadway/Claude Production

In Technicolor & Columbiacolor

Wrapped 23 June 1967. Duration 102mins

Released December 1967 (USA); 1 January 1968 (UK)

HOW TO SAVE A MARRIAGE -- AND RUIN YOUR LIFE

David Sloane (Dean Martin); Carol Corman (Stella Stevens); Harry Hunter (Eli Wallach); Muriel Laszlo (Anne Jackson); Thelma (Betty Field)

Director - Fielder Cook; Producer - Stanley Shapiro; Screenwriters - Stanley Shapiro & Nate Monaster

A Columbia Pictures Corporation Release

In Panavision & Technicolor

Wrapped December 1967; Duration 103mins

Released January 1968 (USA); 30 May 1968 (UK)

BANDOLERO!

Mace Bishop (James Stewart); Dee Bishop (Dean Martin); Maria (Racquel Welch); Sheriff Johnson (George Kennedy); Roscoe Bookbinder (Andrew Pine); Pop Chaney (Will Geer); Babe (Clint Ritchie); Muncie Carter (Denver Pyle)

Director - Andrew V McLaghlen; Producer - Robert Jacks; Screenwriter - James Lee Barrett

A Twentieth Century Fox Film Corporation Release.

In Panavision. Colour by Deluxe

Wrapped June 1968. Duration 106mins

Released July 1968 (USA); 4 July 1968 (UK)

FIVE CARD STUD

Van Morgan (Dean Martin); Rev. Rudd (Robert Mitchum); Lily Langford (Inger Stevens); Nick Evers (Roddy McDowall); Nora Evers (Katherine Justice); Marshal Dana (John Anderson); Little George (Yaphet Kotto)

Director - Henry Hathaway; Screenwriter - Marguerite Roberts

Based on the novel by Ray Gaulden

A Paramount Release. A Hal Wallis Production

In Technicolor

Wrapped July 1968. Duration 102mins

Released August 1968 (USA); September 1968 (UK)

THE WRECKING CREW

Matt Helm (Dean Martin); Linka Karensky (Elke Somer); Freya Carlson (Sharon Tate); Yu-Rang (Nancy Kwan); Count Massimo Cantini (Nigel Green); Lola Medina (Tina Louise); MacDonald (John Larch)

Director - Phil Karlson; Producer - Irving Allen; Screenwriter - William McGivern

Based on the novel by Donald Hamilton

A Columbia Pictures Corporation Release. A Meadway/Claude Production

In Technicolor & Columbiacolor

Wrapped July 1968. Duration 105mins

Released February 1969 (USA); 12 March 1969 (UK)

AIRPORT

Mel Bakersfield (Burt Lancaster); Vernon Demerest (Dean Martin); Tanya Livingston (Jean Seberg); Gwen Meighen (Jacqueline Bissett); Patroni (George Kennedy); Ada Quonsett (Helen Hayes); D O Guerrero (Van Heflin); Inez Guerrrero (Maureen Stapleton)

Director - George Seaton; Producer - Ross Hunter; Screenwriter George Seaton

Based on the novel by Arthur Hailey

A Universal Pictures/Ross Hunter Production

In Todd-AO Technicolor

Wrapped March 1969.Duration 136mins

Released March 1970 (USA); 23 April 1970 (UK)

SOMETHING BIG

Joe Baker (Dean Martin); Col. Morgan (Brian Keith); Mary Anna Morgan (Honor Blackman); Dover MacBride (Carol White); Jesse Bookbinder (Ben Johnson); Johnny Cobb (Albert Salmi); Chief Yellow Sun (Paul Fix); Tuffy (Scruffy)

Director – Andrew V McLaglen; Screenwriter – James Lee Barrett from his original story

A Twentieth Century Fox Film Corporation Release. A James Lee Barrett/Andrew V MacLaglen Cinemacenter Production

In Technicolor

Wrapped September 1971. Duration 108mins

Released January 1972 (USA); 16 December 1972 (UK)

SHOWDOWN

Chuck (Rock Hudson); Billy (Dean Martin); Kate (Susan Clark); Art Williams (Donald Moffat); P J Wilson (John McLiam)

Director/Producer – George Seaton; Screenwriter – Theodore Taylor

From the story by Hank Fine

A Universal Pictures Release.

In Todd A-O 35 Technicolor

Wrapped February 1973. Duration 99mins

Released July 1973 (USA); 23 July 1973 (UK)

MR. RICCO

Joe Ricco (Dean Martin); George Cronyn (Eugene Roche); Frankie Steele (Thalmus Rasulala); Irene Mapes (Denise Nicholas); Jamison (Cindy Williams)

Director – Paul Bogart; Screenwriter – Robert Hoban

From the story by Ed Harvey & Francis Kiernan

A Metro-Goldwyn-Mayer Release. A Douglas Netter Production

In Panavision & Metrocolor

Wrapped January 1975. Duration 98mins

Released January 1975 (USA), March 1975 (UK)

THE CANNONBALL RUN

JJ McClure (Burt Reynolds); Victor Prinzi (Dom DeLuise); Seymour Goldfarb Jr (Roger Moore); Jamie Blake (Dean Martin); Fenderbaum (Sammy Davis Jr); Pamela (Farrah Fawcett); Jackie (Jackie Chan); Sheik Abdul ben Falafel (Jamie Farr); Dr Van Helsing (Jack Elam); Mel (Mel Tillis)

Director - Hal Needham; Screenwriter – Brock Yates

A Twentieth Century Fox Film Corporation Release. An Albert S Ruddy Production

In Panavision & Technicolor

Wrapped May 1981. Duration 95mins

Released June 1981 (USA), July 1981 (UK)

CANNONBALL RUN II

JJ McClure (Burt Reynolds); Victor Prinzi/Captain Chaos (Dom DeLuise); Mr Sinatra (Frank Sinatra); Jamie Blake (Dean Martin); Fenderbaum (Sammy Davis Jr); Sheik Abdul ben Falafel (Jamie Farr); Ricardo Montalban (King Abdul ben Falafel); Dr Van Helsing (Jack Elam); Sister Veronica (Shirley MacLaine); Mel (Mel Tillis); Sheik's Servant (Doug McClure)

Director – Hal Needham; Producer – Albert S Ruddy; Screenwriters – Hal Needham, Albert S Ruddy & Harvey Miller

A Golden Harvest/Warner Brothers Release. In Technicolor

Wrapped September 1983. Duration 108mins

Released June 1984 (USA), August 1984 (UK)

Stage, Radio & TV Appearances

While this list is not exhaustive due to the exceptional number of events throughout Dean's career, it hopes at least to document many of his well-known and/or important appearances. Any omissions or errors in the data hereunder are accidental.

1940	Reeds Mill Warehouse & Walkers Nightclub, both Steubenville ;Hollenden Hotel, Cleveland
1941-1944	various radio appearances, inc. Manhattan & Kentucky
1944	Club Riobamba [debut], Loew's Theatre, both New York; earliest known recorded radio item, Chicago
1945	Bryant Hotel, Belmont Plaza, The Glass Hat, all New York [served in US Military in Akran, Ohio, 14 months]
1946	500 Club (first public appearance with Jerry), Atlantic City
1947	Latino Casino (as Martin & Lewis), Philadelphia
1948	Copacabana,New York [Martin & Lewis' television debut]; Chase Club, St Louis; Slapsie Maxie's, Hollywood; signs as solo recording artist with Capitol Records
1949	*The Milton Berle Show* [as Martin & Lewis]
1949-1951	*The Martin & Lewis Radio Shows*

1950-1953   *Colgate Comedy Hour* [as Martin & Lewis]

1951   *Bing Crosby Radio Show* [as Martin & Lewis]

1952   Hollywood Fun Festival [as Martin & Lewis]

1953   Glasgow Empire Theatre, Scotland; The London Palladium [both as Martin & Lewis]

1955   Academy Awards, Hollywood [as Martin & Lewis]; The Martin & Lewis Muscular Dystrophy Benefit

1956   *This Is Your Life*: Milton Berle; *The Perry Como Show*; *Here's To Veterans* [US Army Personnel Benefit] radio show

1957   'City of Hope' New York Benefit [24hr Telethon]; *Ten Thousand Bedrooms* Press Interviews

1958   *The Eddie Fisher TV Show*; Club Oasis Chesterfield TV Special

1958-1967   *Dean's Jubilee Time TV Special* [intermittent, not annually]

1959   *The Frank Sinatra Timex Special*; Academy Awards; *Boomtown Show TV Special*

1960   *Frank Sinatra Jubilee Time TV Special*; *Dean Martin TV Special*; *The Lucille Ball Show*; Friar's Club Testimonial Dinner; *Share Benefit Boomtown TV Special*

1960-1967   The Sands Hotel, Las Vegas [some of the live shows recorded by Reprise]

1961   Cal-Neva Lodge

1962   *Judy Garland TV Show*; Summit Meeting Special

1962-1963   Chicago-Villa Venice [some of the live shows recorded by Reprise]

1963	*Bob Hope TV Show*; Frank Sinatra Golf Tournament, Palm Springs; *NBC TV Spectacular*; *Bob Hope Spectacular*
1964	Dick Powell Theatre; *Bing Crosby TV Show*; Perry Como Music Hall; *Bing & Rosie Show* [Bing Crosby & Rosemary Clooney]; *The Dean Martin Show Special*; cement imprints at Grauman's Chinese Theatre; *Rawhide*: 'Canliss', guest spot; stand-in for Nat 'King' Cole at the Sands, Las Vegas
1965-1974	*The Dean Martin Television Show* [known alternatively as *The Dean Martin Variety Show*] [264 episodes]
1965	*National Guard Sessions Radio Show*; *Sinatra – An American Original*
1966	*The Lucille Ball Show*; *The Tonight Show*; *TV Charity Special* [Dean donated $500 for Bobby Darin to sing]
1967	'Man of the Year' accolade from the Boys Club of Italy; 'Music Man of the Year' award from the Academy of Country and Western Music, Beverly Hilton Hotel, LA; *Movin' With Nancy*; Christmas TV Special [featuring the Martin & Sinatra families with Sammy Davis Jr]; American Federation for the Blind interview
1969	'The Total Entertainer' accolade from Billboard; *Sammy Davis Jr Special*; *Ann-Margret: From Hollywood With Love*; Roger Baldwin Foundation for American Civil Liberties Union [Dean raised $200,000]; 'Dino Golf Balls' TV commercial
1970	*The Jack Benny TV Show*; Pro-Am Golf Tournament; *Bing Crosby - Cooling It TV*

Special; Love Letter to Jack Benny TV Special; Joe E Lewis Tribute, Riviera Hotel, Las Vegas; *New Year's Eve TV Special;* Ronald Reagan Campaign Concert

1972	The first Dean Martin Gold Tournament, Lake Tahoe
1973-1992	MGM Grand Hotel (live shows), Las Vegas [MGM Grand becomes Bally's in 1988]
1973	*Jack Benny: First Farewell Special;* host of International Radio & Television Society TV Special;
1974-1978	*The Dean Martin Celebrity Roasts* [54 specials and shows]
1974	*Dean Martin's Comedy Classics*
1975	*Dean's Place TV Special; The Dean Martin Christmas TV Special*
1976	*Bob Hope 25th Anniversary Special; The Lucille Ball Show; What's My Line?; Dean Martin's Red-Hot Scandals of 1926* (Part 1); *The Jerry Lewis Muscular Dystrophy Telethon; NBC – The First Fifty Years TV Special;* Flamingo Hotel, Las Vegas
1977-1979	*Dean Martin's Christmas In California*
1977	*Bob Hope TV Special; Sinatra & Friends; Paul Anka: My Way TV Special; Music Country USA TV Special;* New York State Lottery Draw; *Dean Martin's Red-Hot Scandals of 1926* (Part 2); *Bob Hope 40th Anniversary Special; NBC TV – Fifty Years: A Closer Look TV Special*
1978	*Milton Berle Tribute Special; George Burns' 100th Birthday Special; Bing Crosby Tribute Special; Charlie's Angels:* 'Angels In Vegas', guest spot; Circle Theatre, San Francisco

1979-1980	The Dean Martin Television Show [known alternatively as *The Dean Martin Variety Show*] [re-runs]
1979	*The Best of Dean TV Special*; Academy Awards; *Vega$*, guest spot; *The Misadventures of Sheriff Lobo*: 'Dean Martin & the Moonshiners', guest spot; Ronald Reagan Campaign Concert; *Sinatra – The First Forty Years*
1980	*The Big Show*; *Dinah Shore Talk Show*; *The Joe Namath Show*; *Shirley MacLaine: Every Little Movement*; *McVicar*, excerpt from *The Dean Martin Television Show*; Ronald Reagan 'Prelude to Victory' Presidential Campaign Concert; Absecon Fields Softball Match
1981	*Bob Hope TV Special*; President Reagan's Inaugural Gala; *Ladies & Gentlemen, Bob Newhart*; AT&T TV commercials; Paul Anka Cerebral Palsy Telethon; *Comedy Classics TV Special*; *Dom DeLuise & Friends*; *Dean Martin's Christmas at Seaworld*
1982	*Portrait of A Legend* [TV documentary]; Jerry Lewis interview; *The Big Event – The First Fifty Years*; *Bob Hope Presents the Great Singers*; *Dean Martin at the Wild Animal Park*; *Bob Hope Special: 'Pink Panther' Tribute to Peter Sellers*
1983	NBC TV Tribute to the Dean Martin Television Show; Palm Springs Benefit Concert; *Dom DeLuise TV Show*; *Dean Martin – Wine, Women & Song*; Royal Invitation to Dean's Birthday Luncheon, London; the Apollo Victoria Concerts, London; *Nationwide* [UK] feature; Golden Nugget, Atlanta
1984-1985	*Half Nelson* [6 episodes]

1984	*Dom DeLuise & Friends* (Parts 2 & 3); *Foul-ups, Bleeps & Blunders*; *Bob Hope: Who Makes the World Laugh?*; the Moulin Rouge Concerts, Paris; 'L.A. is My Lady' music video [cameo]; *The Classic Sinatra TV Tribute*; 'Friar's Club Man of the Year' awarded to Dean Martin; 'Since I Met You Baby' music video [unreleased]
1985	*All Star Party for Lucille Ball*; *Entertainment Tonight* [UK] feature; *Motown Revue*; *All Star Party for 'Dutch' Reagan*
1986	*Dom DeLuise & Friends* (Part 4); 'Friar's Club Man of the Year' awarded to Roger Moore; *Shirley MacLaine TV Special*
1987	'Together Again' press/media spots [with Frank Sinatra and Sammy Davis Jr]; London Palladium concerts; *Dom DeLuise All-New Show*; *Las Vegas All-Star 75th Anniversary*
1988	'Together Again' tour commences, Oakland, California & Chicago
1989	*Sammy Davis Jr's 60th Anniversary Special*
1990	*Crooners of the Century* [hosted by Jerry Lewis]; *Sinatra 75 – The Best is Yet to Come*
1995	Obituaries [global]

Timeline: The Dean Martin Association

Notable events, year-by-year, of the DMA. Any omissions or errors in the data hereunder are accidental.

1960	Founded by Dean Martin and Bernard Thorpe as 'Dino's Fan Club'
1961	Dean starts regular contact with Bernard, sharing career information and insights into his life as the years progress; Dean's office begins regularly supplying merchandise to the club as and when it is released.
1962	Dean makes Frank Sinatra, Sammy Davis Jr, Joey Bishop and Peter Lawford honorary members; Dean closes unofficial fan-clubs in Germany and Chicago, transferring membership to the club, as he wants only one world-wide official organisation.
1963	January 19th, club featured in pop magazine 'Cherie'.
1963	Dean requests Bernard's position within the club to be as President with Dean himself acting as Honorary President.
1964	June, "Let's Be Friendly" album from EMI Records, compiled, produced and sleeve design by Bernard. Bernard interviews Dean for World Record Club magazine (reproduced below).

1966   Dean changes his title from Honorary President of the club to Chairman; the club attends UK premiere of *The Silencers* at London's Odeon Leicester Square, with the Matt Helm 'Slaygirls' in attendance; Pop magazine 'Diana' runs article on the club and 'super-agent' Matt Helm.

1967   January 25th, the club attends 20th Century Fox's private showing of *Murderer's Row*; DMA and Pye Records release special 7" single of 'I'm Not the Marrying Kind' with a special introduction by Dean. The club attends UK premiere of *Rough Night In Jericho*.

1968   BBC Radio's 'Roundabout' programme runs major feature on Dean, scripted by Bernard; the club attends UK premiere of *The Ambushers*.

1969   January 24th, Bernard asks Pye Records to release 'Gentle On My Mind' as a single from the album of the same name. It reaches No.2 in the UK charts on 1st March and remains high in the charts for 23 weeks. It is also the most played single of that year; Bernard meets with Dean's recording manager Jimmy Bowen; October, the club holds first ever members' meeting.

1970   Bernard compiles 6xLP box set 'The Dean Martin Collection' for EMI Records; April 23rd, the club attends UK premiere of *Airport* at Odeon Leicester Square.

1972   Dean makes Jack Lord an honorary member; July 31st, BBC Radio starts a 'Dean Martin Week' in which the club features; November, the club is profiled in music publication 'Listen Easy'.

1973	April 2nd, Dean changes the name of the club to the Dean Martin Association [DMA]
1974	July, the club profiled in music publication 'Melody Maker'.
1975	DMA compiles album 'Memories Are Made of This' for EMI Records; Deana Martin contacts the DMA, expressing how pleased the family is with the continued hard work on Dean's behalf; Dean makes his god-daughter Nancy Sinatra an honorary member.
1976	DMA compiles '20 Original Dean Martin Hits', designing the sleeve and producing for Warner Reprise. It becomes Dean's only UK Gold Award album, reaching No. 2 on November 13th.
1979	EMI Records ask Bernard for 16 of his favourite songs by Dean to form the album 'The Classic Dino' (the album goes on to remain in EMI's catalogue for 11 years); August, DMA profiled in both the lifestyle magazine 'Weekend' and local newspaper 'Croydon Advertiser'.
1980	DMA celebrates 20th Anniversary; EMI publicises 'The Classic Dino' as the recommended Dean Martin album of the year; May, Dean gives Bernard the moniker Chief Executive.
1982	July, the last ever members' meeting held (withdrawn because of increasing venue costs).
1983	June: DMA attends Dean's London concerts at Apollo Victoria.
1985	DMA celebrates 25th Anniversary.

1988	EMI Records contacts DMA to co-produce 'The Best of the Capitol Years', Dean's first digital release on CD.
1990	DMA celebrates 30th Anniversary.
1992	Bernard takes part in a 75th Birthday Radio Special in Pennsylvania, USA
1994	DMA compiles Music For Pleasure CD 'Singles' for EMI.
1995	Bernard receives permission from Dean to write his biography and starts in earnest; DMA contributes to *Biography* documentary on Dean for US television production company A&E; Christmas Day, Dean Martin passes away; same, DMA issues notice of Dean's death following the call from his office.
1996	Jeanne, Dean's ex-wife, contacts the DMA thankful for all the support and hard work over the years; August, DMA produces 2xCD box set of original Reprise recordings 'Dean Martin Sings the All Time Hits' for Charly Records; DMA suggests to EMI a 'two on one' CD release of 'This Time I'm Swingin'' with 'Pretty Baby' and 'Dino Italian Love Songs' with 'Cha De Amor'. This format instigates similar highly-successful releases for other artists by EMI.
1998	EMI ask DMA to compile songs for CD release 'The Very Best of Dean Martin: The Capitol and Reprise Years'.
1999	DMA compiles Italian CD release 'Again' for Joker Records.
2000	DMA celebrates 40th Anniversary; DMA compiles Italian CD release 'Someone Like

You' for Joker Records; DMA writes liner notes for concert programme for *Frank, Dean and Sammy: The Rat Pack Live from Las Vegas*; May, DMA writes article on *Frank, Dean and Sammy: The Rat Pack Live from Las Vegas* for theatre magazine 'Encore'; August, DMA selects songs for 'The Very Best of Dean Martin: The Capitol and Reprise Years Volume 2' for EMI.

2003	DMA writes Bob Hope obituary for theatre magazine 'Encore'; November 17th, DMA compiles songs for exclusive HMV release 'The Dean Martin Collection'.
2007	November 25th, DMA attends stage show *Christmas With the Rat Pack* in London.
2009	July, DMA writes for concert programme for Mark Adams' 2009 tour of *That's Amore: A Celebration of Dean Martin and Friends*; August, DMA interviews Mark Adams as part of his promotional material for *That's Amore: A Celebration of Dean Martin and Friends*; August, DMA contributes to concert programme for the 2009/2010 tour of *Frank, Dean and Sammy: The Rat Pack Live from Las Vegas*; September, DMA allowed exclusive access to rehearsals of *That's Amore: A Celebration of Dean Martin and Friends*.
2010	DMA celebrates its 50th anniversary.
2011	DMA publishes its final newsletter and formally closes down as an active membership society.
2014	Discussions begin between Bernard and Elliot regarding the Dean Martin biography that Bernard started in 1995, with a view for

potential publication to tie-in with Dean's centenary year in 2017.

2015   February, Bernard gives permission for Elliot to solely work on the biography; March, Bernard passes away after a short battle with cancer; Chinbeard Books commissions publication of the (as-then untitled) biography.

2017   Elliot relaunches the DMA as an online presence only, without an active membership; Chinbeard Books releases the biography in paperback as 'Just Dino - A Personal Recollection of Dean Martin'.

2018   The rights to 'Just Dino - A Personal Recollection of Dean Martin' revert to the DMA; the DMA website undergoes a redesign; Grosvenor House Publishing releases a revised and expanded edition of the biography in hardback, retitled 'Dean Martin - Recollections'.

Thanks Brad

Din

CPSIA information can be obtained
at www.ICGtesting.com
Printed in the USA
BVHW080630041221
623158BV00011B/355/J

9 781786 233653